Human Resource Management in the Hospitality and Tourism Industry

Second edition

Michael Riley

BUTTERWORTH
HEINEMANN

Butterworth-Heinemann
Linacre House, Jordan Hill, Oxford OX2 8DP
A division of Reed Educational and Professional Publishing Ltd

 A member of the Reed Elsevier plc group

OXFORD   BOSTON   JOHANNESBURG
MELBOURNE   NEW DELHI   SINGAPORE

First published as *Human Resource Management* 1991
Reprinted 1992, 1994
Second edition 1996
Reprinted 1997 (twice)

© Michael Riley 1991, 1996

All rights reserved. No part of this publication
may be reproduced in any material form (including
photocopying or storing in any medium by electronic
means and whether or not transiently or incidentally
to some other use of this publication) without the
written permission of the copyright holder except in
accordance with the provisions of the Copyright,
Designs and Patents Act 1988 or under the terms of a
licence issued by the Copyright Licensing Agency Ltd,
90 Tottenham Court Road, London, England W1P 9HE.
Application for the copyright holder's written permission
to reproduce any part of this publication should be addressed
to the publishers

British Library Cataloguing in Publication Data
Riley, Michael
  Human resource management
  in the hospitality and tourism industry - 2nd ed.
  1 Hotels - Personnel management 2 Caterers and catering -
  Personnel management 3 Personnel management
  I. Title
  647.2

ISBN 0 7506 2729 8

Photoset by Deltatype Ltd, Ellesmere Port, Cheshire
Printed and bound in Great Britain by The Bath Press, Bath

Contents

Preface	iv
1 Introduction	1

Part One   An Anatomy of the Hotel and Catering Labour Market
2 Understanding labour markets	7
3 An anatomy of hotel and catering labour markets	15
4 Overtime and labour costs	26

Part Two   People at Work
5 Stating the problem	33
6 Start Monday – the manager–worker relationship	38
7 Motivation	44
8 Negative behaviour	55
9 Groups and teams	60
10 Feelings about pay	66
11 Organizations and authority	69
12 Attitudes and attitude measurement	74
13 Understanding customer–staff relations	84

Part Three   Some Useful Techniques
14 Labour utilization and productivity	95
15 The measurement of labour turnover and labour stability	106
16 Recruitment and selection	109
17 Appraisal	123
18 Pay administration	127
19 Grievance and dispute management	141
20 Personnel administration	145
21 The costs of training	151
22 Questionnaire design	156

Part Four   Human Resource Management and Quality
23 Commitment, job satisfaction and labour turnover	165
24 Empowerment	171
25 Functional flexibility and the service organization of the future	175

Part Five   Management at the Corporate Level
26 Career management	183
27 Organizational change	194
28 Developing labour strategies	200

Further reading	211
Index	217

Preface

This book is about being a manager in the hotel, catering and tourism industry; it is about managing people and controlling the cost of labour. The book is both focused and comprehensive. It is focused in the sense that it is concerned with one large industry and it is written to explain the opportunities, the constraints, the problems and the solutions that face management at every level in that industry. It is, to use the parlance of the detective novel, an inside job. It is comprehensive in the sense that it is not just concerned with the psychological aspects of managing people, but also with the role of policy in managing a workforce and the central position of labour economics – labour cost, utilization, labour market behaviour and pay. In a labour-intensive industry, knowledge of economics and strategy are inseparable from the skills of managing people.

The book is in five parts, each with a particular realm of fact and theory which build into a coherent body of knowledge.

Part One is called 'An Anatomy of the Hotel and Catering Labour Market'. This focuses primarily on economics but no previous experience of economics is assumed and the reader will be introduced gradually to a portrait of the labour market which explains the skill levels, pay distribution, pay levels, mobility patterns, and conditions of supply and demand.

Part Two is called 'People at Work' and relates the theories of behavioural science to work in the industry. This section forms the essential theoretical background for the remaining sections of the book.

Part Three is called 'Some Useful Techniques' and focuses on personnel administration and labour utilization. This part is about being organized and using techniques correctly.

Part Four is called 'Human Resource Management and Quality'. This recognizes the role of people and work systems in creating and sustaining the required level of quality in a service or a product. It examines the ideas which human resource management has contributed to the issue of quality.

Part Five is called 'Management at the Corporate Level' and is concerned with the process of strategy and policy development and with the particular problems of managing managers.

The book is for students who are studying management in the hotel and catering or tourism fields. It is also relevant to practising managers in the industry.

It begins with a short introductory chapter which outlines what knowledge lies behind successful human resource management. It also deals with the similarities between the diverse sectors of the tourism industry, while suggesting the important differences which exist between the industry and other service and production industries.

The book is not about labour law. This deliberate omission is not intended to diminish the importance of law. The view that labour law is beyond the scope of this book is founded on the recognition of a special expertise and that while the law and human resource management share a concern for reasonableness and the long term, there are many areas of working life where the law stands in the background and where economic imperatives and technological processes are of more immediate relevance.

Michael Riley

1 Introduction

Is hotel and catering management unique?

Every industry thinks it is unique and, in a very real sense, each industry is right. Every technological process and each type of service does present different problems to its managers, probably has its own labour markets and, for those who work in it, has its own culture. What is more, the role of uniqueness can never be underestimated in a person's psychology. We all like to be different!

The case for the hotel and catering industry appears to be a particularly strong one. It has, after all, a lot of conspicuous features. What with all those uniforms, strange sounding job titles, tipping and unsocial hours, not to mention the high levels of entrepreneurship and labour mobility. It is not too surprising to hear a claim for being a bit special. The unsocial hours factor alone suggests that at least as 'a life' hotel and catering management is out of the ordinary.

Well, just when you thought it was safe to declare for uniqueness, along come two contrary arguments which together constitute what might be called the pure management approach. Looked at solely as a 'managerial task' running a hotel, restaurant or institutional establishment can be seen as a set of systems and processes common to managing anything. This approach does not ignore the special features but treats them as things to be measured and analysed and turned into information that will help managers make good decisions. This is the approach of scientific management. It is greatly undervalued, and therefore underused, by hotel and catering managers. Perhaps the argument that is more easily appreciated is that like any other business, hotel and catering establishments have to make profits and maintain cash flow and, therefore, can be run on business principles. What both these arguments are saying is that 'business is business' and 'managing is managing' whatever the industry. They are undeniably true, yet acceptance of them does not really contradict the case for uniqueness. They are not mutually exclusive arguments. In addition to the business thinking and the clinical analysis of data, there is the need to know what you are managing, especially in a service industry. In a manufacturing industry there is usually a time gap between production and selling with several processes and intermediary agents in between. This is not so with service industries. There is an immediacy about service which requires managers to anticipate, adjust or react in a time span. This immediacy flows directly from four features of the industry, which are so all pervasive that they account for most of what might be called the character of life in the industry. These features are:

- *Constant fluctuations in short-term customer demand*   This is often referred to by sales people as short-term sales instability. What it means is that business fluctuates by the week, the day, the hour. For the worker, this means that his or her job has an irregular work flow. For the business, this means a problem of adjusting labour supply to demand and hence the use of part time and casual labour and a pay system which alters earnings by customer demand, i.e. tipping or some appropriate surrogate.

- *The demand for labour is direct* In the hotel and catering industry labour is demanded for what it can produce, people are not machine minders. This means that productivity is based on personal ability and effort. Consequently, there are great individual differences between workers' output. Concepts of productivity are, therefore, about judgements of human capacity.
- *The subjective nature of standards* Concepts like 'hospitality', 'service', 'cleanliness' are all matters of subjective judgement. This means that every worker's output is judged subjectively. This has the effect of making the actual relationships between managers and workers crucial to standards. In a factory this would not be the case at all. There, they would have methods of measuring output formally. When you cannot measure formally it is difficult to build a bureacracy in the organization. Rules always require specified standards. However, subjectivity means that standards are open to interpretation. Bureaucracy can be a blessing in disguise. In the absence of explicit standards there is a potential for conflicts to arise between workers and customers and between workers themselves – housekeeping want the room to be 'perfect', reception want it now; a speed versus quality dilemma.
- *Transferability of skills* The kind of skills that workers in the hotel and catering industry possess are generally confined to that industry. This makes for an efficient labour market between the various sectors of the industry. This, together with the relatively unskilled nature of some of the work, encourages the high labour mobility pattern which is often such a conspicuous feature of the industry.

These features create the immediacy which so characterizes management in this industry. It is not to say that managers simply run around 'coping' but it is to suggest that there is a tendency for the short term to be dominant. Even going up the hierarchy does not escape the sense of immediacy. The product is perishable. A room not sold tonight is gone for ever. Sometimes the fluctuations are of sufficient volume to be constantly developed in respect of the longer view. This is why the thrust of this book is towards managing the present and organizing for the future. Knowing your business means knowing what is possible and what your customer considers to be good. What with all this fluctuation and subjectivity around the one thing you must be is organized! This book argues that the management of labour in the hotel and catering industry has to accommodate the primary characteristics of the industry. Perhaps it would be useful at this point just to list the characteristics that are likely to be found in the hotel and catering industry:

- A set of skills specific to the industry.
- A range of skills for each occupation.
- Subjectively judged standards.
- Unevenly paced work.
- Seasonal employment patterns.
- Lack of bureaucracy.
- Complicated pay systems.
- An in-built speed versus quality dilemma.
- Unsocial hours.
- Part time and casual employment.

Most of these conspicuous characteristics can be explained by the four principal features. Managers are part of the features. It is the context in which they manage. Recognizing this, the book focuses on the *understanding of behaviour* and the *understanding of labour markets* as the two primary educational needs of managers in the industry. It also recognizes that 'business is business' and 'managing is managing' and good practice in management applies everywhere. The immediacy of hotel and catering management does not deny the need for good, or excuse bad, administrative and investigative techniques. For this reason, the book explains relevant and useful *techniques of labour administration* and tackles issues that are crucial to the *corporate management* of labour.

Part One

An Anatomy of the Hotel and Catering Labour Market

2 Understanding labour markets

All organizations live in a labour market environment, it is the sea on which they sail. To complain about the labour market is like the captain of a ship complaining about the sea. Yet labour markets are invariably problematic to organizations because they are mostly invisible things. In order to make sense of Chapter 3, which analyses hotel and catering labour markets, it is necessary to look first at some basic ideas and concepts that appertain to understanding labour markets. These are:

- What are labour markets?
- Is recruitment related to labour turnover?
- The idea of internal labour markets.

What are labour markets?

Labour markets exist on two levels; factual and perceptual. At any one time, people will be seeking employment or trying to change their jobs. Simultaneously, employers will be seeking new employees. Wage rates will be set, recruitment policies implemented, people will need training, people will have to move. This is the daily life of labour markets. Thousands of independent decisions made by employers and employees make up the trends in mobility, the surpluses of or shortages of supply, the excesses or lack of demand. In other words, whatever the state of supply and demand in a labour market, it is brought about by the independent and unconnected decisions of thousands of people.

According to conventional economic theory, supply and demand will be brought into equilibrium by the price of labour, i.e. the rate of pay. However, behind the assumption of a perfect market is a perfect flow of information between buyers and sellers of labour. In a perfect world the buyers would know how many have the skills they desire, how many would like to learn them and where these people are. Conversely, people would know how many vacancies there are, in what organizations and at what rate of pay.

Labour markets run on information, but they are invariably less than perfect mechanisms. What both buyers and sellers are left with is their perceptions and assumptions of supply and demand. We may think that there is no current demand for our skills, yet it may be that there is! An employer may think it is going to be easy to recruit a certain skill and set the rate accordingly, but may find that it is not. In the absence of perfect information and measurement, trial and error is both the decision process and a learning source.

While it is difficult to know a labour market, learning about it is a matter of reading signals in society such as the general level of employment, education trends and major changes in the birth rate. More important however, is to look closer to home at the local labour market and particularly at the rate of labour turnover, competitors' pay rates, the number of vacancies and the number of applicants per vacancy. It is also possible to survey local markets in various ways.

Adam Smith

It would be appropriate to begin with some older wisdom. For Smith, it wasn't just earning more money that made a job seeker choose a particular job, other things entered the equation:

- The agreeableness or disagreeableness of the work, the degree of hardship involved, the honourableness or dishonourableness.
- The easiness or difficulty of learning the job and its attendant cost.
- The degree of security or constancy of the employment.
- The degree of trust and responsibility in the job.
- The probability of success in the job.

According to Smith, all these factors influenced the price of labour because they influenced the decision maker. Carrying no psychological baggage, these ideas have a timeless common sense about them.

Smith, A. (1976), *Wealth of Nations*, Chapter 10, Penguin edn.

Despite the problem of imperfect information, it would be wrong to assume that managers do not have any control over the labour market because they do. For a start, although all organizations are involved in the national labour market, what counts to the health of the organization is the performance of its local labour market and the particular segments of it that are salient. What arbitrates the size of these markets is the degree of specialization of the organization. If the skills required are very specific to the organization, then there is a choice between fishing in a small pond or doing a lot of training. If the skills are generally held in the wider population, then the market will be larger and it is a case of trawling with a large net.

Notwithstanding the size of the labour markets, managers have at their disposal a wide range of tools for meeting the problems of labour markets, e.g. increasing pay, more training, altering hiring standards, promoting from within, plus many more. Increasing pay, for example, might not only attract more people, but may do so by extending the geographical limits of the local market by revaluing 'travel to work costs'.

Labour markets are always an unknown quality, but acceptance of that and a willingness to try to understand what is going on is essential to labour management. All manpower policies, but particularly those relating to recruitment and training are, to a large extent, dependent on labour market factors.

One concept central to labour markets is that of elasticity. It is necessary to understand the economic notion of elasticity. Quite simply, if pay is the driving force of the market, how responsive is the demand for labour to rises and falls in the rate of pay and how responsive is the supply of labour to rises and falls in the rate of pay? If, for example, we could obtain any amount of labour at one particular rate, then we would say that the supply of labour is perfectly elastic. If, however, we need to increase pay to get more labour then the supply of labour is, to a degree, inelastic. The graph in Figure 2.1 illustrates the point.

Understanding labour markets

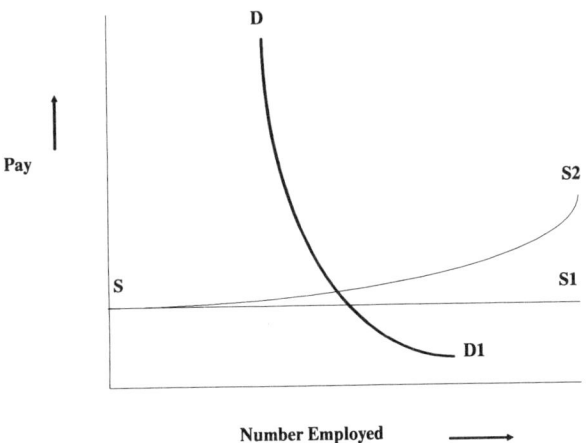

Figure 2.1

Here, pay is plotted against the number of workers – labour supply. The line S–S1 represents perfect elasticity. The line S–S2 represents a degree of inelasticity – in other words this line is responsive to pay. The demand for labour can be expressed in exactly the same terms, only this time the slope is from right to left, as more labour would be demanded at the lower price – line D–D1 represents a particular level of demand. You will have deduced from all this that the slope of the line represents the degree of elasticity.

Is recruitment related to labour turnover?

Having said that labour markets are slightly mysterious unknowable things, it will come as a pleasant surprise to know that there is one aspect of labour market behaviour that is universal enough to be predictable; so reliable in fact that it should enter all calculations of recruitment. What is this potent factor? Quite simply, it is the common sense notion that 'the longer a person stays in a job, the less likely he or she is to leave'. In reverse this reads 'a person is more likely to leave a job the shorter his or her period of service in that job'. The uncertainties of a job and surroundings are likely to be greater when a person first enters a job – does it meet expectations? It is in this early period that a person has a high propensity to leave. Conversely, the longer a person stays in a job the more comfortable it becomes; it begins to fit like an old overcoat.

This behavioural tendency has real significance for labour management because it unites *recruitment* with *labour turnover*. The golden rule is that the rate of each *rises and falls together with just a short time lag*. When recruitment goes up, so does labour turnover. This may astound. Surely when business is expanding people will want to stay? Maybe, but when business is expanding the proportion of new recruits with a high propensity to leave is higher than normal. Thus the number of leavers increases. Some examples of the significance of this will be helpful.

A case of expansion

Suppose a company needs to substantially increase its manpower in respect of one particular occupation. For years it has employed sixty in number and 20 per cent leave every year. Half of these vacancies are filled by promotion from a lower grade and the rest are made up by recruitment from the external labour market. The situation would be:

Existing staff	Labour turnover	Promotion	Recruitment
60	12	6	?

Let's leave the recruitment figure blank for a moment. If the company needed to expand, say, to ninety, then the question of recruitment and a recruitment budget become crucial. An obvious projection of what might be needed would be:

Existing staff	Labour turnover	Promotion	Recruitment	Target
60	12	6	36	90

But it would be wrong, because it assumes that the labour turnover percentage will remain at 20 per cent, when it will not. Expansion means recruiting more newcomers with a higher than normal propensity to leave. In reality, the company will have to recruit more than the thirty-six projected in order to achieve the target of ninety. The real situation might progress differently:

Existing staff	Labour turnover	Promotion	Recruitment	Target
60	25	6	49	90

The recruitment budget would need to be larger to be more realistic. To repeat, as recruitment rises so does labour turnover. It is equally important in a period of contraction.

A case of contraction

An organization wishes to reduce its staff. The plan is to reduce staff from 600 to 300 in five years. In order to do this the organization takes the decision to use only 'natural wastage', estimating that as labour turnover runs at 10 per cent per annum, if they stop recruitment that will reduce the numbers down to roughly the number required – 354. The policy of 'natural wastage' simply lets those who want to leave or retire do the reducing – it is a popular policy. This is perfectly understandable – no one likes making people redundant and it always appears to be an easy option. The question arises, however, of whether it is realistic simply to stop recruitment.

The first objection is that natural wastage occurs indiscriminately, so that parts of the organization will be desperately short, while others will be overstaffed. Unless the organization has considerable occupational flexibility the policy will break down under the pressure of simply keeping the organization going.

However, the second objection is equally powerful. If we apply the relationship between recruitment and labour turnover, it will be obvious that when recruitment has been stopped the rate of labour turnover will decline, because the workforce will simply be getting older in their jobs. Table 2.1 represents a 'length of service' profile of the organization at the start of the period.

Table 2.1

Length of service in years	No. of employees	LT (%)	Actual LT
0–1	150	16	24
1–2	120	13	15
2–3	100	10	10
3–4	130	6	8
4–5	60	5	3
5+	40	5	2
	600		62
			(10.3%)

As recruitment has been stopped the rate of labour turnover will progressively decline. Table 2.2 shows the annual reduction.

Table 2.2

Year	No. of employees	Leaves	Turnover (%)
1990	600	62	10.3
1991	538	44	8.1
1992	494	27	5.4
1993	467	25	5.3
1994	442	23	5.2
1995	419	–	–

The result of 419 is nowhere near what is required.

The point being made in both these cases is that as there is a relationship between the rate of recruitment and the rate of labour turnover this has to be built into manpower planning. In an area of great uncertainty, this relationship represents a valuable aid to realistic planning and budgeting. In fact, it is possible to go further here – the relationship is so important that it infiltrates, in some way, almost every aspect of human resource management.

The idea of internal labour markets

While the conventional wisdom argues that in the external labour market skills are distributed by the price of labour, there may be completely different rules at work within the organization. These rules are known as the internal labour market.

The concept of the internal labour market is based on the idea that sets of rules and conventions form within organizations which act as allocative mechanisms governing the movement of people and the pricing of jobs. Such rules are about promotion criteria, training opportunities, pay differentials and the evaluation of jobs, but most importantly, they are about which jobs are 'open' to the external labour market. It is the concept of openness which represents the interface between what goes on inside the organization and the external labour market.

Management have a choice as to what rules they use to govern internal affairs, but should they choose not to use rules then they open up their organization to the influence of the external labour market. Like everything else, it is a question of degree. It is possible to envisage two extremes – a strong and a weak internal labour market. Figure 2.2 illustrates the dimensions of an internal labour market.

Strong	**Weak**
Structural features	*Structural features*
• Specified hiring standards	• Unspecified hiring standards
• Single port of entry	• Multiple ports of entry
• High skill specificity	• Low skill specificity
• Continuous on-job training	• No on-job training
• Fixed criteria for promotion and transfer	• No fixed criteria for promotion and transfer
• Strong workplace customs	• Weak workplace customs
• Pay differentials remain fixed over time	• Pay differentials vary over time

Figure 2.2 *Dimension of internal labour markets*

It is important to add that the appellations strong or weak, are purely descriptive; there is nothing intrinsically meritorious about 'strong' or pejorative about 'weak'. The question arises as to why managers should direct their policies in a particular direction. The arguments in favour of a strong internal labour market revolve around the benefits of stability.

There are three basic conditions which promote the formation of strong internal labour markets; all are concerned with stability. First, and above all, such markets are likely to form where the technological process decrees that skills in the organization are very specific to that organization. The effect of this is to throw the burden of training on the organization, because at best, the external labour market can only provide a generalized or approximate capability.

Second, where the type of skills lend themselves to being learnt more easily and cheaply by on-the-job training, the burden of training is taken up by existing employees. Hence management will need stability.

Third, where jobs are not easily definable and output not yet open to exact measurement, or where discretion and judgement by employees are unavoidable, then custom and practice with its continuity becomes important. Here again, stability is a desirable state. In these circumstances, in addition to the intrinsic benefits of stability, management also make gains through reduced labour turnover and recruitment costs, together with efficient and cheaper training. For the workforce there is greater job security, open promotion channels, better training opportunities and pay enhanced by training responsibilities.

Such cosiness could be upset by the external labour market supplying better and cheaper people. Basically, if it could it would. It is only when it simply cannot, because the skills needed are so organization specific, that internal labour markets become dominant.

If all these benefits are going to be realized, then it is essential for a strong internal labour market to keep the external labour market out of the picture. If every job in the organization is a 'port of entry', i.e. open to outsiders and there are no hiring criteria, then the organization is totally 'open' to the outside world. Conversely, if ports of entry are restricted to a few jobs and strict hiring standards applied, then the organization is fairly 'closed' to the vagaries and caprice of the external labour market.

Once entry is restricted, then allocation of people and skills within the organization is based on the training capacity of existing resources and on rational progressions strongly related to the technological process. In other words, with restricted and controlled entry the organization can build on the job progressions and promotion sequences based on technological and functional priorities, both arranged with suitable incentives. As long as technological priorities remain the same we would expect to find pay differentials remaining fixed over time.

If, on the other hand, an organization does not need the benefits of a stable workforce, then the merits of a weak internal labour market become apparent. These merits include granting a degree of flexibility of response to fluctuations in demand, a strong emphasis on training the unskilled and the injection of new blood.

If the problem is to assess an organization on the strong–weak dimension, an obvious clue would be the rate of labour turnover. If internal labour markets are about restricting the power of the external, or about 'locking' employees into a bureaucratic employment relationship, we would expect to find low rates of labour turnover associated with strong internal labour markets and high with weak. This, however, can only be a rough indication. Basically, there are five areas of measurability: the specificity of selection criteria; the degree of openness; the extent of on-the-job training; the rate of internal promotions; and the fixity of pay differentials over time. This information could be collected directly using a variety of methods. It is also possible to collect data on management practices in relation to manpower as these are linked to the 'rules' existing in the internal labour market. The rationale for this is that, in theory, management have a complete range of options open to them with respect to the external market, such as:

- Alter pay and conditions.
- Alter hiring standards.
- Alter training policies.
- Use overtime and other forms of increased labour supply.
- Alter promotion criteria.
- Extend ports of entry redesign jobs.

There are others, but the point here is that choosing to foster a strong labour market may subsequently constrain management's use of these alternative options. In this way, management behaviour at the interface of two labour markets is a good general indicator of the character of the organization's internal labour market.

Summary

The intention has been to introduce some basic ideas about labour markets in order for the reader to understand the anatomy of hotel and catering labour markets which follows in the next chapter. Of particular relevance will be the notion of elasticity and the concept of internal labour markets.

3 An anatomy of hotel and catering labour markets

Introduction

If you were lost in a dense forest of pine trees, which would you prefer to have – a compass or knowledge of the maximum width of the forest? The first would keep you on a straight line, but the second would be more reassuring and comforting, because it would define the limits of your problems. It is the big picture which really helps. The purpose here is to paint a portrait of a labour market in such a way as to show how its economic imperatives and technical imperatives are integrated by structures and behavioural patterns.

The mere fact that we can speak of a hotel and catering labour market means that in some way the market has been defined. Usually markets are defined by a set of skills represented by occupations and supplied to particular organizations. In the case of the hotel and catering market, the market itself is fairly conspicuous. You don't have to be in it to recognize certain obvious features, such as:

- A fairly large proportion of unskilled occupations.
- The transferability of skills at any level between a broad range of hotel and catering establishments.
- Often, but not invariability, high levels of labour turnover.
- Low levels of pay, particularly for unskilled work.

These four features are not unconnected. A large proportion of unskilled or semi-skilled occupations means that these jobs are connected to the general unskilled labour market. Because they can be learnt quickly on the job, such jobs are available to the unskilled workforce. Parts of that unskilled workforce will not be permanently attached to the labour market at all. In other words, hotel and catering recruitment is not just concerned with competing with other firms, it is also a matter of inducing people into the labour market from domestic life. The effect of the unskilled nature of the work is to create a surplus supply, which in turn has the result of depressing the rate of pay.

The fact that a cook can ply his or her trade in a hotel, a restaurant, a pub, a hospital, a school, an industrial canteen, a ship or anywhere else that might need cooking, and the fact that such a cook may perform anywhere between the highest and lowest levels of this skill, means that such a person would have a wide range of establishments in which to look for work. In other words, he or she could transfer their skills widely, but only within the hotel and catering industry. Such a person would have to retrain to enter the building industry, for example. What all this means, is that hotel and catering skills are specific to a particular industry and in such circumstances we expect to find mobility mainly *within* the hotel and catering industry with mobility into and out of the industry confined to unskilled jobs and to questions of attachment to the labour market itself. Broadly speaking, this is what we find.

As pay is deemed to be the market mechanism, analysis of any labour market must focus on explaining the general level of pay. However, in the case of the hotel and catering industry we have a market very clearly determined by a set of skills, therefore the task of describing the market mechanism is mainly one of explaining *how the pay structure and skill structure integrate*. The purpose will be to identify and differentiate the behaviour of the market participants, that is both employers and workers, and then to explain the measurable activities of the market itself, such as: pay levels, pay differentials, patterns of mobility and market segmentation.

What follows is an attempt to build a model which will meet this requirement. It is founded on the identification of three major influences on the market. These are:

- The nature of the skills involved – a skill model.
- The constantly fluctuating nature of consumer demand.
- The existence of market segmentation, founded upon social and unsocial hours of work.

The nature of the skills involved – a skill model

The construction of a skill model is in three stages, each with its attendant problems. The first stage is actually to describe and differentiate skills. The problems here are:

- Hotels employ a large range of occupations and skills.
- Occupational titles only describe a type of skill, not a level of skill. The term 'cook' conveys only an activity.
- Skill levels overlap other sectors of the industry.
- The problem of drawing a line between what is skilled and unskilled.

The difficulty is to unhinge the concept of skill from the mask of occupation. To do this, an occupational classification has to be represented by a skill classification. The work of the UK Hotel and Catering Industry Training Board is helpful here. They used a skill classification of four tiers, which were:

- Managerial
- Supervisory
- Craft
- Operative

Accepting that managing and supervising are skilled activities, the difficulty comes in separating craft from operative. The HCITB use craft qualifications to define craft. Thus, vocational qualifications in cooking, silver service waiting, wine waiting and reception determined the craft category. Here, the distinction used is very similar, i.e. that craft represents skilled, and operative semi-skilled and unskilled. The distinction between skilled and unskilled is that skill requires some form of formal training or education and cannot be solely learnt by on-the-job training. Consequently, unskilled implies that work can be learnt solely on the job.

The second stage is to estimate the proportion of skilled to unskilled per unit. There are two questions here. First, are there occupations that vary in their classification of skilled or unskilled by the type of establishment? Second, does the proportion of skilled to unskilled vary?

The place to start here is with the occupational structure of establishments. Table 3.1 is an example of the occupational structure of a hotel and an institutional catering establishment (industrial, hospital, school etc.). There are, of course, other sectors of the industry, but these two are always present and are always large sectors.

Table 3.1

Hotel	Proportion (%)	Institutional establishment	Proportion (%)
Managers	7	Managers	7
Chefs	12	Chefs	18
Kitchen hands	8	Kitchen hands	28
Waiter/ess	21	Counter hands	15
Bar	13	Waiter/ess	12
Hotel porter	6	Cashiers	3
Housekeeping supervisor	2	Other	2
Maid	12		
Reception	8		
Clerical	2		
Cleaning	3		
Maintenance	6		
Other	2		

Source: Knight, I. B. (1971), *Patterns of Labour Mobility in the Hotel and Catering Industry*, HCITB.

In respect of the first question, is it possible to pick out which occupations might vary in skill status by type of establishment? Some reasonable assumptions are necessary here.

If we assume that managers and supervisors are skilled, what of the others? The candidate for the category 'sometimes skilled' are chefs and waiters. It would depend on the class of establishment. Receptionists are more likely to be skilled, irrespective of the class of establishment. The rest could be allocated to the unskilled or semi-skilled category, which equates in our classification to operative. Accepting that there must be exceptions, the guiding principle for the skill model is that the occupations which can vary between operative and craft classifications are chefs and waiter/ess. Table 3.2 is a summary of how the HCITB resolved the conversion of occupational structure into skill classifications. They used five sectors of the UK industry here, three are reproduced.

Table 3.2

	Hotel (%)	Restaurant (%)	Industrial catering (%)
Management	5	15	7
Supervisory	9	6	8
Craft	20	27	17
Operative	66	52	68

Source: HCITB (1984), *Research Report: Manpower Flows in the Hotel and Catering Industry*, Table 1, p. 5.

Thus an estimated model of the skill composition of a unit might be as shown in Figure 3.1.

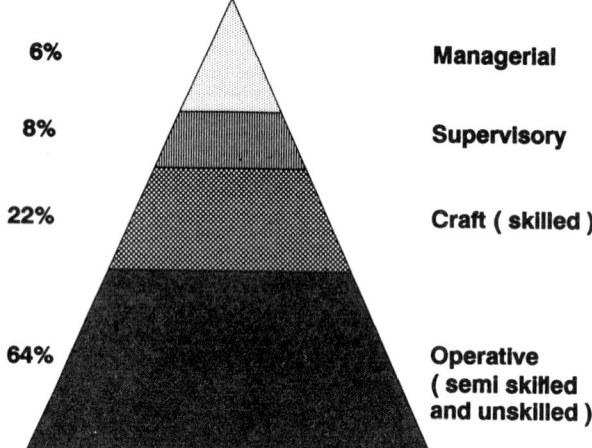

Figure 3.1

The question which is yet unresolved is – do the proportions vary with size of unit? Again, some reasonable assumptions are necessary here. There is a prima facie case for saying that the skill proportions don't change with size. Surely as hotels get bigger they need more unskilled maids, but larger hotels tend to have more function rooms and higher levels of service creating more chefs and every housewife knows more elaborate cooking means more washing up! In this way, skill breeds unskilled work. It would not be taking too much licence to say that the skill proportions are linear and like a nest of Russian matryoshka dolls, they are the same whatever the size.

What the proportion triangle doesn't capture is that there must be graduations of skill within the skill category. The third stage, therefore, is to conceive the industry as a hierarchy of units with the same skill proportions but with the absolute value of skill rising as the hierarchy ascends.

While it is perfectly legitimate to analyse the industry by its component sections such as hotels, restaurants, industrial catering, hospitals etc., what has to be realized is that each of these contains a hierarchy of standards representing a range of customer or contract spending. To simplify matters, the industry can be visualized in two broad components – on the one hand, hotels and restaurants and on the other, all forms of institutional catering. This division emphasizes different forms of commercial trading but, perhaps more important to the market, different demands on labour in terms of working hours. Figure 3.2 represents the industry skill structure. The pyramid for the hotel and restaurant sector is taller than for the institutional sector on the assumption that the higher end of the price range demands the highest standard of skills.

This model assumes that the mobility pattern is in three streams; unskilled entrance at all levels, skill is accumulated by mobility up the pyramids and a movement of skilled labour from hotels and restaurants to institutional catering. This mobility pattern is founded on certain crucial assumptions about the capacity of units to train. In terms of capacity of any one establishment, we assume that:

- Every establishment has an *upper limit to its capacity to teach*. Standards are for guests

An anatomy of hotel and catering labour markets 19

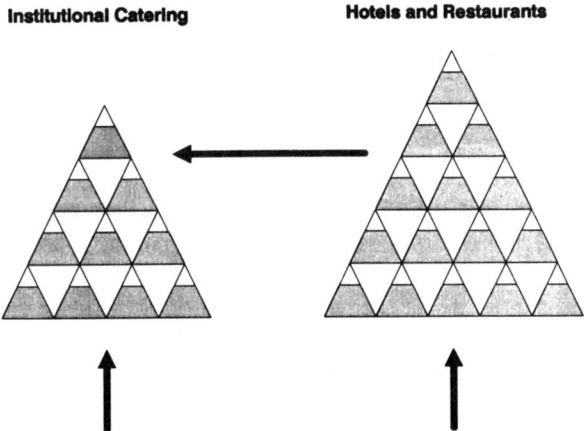

Figure 3.2

not staff, and they do not change overnight. Any movement upwards tends to be gradual. Once the skills have been mastered, further acquisition must be through moving to an establishment with higher standards.
- Although skills are transferable, there are barriers within the establishment to changing occupations. A waiter cannot simply change to a receptionist, a receptionist cannot become a cook etc. This *occupational rigidity* is not solely confined to the skilled occupations.
- Every establishment has a capacity to undertake on-the-job training and formal training to cope with the influx of unskilled and semi-skilled people.

It has also been assumed that there exists two labour markets segmented into one which works the same hours as the general population and one which works different hours. These are termed social and unsocial hours markets. This is subject to cultural variations, but what is important here is that if it is assumed that both markets offer the same pay and are in other respects the same, one has an advantage in hours. If Figure 3.2 is correct, people can transfer from hotels and restaurants to institutional catering without loss of material benefit, depending on the pay differentials between the two sectors. Given the circumstances of a hierarchy of establishments and an alternative market with social hours, it follows that:

- Individuals in the craft, supervisory and managerial categories seeking to learn will use the hierarchy of establishments to acquire more and higher skills.
- Skilled individuals will sometimes work at levels below their skill capacity.

The contribution of the skill model is that it puts forward enabling conditions which create pressures to be mobile such as:

1 The transferability of skills across all sectors of the industry.
2 The non-transferability of skills across occupational boundaries.
3 The 'skill pyramid' structure of the industry offering mobility as a means of skill acquisition.
4 On-the-job training capacity.

5 The existence of a top limit to the capacity for skill and knowledge learning in each unit.
6 The opportunity to work at below the maximum skill level without loss of material benefit.

Thus, for both the individual wishing to acquire skills and the individual looking to use less of their skill, mobility offers a means.

So far, the emphasis has been on the skilled, but before we conclude the skill model, some discussion is required on the nature of the unskilled work. It is one thing to say that as the unskilled proportion is the greater the industry will always have a surplus supply because it is connected to the general unskilled labour market and can quickly train people, but is quite another to actually get them. Three aspects of hotel and catering unskilled work are important here:

- Unskilled jobs are not machine minding, they are a bundle of low level tasks which, no matter how menial, require a degree of self-organization.
- The effort and character of individuals actually counts in performance, therefore there will be individual differences in performance.
- Productivity does not depend on job tenure to any large degree.

The skill model and pay

The influence of the skill model on pay is as follows:

- The higher proportion of unskilled job tends to create a surplus supply which depresses rates of pay.
- Competition is encouraged by the hierarchical skill structure and by the fact that individual attributes actually count.
- The skill structure encourages mobility.
- As productivity does not depend on job tenure, there is no incentive to reward long service.
- The existence of alternative markets, with different hours of work, allows workers to trade off skill and hours.

By far the most important of these influences is the encouragement of a surplus of supply by the unskilled nature of the work. This has significance for both managerial and market behaviour. If the surplus keeps pay down, then it is *always in the interests of managers to de-skill*. If there is always a surplus, then supply will be elastic. Figure 3.3. illustrates the probable relationship between supply and demand in the hotel and catering industry.

In Figure 3.3 supply is considered to be very elastic but demand fairly inelastic. The thought here is that only in the long run would more people be employed the lower the pay. However, if the large picture is substituted by a portrait of a single unit, differences appear.

An anatomy of hotel and catering labour markets 21

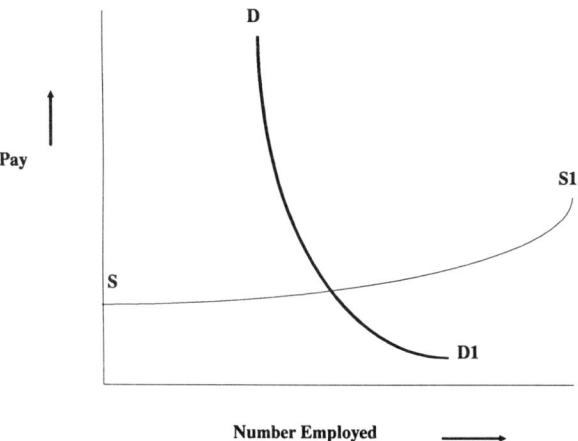

Figure 3.3

The constantly fluctuating nature of consumer demand

It is a universal characteristic of hotels that there will be short-term variations in demand. This produces the need to make adjustments in short-term labour supply if labour costs are to be controlled. This aspect is portrayed in Figure 3.4.

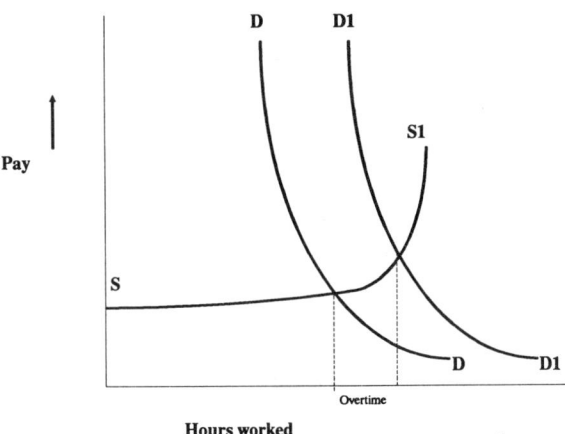

Figure 3.4

Figure 3.4 represents one establishment. The demand increases from D–D to D1–D1 for just one day.

Just as in the macro picture, the supply of labour is elastic, but only up to the point where a small surge is required by the pattern of demand. When this happens, managers increase labour supply by a variety of means such as overtime, employing casuals and bonus payments. In other words, extra supply is responsive to pay at the micro level. By making these adjustments at the micro level through pay incentives, the general supply of labour during normal hours of work is unhinged from the influence of pay. Thus only part of total earnings actually fluctuates with demand. We are left with a supply side which is still very elastic.

When business fluctuates, the commonest approach is to set up a buffer consisting of part-time workers, casuals, overtime and bonus incentives. Productivity is essentially the management of labour supply.

We will consider now the skill model and the nature of consumer demand together. It has been suggested that the proportion of unskilled work is responsible for surplus supply which depresses the level of pay and that the need for short-term adjustment shows the same direction of influence. However, they are not discrete concepts – they work together. As it is easier to adjust the supply of unskilled labour to that of skilled, it is always in the interests of management to de-skill. The ever-present fluctuation in customer demand creates an ever-present incentive to de-skill. De-skilling does not necessarily mean replacement with a machine. It can mean simply a change of work practice, e.g. silver service to a buffet.

Demand fluctuations on the organization

Given the need for flexibility, a high proportion of unskilled labour and transferable skills, what kind of organization does this produce?

The most powerful motive for constructing a strong internal labour market is to retrain staff, because their skills are unique to your organization. We have seen already that skills are transferable across the industry. Therefore, there is no real incentive to do so. Why go to all the trouble of constructing the left-hand side of Figure 2.2 if the largest proportion of your staff are unskilled and you need numerical and pay flexibility?

Are there any circumstances which would induce managers to go for retention and a strong internal labour market? One speculation is important to this question. If managers could achieve functional flexibility, by which is meant that people can easily change their job within the unit, then that would lessen the need for numerical flexibility and it would be worth retaining these multiskilled staff. Alas, one of the most conspicuous features of hotel and catering life is functional or occupational rigidity. People change jobs only by changing employer. There are perfectly legitimate reasons for this, it takes time to train people into an occupation.

Surely the skilled are worth retaining? The problem here is that the skilled are necessary and important, but they are in a minority and it is very difficult to operate two management strategies in the same unit. This task is made even harder if the unskilled can become the skilled in the same unit. One of the strange ironies of weak internal labour markets is that the very absence of any specific criteria for promotion often leads to a high rate of promotion from workers to supervisors. This is the case with the hotel and catering industry. However, the most pressing case against building a personnel policy around the skilled instead of the unskilled, is that the unskilled produce more revenue and profit. Think of how many meals a skilled chef has to cook to make the same revenue or profit that a room cleaner can make by cleaning rooms for eight hours!

Although all the evidence points to hotel and catering organizations running weak internal labour markets, there are circumstances where a case could be made for strong markets. Three further circumstances make such a case: where there is no variation in consumer demand; a genuine skill shortage; and where considerable time is needed to train the unskilled. It is well worth noting that it is all too easy to label a job unskilled. It may still need a considerable amount of training and experience.

Weak internal labour markets and vocational education

The skill model presents a conflict over who teaches skills. The argument is that the interests of the unit are to de-skill while the interests of the industry as a whole are to maintain and enhance its qualitative capacity. Weak internal labour markets in a unit throw the responsibility for teaching skills on to individuals who use mobility around the hierarchical structure and vocational education.

The relationship between the industry and vocational education is focused at one point – junior management and supervisor level. If units are promoting from within, the rate needed to induce unskilled workers to learn more and take responsibility, becomes the rate at which the products of vocational education enter industry. This rate, formed by internal pressures, may not be sufficient to induce people to undertake vocational training. In other words, people building careers on the job compete with those using vocational qualifications to start their careers, and the level of pay that arbitrates this relationship is umbilically linked to the rate for unskilled staff.

It would follow from this that the influence on managerial pay would be the output of vocational education and the rate of promotion from unskilled to skilled.

Market segmentation

One thing is obvious, everybody working is not in the same market. If they were, then everyone could move into any job which is clearly not true. There are many divisions within the overall labour market and it is worthwhile seeing these divisions so that we can understand patterns of mobility and recruitment opportunities and constraints.

So far, the emphasis of this analysis has been on what goes on in the unit and this is an appropriate starting point to understand segmentation in the actual labour market. Already we have suggested that there are two types of job in the unit – skilled and unskilled. This division suggests that the market may have a dual character with a primary and a secondary sector. Primary markets are usually described as requiring education, having careers and being well paid in contrast to secondary markets which contain jobs not careers, low levels of attachment, plenty of mobility and low pay. This picture does not quite fit the hotel and catering industry, but there are certainly two markets.

The skill model suggests a hierarchy of skills within the unit and a hierarchy of units. In such circumstances one would expect the skilled to be paid more than the unskilled in each unit and the skilled to be paid more the higher the unit in the hierarchy. The factor which determines the pay differentials between skilled staff is the level of service, that is the level of skill demanded by the customers' ability to pay. This factor is crucial to understanding the relationship between the two markets. If, for some reason, customers demand a lower quality product, then the skills required would be less. This would tempt management to de-skill the job which means that they would then recruit in the lower, cheaper secondary market. In other words, the proportional size of the two markets is dependent on the tastes and ability to pay of customers.

By far the strongest influence on segmentation is the functional or occupational rigidity within the unit. While most skilled jobs require a period of training and it is, therefore, reasonable for people to want to recoup their investment by staying in the occupation. What is surprising is that occupational rigidity also applies to unskilled jobs. The effect of this is to make those who want to change their occupation compete in the external market where there is likely to be a surplus supply anyway. It simply keeps people in one job type.

The important question of the division of the market by social hours has already been discussed, but its contribution is mainly in inducing mobility. There are three major ways in which hotel and catering labour markets can be segmented as shown in Figure 3.5.

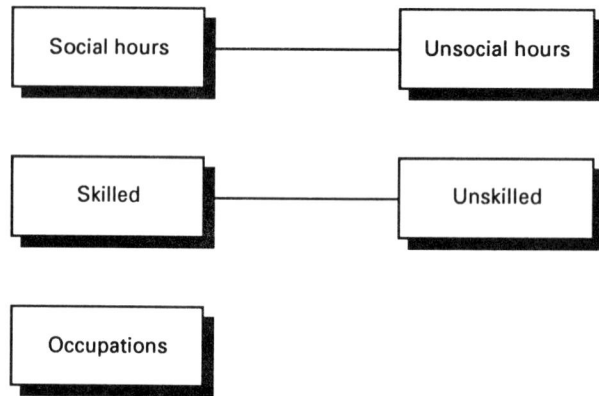

Figure 3.5

Finer graduations of these divisions and their practical implications will be discussed in Chapter 16 on recruitment.

Summary

In summary, it would be appropriate to identify clearly the influences on the rate of pay and pay differentials (Figures 3.6 and 3.7).

- The likelihood of a surplus supply caused by the high proportion of unskilled labour required.
- The need for short-term adjustment in labour supply connecting earnings rather than pay to demand.
- The ample opportunities available to de-skill labour with or without technological substitution.
- The opportunity to use mobility to accumulate skills.
- The supply of skilled labour from vocational education.
- The transferability of skills between sectors of the industry with different employment conditions.
- As productivity is not related to job tenure, there is no incentive to reward long service.
- Promotion opportunities is an alternative reward system to pay.

Figure 3.6 *Influences on the rate of pay*

- Levels of service – pay differentials are created by skill differentials which follow directly from levels of service demanded by consumers.
- Functional or occupational rigidity – apparently operating for both skilled and unskilled labour. If there is a weak internal labour market people are forced out on to the external market where segmentation reinforces the differentials.
- For all types of work, personal effort and character actually count producing individual differences.
- Different training and education duration for different occupations.

Figure 3.7 *Influences on pay differentials*

One thing is clear from the analysis of pay influences and the skill model and that is that *the economic interests of each unit conflict with the overall skill needs of the industry*. It has been argued that in all but a few circumstances it is in the interests of management to form weak internal labour markets. That being so, skill development is left to either vocational education or mobility around the hierarchically-structured units.

Figure 3.8 conceptualizes the motives for forming a type of internal labour market and the consequent effect on the external labour market.

Influence towards weak ILM
- Fluctuating consumer demand.
- High proportion of unskilled workers.
- Surplus supply of unskilled workers.

Influence towards strong ILM
- Skill shortage created by consumer demand (de-skilling not an option).
- High proportion of skilled to unskilled workers.
- Long duration for unskilled training.

Consequent behavioural characteristics of ELM
- High labour turnover.
- Skills accumulation mobility.
- Wide distribution of pay.
- Dependency on vocational education for basic skills training.

Consequent behavioural characteristics of ELM
- Low labour turnover.
- Greater differential between skilled and unskilled labour.
- Low dependency on vocational education.
- Greater unionization.

Figure 3.8

4 Overtime and labour costs

It would be appropriate at this point to highlight a problem that stems directly from management's strategy towards the external labour market. When adjusting labour supply, of all the options open to management, perhaps the easiest to arrange is overtime – a couple of telephone calls and it is done. It is this very ease which makes overtime such a potentially dangerous commodity and one which management must keep control over. There are three basic dangers, especially when labour turnover is high. First, it can run out of control, second, it can undermine recruitment and third, it can undermine supervision and therefore the quality of the service.

The behavioural implications of overtime

The cause of this potentially disruptive power lies in the behavioural reaction of people who receive their overtime. Put simply, people like the enhanced earnings, but they get tired by the extra work, so they make a short-term adjustment in their method of doing the work. This short-term adjustment is relatively harmless unless it becomes a longterm adjustment and a cycle sets in. An example would help to illustrate the point.

A brigade of five chefs is reduced to four when one chef decides to leave. The pay system automatically grants premium pay, such as overtime, to the remaining four chefs. They have to work hard, but the thought of the extra pay compensates for that. If this situation persists, two things will happen. First, they will get used to the enhanced pay and second, they will find ways of readjusting their working practice to reduce their effort (short cuts). The effect of the latter is to make supervision harder and to put quality standards at risk. However, working together, more money and short cuts present a problem for recruitment. The longer the vacancy exists, the more the workers will get used to the extra pay and the more they will adapt their methods to cope with the pressure.

This means that any newcomer becomes a threat both to their earnings and to their new-found methods. In such circumstances, when a new recruit arrives he or she is not welcome, which may cause them to leave thus perpetuating the situation. This is the rejection effect of overtime. The person who has to bear the brunt of this cycle is the supervisor. The supervisor is having to cope with staff shortages and stem the temptation to lower standards.

A conceptual framework may help here. In Figure 4.1 the two circles represent the product market and the labour market.

The high fluctuation in demand in the product market and the volatility in the labour market both cause fluctuations in the demand for labour. In the case of increased labour supply the pay system automatically enhances earnings when effort needs to be increased. If more customers turn up or if there is a vacancy in the work department or if both occur, then the result will be a demand for more effort – more labour supply.

The point here is that because reward is automatic, it buys time for the recruitment function to do its job. The danger is that it allows *too much time*, time in fact for the

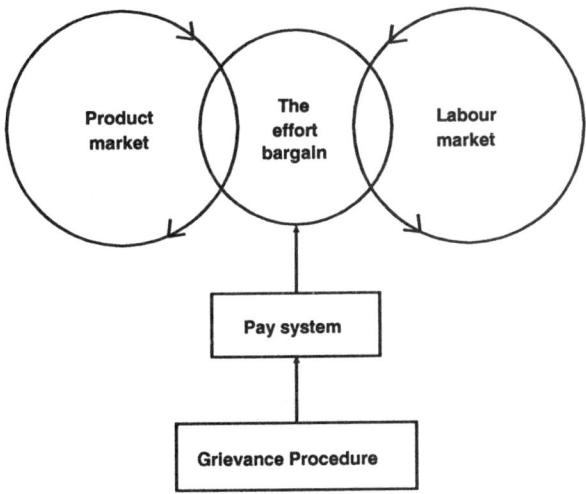

Figure 4.1

rejection effect to take place. The key element to managing overtime is rapid recruitment and the key measure for keeping control of overtime is not simply the amount of overtime given, but the number of vacancies *and their length*! The danger signals which tell when this kind of effect has taken hold, is when recruitment and labour turnover are declining but premium pay rising.

Labour costs and labour turnover

It has already been stated in Chapter 2 that recruitment and labour turnover rise and fall together with a small time lag. In which case it would be reasonable to assume that the associated costs would rise and fall in the same way. If, however, the effect of the behavioural ramifications of overtime are considered a slightly different possibility emerges. Labour turnover generates two types of cost which can get very confused – some costs come directly from the *rate of labour turnover* but others come from the *length of the vacancy*.

When it comes to the measurement of labour turnover costs, the conventional wisdom tends to be polarized. On the one hand, there is the comprehensive approach which tends to heap everything but the kitchen sink onto the rate of turnover. On the other hand, the simplistic approach merely measures the cost of recruitment. The rationale behind the comprehensive approach is not difficult to see. What better way to beat managers into doing something about their turnover than to present them with the 'real' costs. To this end, costs are estimated to include not just direct recruitment costs nor simply the cost of keeping the vacant job going but also the time and documentation of the personnel department, and the time and cost of training, added to which there is the supervisor's time, low productivity of newcomers, cleaning uniforms, even changing the sheets at the staff house, etc. Without wishing to be scornful, a little water needs to be poured on such 'realism' for while correct, such definitions are redundant in the sense that they offer no assistance in control. The basic criticisms of such methods are that many items would not vary with the rate of turnover. In other words, the decision to incur such costs is not solely a function of the rate of labour turnover (e.g. salary of personnel staff). Furthermore, even those items which do vary with the rate are too numerous for accounting to spend time collecting (e.g. documentation, uniform cleaning, etc.). This approach can get out of hand and become impractical.

At the other end of the spectrum is the simplistic method of only measuring direct recruitment costs (advertising, agencies, transfer costs, etc.). Apart from the merit of simplicity, when compared with actual rates of labour turnover it does give a rough guide to the efficiency of the recruitment function.

Notwithstanding the merits of either approach, they both assume that the result of their measurement is derived from the rate of labour turnover. As such, both are flawed, because they do not recognize that costs are derived from two separate sources: the cost of replacement, which springs directly from the recruitment–labour turnover relationship and the cost of meeting the workload that has been vacated. This can be called job continuity costs – that element of increased labour supply and therefore costs (overtime, premium pay, casual labour) which is attributable to labour turnover. What is important is that it is derived from the length of a vacancy not the rate of labour turnover. Figure 4.2 illustrates the different allocation of costs for both tangible and intangible items across the two forms of cost constituency.

	Derived from the rate of labour turnover	**Derived from job continuity**
Tangible costs	• Cost of recruitment • Cost of training • Documentation for recruitment • Documentation for training	• Premium Pay (overtime, bonuses, casual labour etc.)
Intangible costs	• Low productivity of newcomers • Time for recruitment • Time for training	• Short cuts • Lower standards • Supervisory problems

Figure 4.2

If it is accepted that there are two costs involved in labour turnover, the reason why they should be measured separately is based on the relationship between recruitment costs and the length of a vacancy. If the assumption is made that the more you spend on recruitment the shorter will be the length of the vacancy, then there is a direct trade off between the two types of cost. In these circumstances, as recruitment costs rise, job continuity costs decline. In this case, it is recruitment costs which are dictating job continuity costs. However, circumstances may arise when it is job continuity costs which drive both recruitment costs and the rate of labour turnover. To be precise, the circumstances in question are the behavioural implications of overtime described earlier.

Where staff have enjoyed enhanced earning from overtime or premium pay it is not uncommon to find that they reject newcomers because of the threat to their earnings.

Here, one would expect to find the rate of labour turnover, recruitment costs and job continuity costs all rising at the same time.

However, these circumstances can persist with the acquiescence of management who begin to 'get used to' job continuity costs and consequently undertake less recruitment and thus labour turnover goes down. It is in this sense that labour turnover costs could rise while labour turnover declines. Unless these two types of costs are measured separately, compared and separately compared with the rate of labour turnover, it is impossible to spot where the driving force is coming from. It is possible to suggest that when job continuity costs start to drive labour turnover and recruitment, management have lost a great deal of control. Management have a choice between the two types of costs at any rate of labour turnover requiring management to ask – which is the most expensive?

The temptation for management is to let job continuity cost run on because it saves money on the basic wage bill despite the premium pay. Against this has to be judged the cost to productivity and quality standards of employees working on permanent overtime. This kind of situation can 'creep up' on management. Labour turnover is declining, recruitment costs are going down, the wage bill is down and only overtime is up – all looks rosy. But it can get out of hand so quickly and so easily.

Part Two

People at Work

5 Stating the problem

The problem can be seen everywhere. Here a manager tries to persuade a worker to do something, there a manager issues a reprimand, another worries over the performance of a group, yet another listens to a gripe. Meanwhile, someone else is designing a new control system, while a colleague contemplates redesigning a form. They all have something in common. Everyone is making assumptions about how people will behave. Here then is 'the' problem. We cannot look into the feelings and motives of our workforce, we have to work with the only clue available – behaviour. Whether we are aware of it or not, in everything that we do we are constantly making assumptions of cause (what lies behind it) and deductions about consequences (what it will lead to). In other words, everything in management, even when it doesn't involve dealing with people, involves making assumptions about how people will behave. There are a few guiding stars – experience is certainly one – but theoretical knowledge is another. The heart of the problem is not merely the fact that you can only work from behaviour but also the *sheer complexity which lies behind that behaviour* – people are impossible to understand!

Are they? Well, yes and no. Remember there are limits to what you, as a manager, need to understand: you are not a psychiatrist. Within limits, people can be understood, but many people give up. For them, the human aspects of management are seen as 'impossible', since it is claimed that 'we are all different, anyway'.

This is the original sin of human resource management. A moment's thought, however, tells us that that statement is both true and false. We are all different, but it is plainly obvious that we are also the same. We all have, to varying degrees of efficiency, the same mental processes (motor drives, memory, cognitive mechanisms, reasoning processes etc.) and what is more, a great deal of our behaviour is in fact similar and predictable: social life would be intolerable were that not the case. The idea of 'common' behaviour is a helpful clue in attributing the cause of some behaviour we see.

Common behaviour is behaviour that recurs irrespective of the people involved and as such can be seen in various unconnected situations. If behaviour can be seen in various locations, at various times, involving different people and yet be essentially the same, we might assume that the cause of such behaviour could be something external to the participant rather than internal within them. We then must look for what that might be – a common situational variable. This is where experience comes into interpreting behaviour. If you've seen it all before with a different case, then some external factor is likely to be at work. A chef and a waiter having an argument at the hotplate can be seen everywhere. Speed versus quality conflict? Even if you don't fall for the original sin, there is another line of resistance and that is to keep it simple. It's natural but often wrong.

There are no universal principles of management in respect of managing people. If there were, we would all simply learn them and be good at it. Acceptance of this alone is the springboard for learning about the relationship between people and work. There is a difference between keeping it simple and being simplistic. No one can doubt that as managers get older they find an approach to people which 'works for them'. A kind of melding of authority with personality. This is natural and good but simplistic approaches are invariably wrong. This is not to say there aren't techniques which can be learnt and which will help managers in their tasks. There are, and some of them are addressed in Part Three of this book. After all, the management of people is not a tea and sympathy exercise and just because things are complex doesn't mean we shouldn't approach them with professional skill.

Perhaps a more attractive line of resistance to complexity lies in 'common sense'. Everybody has common sense theories about what makes themselves and others 'tick'. You will find that these are not too far adrift from the writings of eminent psychologists. Let's put theory into perspective.

The best way to see theory (your own or academic theory) is as a Sherpa. He will carry some of your bags and guide you up most of the mountain, but doesn't do the climbing for you and won't take you to the top. As there is no general theory of behaviour, it would be more realistic to see theories as a bunch of rather truculent Sherpas, each with their own ideas about best routes to the top, most of them at variance with each other. But they are necessary and helpful. Remember, the purpose of theory is to explain practice. The first thing you have to do when confronted with a theory is make sure you know what piece of behaviour it is supposed to be explaining.

If there are any golden rules, then being seen and taking in what is going on are essential for the understanding of your workforce. Not that the evidence of your own eyes is always helpful. What does a motivated person look like? Workers trooping round singing 'hi ho, hi ho, and off to work we go' is a somewhat rare occurrence. To make matters worse, the productive often 'look' lazy. It is not easy, but theory can help you to expand your understanding of your own perceptions of what is going on. To illustrate this, it is probably best to start with our own behaviour.

Theory can help us to understand situations and our own behaviour. This clarity can only aid our judgements and decisions by giving them a coherence and logic.

By way of illustration, let us take three incidents in the day of a hotel manager.

- A group of rugby players smash up the disco bar.
- A sous-chef and a waiter have a blazing row across the hotplate in the middle of service.
- A young man applying for a front office position appears to be very nervous at the interview.

Three discrete pieces of behaviour. For our purposes, you are the hotel manager. Are these incidents related? Is there some way that we could perceive these incidents in a coherent unified way? Our decision making, in these three situations including whether or not we make one, will depend on how we 'read' the situation. Part of that 'reading' of the situation is the key process of attributing the cause. We make assumptions about the cause of something (what lies behind it) and deductions about consequences (what it will lead to). Once made, an attribution gives direction to our thinking. In fact, we don't normally notice this process unless someone else disagrees with our assumed attribution. When there is a general consensus about the cause of something, this forms part of what we call common sense.

Attribution theory

In fact, the process of attribution rarely actually goes as far as seeking the *actual cause* of something instead it points out the *locus of cause*, i.e. where the cause lies. For our analytical convenience, we can map any behaviour into three aspects:

Actors – who took part.
Action – what happened.
Situation – what are the circumstances.

So in our incidents, we have:

Actors	*Action*	*Situation*
Rugby players	A fight	A disco bar, late at night
A chef and a waiter	A row	At the hotplate in the middle of service
An interviewer and an applicant	Fidgeting and stumbling over words	A selection interview

When confronted with these incidents we don't run through every possible explanation for what is in front of our eyes, we make our first cut – is it something *internal* to the actors or *external* to them? Is it something about the people or the situation? Simultaneously with this cut comes a process of generalization, bringing with it the possibility of suggesting either that all sorts of people do that or that that sort of behaviour occurs in other situations. The first generalizes across actors, the second across situations. These two types of generalization are called *consensus* and *distinctiveness* respectively. A third generalization is possible – one across time – that behaviour rarely happens or it always happens. This is called *consistency*. Thus, we can perceive an incident as having high/low consensus, high/low distinctiveness and high/low consistency depending on how we generalize, and in turn this will determine how we attribute. Some definitions will help.

Consensus   Means people behave in the same way in a particular situation. Thus high consensus means a generalization across actors – all sorts of people behave like that.

Distinctiveness   Means that people will not behave like this in other situations. Thus high distinctiveness means that the action is specific to the situation. Low distinctiveness means a generalization across situations so that this behaviour occurs in other situations.

The argument of attribution theory is that the way we generalize points us to an attribution which can either be *dispositional* (actor) attribution or *situational* attribution. To put it another way, internal or external.

If we say an incident is specific to the actor involved (low consensus) and say that this behaviour will occur in other situations (low distinctiveness) then we will make a *dispositional attribution*.

Returning to the three incidents, we might think we can make a dispositional attribution on the following lines:

Low consensus
- We don't get trouble with other groups of young men.
- Nobody else argues at the hotplate.
- Few people are nervous at interviews.

Low distinctiveness
- These rugby players cause trouble in all bars.
- Those two would fall out on a desert island.
- This young man would be nervous in all situations.

Thus, the behaviour results from – being rugby players, not getting on and being nervous. Nothing to do with being in a disco bar, at the hotplate in the middle of service, or being at an interview. Attributing in this way, we might think twice about accepting bookings from rugby clubs; knock the head of the chef and waiter together; and politely let the young man go.

If we say an incident could involve anybody (high consensus) but only in a particular situation (high distinctiveness) then we are likely to make a *situational attribution*.

So that we might think:

High distinctiveness	• Groups of young men always cause trouble in disco bars.
	• Most chefs and waiters argue at the hotplate.
	• Everybody is nervous at interviews.
High consensus	• Rugby players don't cause trouble elsewhere.
	• They get on well away from the hotplate.
	• He is not normally nervous.

Thus, the behaviour results from – something that happens in the bar; the chef wanting perfection, the waiter wanting it pronto, interviews being inherently intimidating.

If we attributed in this style, we might start thinking about our 'door policy' at the disco, we might just accept that chef/waiter conflict is constructive, and we might make changes in our interviewing style and give the young man the benefit of the doubt. It could, of course, be both. The locus of the cause could be dispositional and situational. Here we would expect low consensus and high distinctiveness.

Low consensus	• We don't get trouble from other groups of young men (low consensus).
High distinctiveness	• These rugby players don't cause trouble elsewhere (high distinctiveness).

Thus the trouble results from the fact that they were rugby players (who probably lost) and that they were in a bar (with something amiss). No more rugby groups? A relook at the door policy?

Sometimes either will do and it doesn't matter which. In this case, we would expect high consensus and low distinctiveness.

High consensus	• Groups of young men cause trouble in bars.
Low distinctiveness	• These rugby players cause trouble in any bar.

Thus it could be either that they are rugby players or that they are a group of young men.

To all of these alternatives is added the dimension of continuity. Continuity suggests the person normally behaves like this or does not normally behave in such a manner. If you are suspicious of the above because it is all too rational, you would be right. Attribution processes are subject to biases. These will strike a chord.

- *Self-serving bias* is the tendency to attribute desirable outcomes to oneself and undesirable ones to the situation.
- *Actor–observer* bias is the tendency of people in the action to explain it by the situation, whereas those outside attribute it to personal characteristics of the actors.

- *Fundamental attribute error* is the tendency to simply underestimate situational variables. In other words, the fault always lies with those involved, not in the situation they are in.

The principle at stake in attribution theory is that the direction of our attribution of causes is a result of the way we generalize. The practical point here is that the way we attribute directs our consequent thinking. It defines the area of our decision making – not taking bookings from rugby clubs and altering your 'door policy' are very different consequences following from different attributions. The point being made is that theory is relevant and can help us to self-awareness of our own behaviour.

6 Start Monday – the manager–worker relationship

Almost everyone at some time has been surprised by someone they thought they knew well – a close friend perhaps. 'That's not like them', 'That's out of character', are the kind of sentiments that follow. Yet the possibility exists that whatever our friend has done may be perfectly in character, it is only that our assumptions and expectations of them were wrong. All relationships have a taken for granted element to them. Things are not said, just understood to be so. The manager–worker relationship is like any other in this respect.

The moment at an employment interview when the manager says 'start Monday' and the applicant says 'OK' is the moment when a relationship begins between a manager and a worker. From that moment on it becomes 'necessary' for each to have an opinion of the other. From that moment, each will influence the other's behaviour. Of course they are not equal, but nevertheless, each will affect the other's behaviour. As soon as the 'OK' is spoken, a psychological contract has been made which will change as the relationship develops but will last until one of the parties leave.

The psychological contract usually referred to in behavioural science as the labour contract (note – nothing to do with employment contract) has two principal dimensions which are:

- Effort – reward
- Obedience – discipline

The so-called effort, bargain and authority relations. How much effort do I put in for the expected reward? Which orders do I obey? How conditional is my willingness? How much discipline will I accept? These are the trade offs and balances that form the heart of the contract – they are universal but they exist for the most part in the realm of private thought rather than explicit behaviour. To see the importance of this, it is perhaps best to start at the beginning.

The original bargain is struck at the selection interview. The interviewer tries to assess the capacity of the interviewee in terms of effort and general willingness. The applicant's past record and references help in this process. The interviewee is trying to assess what is going to be required of them in terms of effort and obedience and whether or not it is worth the reward being offered. Both are really fishing and dealing in imprecise quantities. The agreement they finally make is, at that 'start Monday' point, very imprecise. Like anything which is imprecise, it is open to misinterpretation and is, as any agreement, potentially unstable. What keeps a psychological contract stable is the mutuality of the assumptions that lie behind it. If the amount of effort expected by the interviewer is the same as that anticipated by the interviewee, then that part of their relationship is stable. If they aren't the same, it is potentially unstable. This does not mean that it will necessarily lead to manifest conflict, because assumptions can be adjusted.

Suppose on Monday morning the worker finds the job harder than he/she anticipated, but the manager less severe than expected. Similarly, the manager finds the worker less skilled and slower than thought, but seems more willing than he/she expected. It could lead to conflict, but it could simply be a case of adjusted assumptions on both sides. If the latter occurs, then what both have done is simultaneously and secretly adjusted their contract. They will go on adjusting expectations of each other as long as the relationship exists.

At this point, it is worth taking a rain-check. Surely the role of personnel management in the selection process is to make everything explicit and precise? True, but it can never entirely succeed. In other words, the labour contract is always and everywhere, but to a varying degree, imprecise. To understand this, it is necessary to look again at what is being exchanged in the initial bargain. On the one hand, the employer is buying an unspecified potential and the employee is taking on an indeterminate amount of work. Good interviewing practice, job descriptions, previous experience of the same work and clear references can all help to make the assumptions of the parties more precise and mutual, but a job description cannot describe what effort will be required and therefore at the point of agreement even the tangible wage offered becomes subjectively evaluated. This is why, despite good personnel practice, the agreement is always imprecise.

There are, however, degrees of imprecision which are determined by the nature of the technological process in which the job exists. In other words, some jobs make for very imprecise labour contracts and other jobs attract more precise contracts and the determinant of both is the nature of the job itself and how far management can apply formal controls. To illustrate this, it is helpful to contrast two jobs of widely differing technological mode. Suppose we have a job of pencil sharpener. A person sits at a lathe all day and picks up a pencil, runs the end across the lathe and places it in a box. Management could do a pretty good description of this simple task. They would specify the number to be sharpened per hour, the tolerances of the point and the number of breakages allowed. All this could be discussed at the selection interview to make things explicit. Contrast this with the job of a waiter. All the usual conditions such as hours of work, shift times etc. can be specified. The person is supposed to look smart and give good service. While it is possible to specify smartness, it is much harder to say what good service is. It is possible to lay down specific routines for the customer–service interaction, but the only person who can justify whether or not it is good, is the guest. Management don't have the same degree of control.

What is being said here is that different jobs imply a different form of managing the people who do those jobs. Where the job allows management to measure the output precisely they will use formal controls, but where the output standards can only be specified subjectively other forms of managerial control become necessary. An illustration may help here. Figure 6.1 represents two jobs of contrasting technological mode. The shaded area represents the degree to which management can lay down formal standards and use measure as controls.

Notice that every job, no matter how precise the contract, has an element which cannot be laid down.

With care and caution and with respect to generalization, it is suggested that automated mass production industry work produces fairly precise labour contracts with tight formal management control, but service industries contain many jobs where very imprecise labour contracts exist and consequently more informal control processes

JOB A	JOB B
Fairly precise control	Very imprecise control

Formal control	Normative control
Set quantity and quality standards	Vigilance, example and group norms
Performance measured against	

Figure 6.1

are needed. It follows that labour management in manufacturing and in service industries is a different task. The argument here is that the more imprecision the greater will be the significance of the labour contract to the manager–worker relationship. What this actually means, is that more of the relationship will be based on assumptions and unspoken understanding rather than overt control measures.

The covert side of the manager–worker relationship

One of the traps that managers so often fall into is to use the satisfaction–dissatisfaction frame of reference as the principal method of interpreting employee behaviour. It is important, but it is not the sole frame of reference available. There are other ways of seeing.

What the notion of the labour contract tells us is that as the relationship is based on unspoken assumptions, much of what is so important is actually secret. The nature of these assumptions can only become manifest by being triggered by some behavioural event. For example, suppose that A, B and C work for you all with apparent satisfaction, then A leaves for a better job and you give A's job to B. Your relationship with C may well have been based on two incorrect assumptions. C may always have thought that he would get A's job if she left. You never intended to give it to C but to B. Only now can you and C know that your assumptions were never mutual and that, despite years of satisfaction, your contract was always unstable. Conflict may ensue.

Another example, this time on the obedience-dicipline dimension. Suppose four people work together and one day the manager is unusually severe on one member of staff. Either intentionally or not, such action may signal to that employee and to the other employees that their future expectations of discipline may have to change.

This little example may be a trivial incident in daily life, but it illustrates three things. First, that whether they intend it or not, all managerial behaviour may be symbolic. Second, that symbolic communication impacts directly on the psychological contract and third, that labour contracts are not simply individual, they can be interrelated with others. Each action by managers is judged against the currently held assumptions.

Gouldner

Organizations tend to use the bureaucratic principle of formal rationality to organize work and apply power. However, one of the means of production, labour, has a mind of its own, is creative, assertive and can initiate its own behaviour. It also, like capital, has interests. The paradox of impersonal rules is that they tend to be taken as 'official minimum standards' so that while power relations between managers and workers are discounted by the obedience to rules, productivity hovers around the official minimum and no more. The response of management is to tighten the control procedure and exert more discipline which brings conflict between managers and workers. However an unofficial response to rules often achieves the objectives for which the rules were intended but by unofficial and often covert means. Gouldner coined the phrase 'indulgency pattern' to mean the practice by managers of turning a blind eye to worker rule breaking as a tactic to get more than truculent cooperation and higher productivity. It was understood that managers would allow a degree of licence in timekeeping, tool utilization and other union rule infringements in return for cooperation beyond the rules. In other words, trade offs were taking place not just along the two dimensions of the labour contract, but between them as well.

Gouldner, A. W. (1964), *Patterns of Industrial Bureaucracy*, New York Free Press.

The following statements can be made now in respect of how managers and workers relate to each other:

- A relationship exists at a level of unspoken understandings and assumptions, as it were, below any consideration of satisfaction or manifest behaviour.
- The true nature of the psychological contract remains secret unless triggered by some event which questions an assumption held by either partner.
- The two dimensions of the contract can be traded off.
- Stability may sometimes be achieved by illicit means amounting to collusion.
- The scope for these assumptions is determined by the nature of the job.

Managerial behaviour as a form of communication

In many respects, it is a frightening thought that all managerial behaviour sends signals – yet it is true. All behaviour communicates but it is only symbolic where matters are not explicit. It is in areas of ambiguity that symbols play such a large part.

> **Orwell**
>
> George Orwell published his study of a hotel in 1933. It is dated in its descriptions of what people do but timeless in its evocation of the wavelike fluctuation in the pressure of work complete with tidal extremes and of the dominance of normative relationships between the roles of the employees. By some mysterious means, everybody knows what to do and where they stand in relation to others. All, that is, except the author narrator. In his ignorance, he keeps tripping over unspoken agreements on standards, territory and illicit practices. Everyone and everything is communicated by symbols.
>
> Orwell, G. (1933), *Down and Out in Paris and London*, Penguin edn, 1940.

Things have changed. Matters are more explicit – good management and technology have seen to that – but in a sense, managers always have an indulgency pattern with employees. The hotel and catering industry is full of such ambiguity with lots of jobs where the output is subjectively defined. What this means is that if you unintentionally pass a crumpled tablecloth in the restaurant you may be sending a message that you don't care! What you do and what you do not do, speak directly to your workers by helping them to reinterpret their contracts with you. What is at stake here is your authority – a subject to be discussed in Chapter 11.

In conditions where standards are subjective, managers always try to overcome this subjectivity by standardization, checklists and other aids which make what is required more specific. In other words, they try to improve formal methods of control. The problem is that these can never be totally successful. What the hotel and catering industry manager has to realize is that the effective weapons are personal. Example and vigilance with the objective of achieving a shared value with the employees as to what constitutes 'good' in the various circumstances of the operation are effective controls. It is a trust relationship. This relationship between the nature of a job and how management can control it, leads to an important issue for the industry – control versus personal service.

In a bureacracy, if your problem does not fit the remit of the person you approach, you will simply be passed on until either you find someone whose remit embraces your problem or you are left in high dudgeon. Hotel and catering services are not natural bureaucracies. The concept of personal service is about being flexible enough to respond to whatever problem a guest brings to the desk. To make this response the employee's job must be defined in wide scope and that means a problem for management, because the greater the scope of an employee's job, the harder it becomes to exert control. *Here is a dilemma and issue for management*:

> If I want customers to have personal service, how much control can I exert before I stifle the initiative essential to personal service?

To understand how control might stifle initiative, it is necessary to return to the idea represented by Figure 6.1 of different jobs allowing different degrees of formal control. The first law of control is to make whatever it is controllable. Managers with responsibility for a particular area of activity will want to make it controllable. This is inevitably a process of standardization involving putting constraints on the scope of jobs. Thus, management will try to define the job and reinforce standards by such devices as procedure manuals, training, reports and incentives. Technology allows management more and more opportunity to develop formal controls. This is a natural and correct process, yet it brings with it certain problems. It is a question of role expectations. Management have expectations, but the guest may have different expectations. The incumbents themselves will also have expectations and will interpret their role under pressure from both managers and guests. The approach of marketing to this problem would be to suggest that a 'level of service' can be defined. This is only true up to a point. Customers have a way of not conforming to artificial limitations. The real alternative to personal service is self-service, but once roles exist that deal with people, it becomes difficult to limit the demands on those roles without incurring a reputation for poor service. It is a question of priorities. There are four natural pressures on job priorities:

- To do what is required of you by the control system. In other words, give priority to what management will see.
- To do what you are naturally good at or find cosy in the job.
- To do what you really like in the job.

  And for service employees:
- To do what the customers think is important.

The first three dynamic pressures take place in all jobs, but the fourth, exclusive to personal service workers, can often be a countervailing pressure to the demands of management. If you want personal service, and that is an important qualification, then the danger is of overcontrolling.

7 Motivation

What gets us up in the morning – habit, routine, a sense of purpose? We make promises to do things and promises to decide things. Some of these intentions we fulfil, others we don't – why? Some people get more done than others; some set goals while others drift along; some can't get started, others can't be stopped. We are in the realms of motivation. Look at any group of people performing the same task and the observer will be obliged to conclude that some perform better than others. Such individual differences are often most marked with wide discrepancies between the best and the worst. This can be true even when selection has been careful and abilities assessed as uniform. Think of your local football team! Yet cannot differences between individuals be explained by differences in natural ability, training and experience? Yes, they can, but it isn't enough. There is another quality present. That quality is called motivation.

It is the very conspicuousness of individual differences that has led to motivation taking up a central position in management thinking and led to a primary focus on performance. Seeing differences in performance which is attributed to motivation has made management interested in influencing motivation in order to increase performance and in trying to select on the basis of identified motivation. Not surprisingly, therefore, management is interested in 'what motivates' and in using the answer to actually alter employee behaviour. Hotel and catering management has a real investment in motivation because most of its jobs require input where effort and personal character actually matter.

As one might imagine with something so important, theories abound. These theories fall into two broad categories: those about what motivates; and those about the process of motivation – how it works. What most theories assume is that the best way to describe what motivation is is as an inner drive – some kind of decision mechanism which incorporates the will so that things aren't just decided upon but acted upon as well. What will become apparent is that there is a huge element of chance in motivating others. This is the message the theories tell us when the content and process are taken together.

What motivates?

If two managers are left alone for a minute they will talk shop. After five minutes of sharing problems they will end up talking about motivation. What is more, the conversation will turn into a debate about whether money or job satisfaction motivates! This is a legitimate argument but it is flawed. Maybe they are not alternatives, maybe both motivate, maybe neither, but above all it is simply too generalized. Motivation has to be debated at a much more detailed level. A spot of theory.

Maslow

A very influential writer, Maslow's theory is based on the idea of human 'needs'. We have, he argues, physiological and psychological needs and these needs are motivations when they are unsatisfied.

Maslow categorized human needs as follows:

- A need for self-actualization (personal growth).
- A need for self-esteem.
- A need to belong and be loved.
- A need for safety and security.
- A need for food, drink, health, sleep (physiological need).

He argues that these needs emerge as motivations in the hierarchy as listed above so that as the need below is satisfied, the next need emerges as a motivation capable of being fulfilled. This puts a premium on the higher needs because they are more open-ended and don't have an obvious finite limit. When you have eaten you have eaten; if you have a house you have a house; if your friends love you they love you and too much praise can inflate the need for self-esteem but personal growth has no obvious limits, although there must be some. It is this last notion that is so supportive to the advocates of job satisfaction. If people can grow at work, then as this need can never be satisfied it will always be a motivator. To do justice to Maslow, he does recognize there is some overlap in his hierarchy and that self-actualization may have limits.

Maslow, A. A. (1943), 'A Theory of Human Motivation', *Psychological Review*, vol. 50, pp. 370–396.

Maslow's theory belongs to a humanistic school of thought which is optimistic in its view of human life and which is concerned with human potential. This brand of psychology focuses on what individuals are capable of and how they can realize their potential. Maslow created a theory of motivation in life not just in work. The fact that this theory has been so widely acknowledged in the world of work could be because it represents a humanistic justification for the job satisfaction movement in the face of the realities of so much boring, mundane and menial work. If human beings are growth seeking, potential realizing animals, then industry should not stultify this process – so the argument goes. The interest of management in Maslow's thinking is that the idea of 'needs' which can be fulfilled offers a target and a direction to the application of stimuli like money, interesting tasks or recognition. This unfortunately carries with it an unfortunate blight and that is that in trying to stimulate satisfaction managers tend to see motivation solely in terms of satisfaction and dissatisfaction and to see them as one continuous dimension. It is a matter of degree the argument goes.

Herzberg

Seeing motivation in terms of a continuous dimension of satisfaction or dissatisfaction has the effect of suggesting that all facets of the work situation have the capability of being both satisfiers or dissatisfiers and therefore of being motivators. Not so, suggests Herzberg. Usually known as the two-factor theory, he argues that the work situation can be divided into dissatisfiers, that is elements that cause dissatisfaction but which when satisfied don't motivate – he calls these elements hygiene factors. Alternatively, there are satisfiers, that is elements of the work which when satisfied actually motivate.

Note what he is saying here. Elements which satisfy and those which dissatisfy are not opposites. Elements such as conditions of work, supervision, pay and physical conditions can cause dissatisfaction and need to be attended to but they do not motivate people to work harder.

Elements that do that are the work itself, responsibility, recognition, achievement and advancement. By separating satisfiers from dissatisfiers he creates a zone of neutrality so that an individual's feelings can go from neutral to satisfaction and from neutral to dissatisfaction.

Herzberg, F. (1966), *Work at the Nature of Man*, World Publishing Company.

The unique contribution of Herzberg is in breaking the mould of one continuous dimension and at least introducing the idea of neutrality which also opens up the possibility that we may be indifferent to certain aspects of work. Herzberg is, however, firmly in the job satisfaction camp. Note that his motivations are very much to do with recognition needs and growth needs.

It could be argued that all this human potential stuff fades when put against the moral simplicity of having to earn a living. This imperative argument underpins the 'pay as the only real motivator' school of thought. It is all a bit too simplistic. The arguments against the job satisfaction advocates don't actually need an alternative source of motivation and should be taken on their own. There are two broad arguments, which are, first, that there appears to be no great call for job satisfaction in that a lot of people do fairly mundane and boring work without conspicuous dissent. The second argument is that, however one might feel about human potential, much work simply cannot be organized to meet human potential needs. Dishwashing and room cleaning cannot be constructed other than for what they are – mundane work. However, the detective in you will have noticed that as alibis, these broad arguments don't add up. No possibility of reconstructing the work to make it interesting and no dissent. True, many people must be abstracted out and feel like robots but the very lack of dissent suggests most people have endlessly subtle adaption systems which can turn moronic work into something, at least worth possessing, if not even cherishing. Here then is the dilemma of job satisfaction – the range of elements from which satisfaction can be gained extends beyond the normal list of job itself, pay, boss, work group, organization, working conditions, achievement, advancement, etc. The experience of retired people and the unemployed shows not just that work itself makes people valuable to themselves but that individuals 'latch on to' an array of elements, some of which might seem strange to the outside observer, some of which are known only to the incumbent of the job. If managers are seriously interested in tapping job satisfaction the message is that it is a matter of detail. First find your satisfiers. One interesting example of the damage which can be caused by concentrating on work as the source of job satisfaction is the neglect of the power of the actual finished product or service to motivate. Previously, it had always been assumed that only craftsmen like chefs could derive any satisfaction of this kind because of the pride in their skills and achievement. It was, to some, astonishing that people who contributed a fragment, or only indirectly, to a product or service could find the result satisfying. This example also suggests that a sense of purpose might be heavily implicated in satisfaction.

The problem with theories based on satisfaction of needs is that sometimes we come across people who appear to be denying themselves fulfilment. Altruism, self-sacrificing behaviour, even self-destructive behaviour don't, at least, appear to be need satisfaction activities – yet they might be? A theoretical framework which might help here is known as self-theory. The argument here is that we construct a subjective world giving everything meaning in relation to the self.

Snyder and Williams

One of the problems of need theories is that while it may be obvious why we need food, drink and security, it is not obvious why we need recognition, advancement and growth and this they do not explain. We all possess a unique view of the world and a unique view of ourselves. How we see the environment and ourselves in it becomes the essence of our individuality. We develop ways of seeing the environment which enable us to understand everything we see and like a scientist devise ways of predicting and controlling our world. We are not new every morning we awake with knowledge, experience, a mental filing system for information and above all, an identity.

The essence of yourself needs to develop but also needs to be maintained in a stable way. It's this maintenance function that is, for self theory, the overriding need. Needs emerge because they maintain our conception of ourselves. People who see themselves as slim adjust their physiological needs. People who are not sure of their ability seek recognition. It is the image of the self which is regulating the emergence of needs. It is easy to envisage that in the world of work an essential branch of our self-identity would be our occupational identity.

Snyder, R. and Williams R. (1982), 'Self Theory: An Integrative Theory of Work Motivation', *Journal of Occupational Psychology*, vol. 55, pp. 257–267.

Fundamentally, what self theory is saying is that it is our need to define ourselves that regulates our needs. In management terms this might be considered a further complication.

Perhaps it would be appropriate to conclude the discussion of what motivates by considering the case of Japanese organizations who answer the question by saying everything does – *as long as it all makes coherent sense*! Western writers have concentrated on particular aspects of Japanese management such as quality circles and culture, but have neglected the point that everything about employment is deliberate. In other words, every aspect of the individual environment is planned in a coherent way. The approach embraces needs theory and attempts to influence the self concept by designing an environment that tells a coherent story. *The debate about what aspects of employment motivate may well hide a truth that they all do when held together.*

How does motivation work?

The simplest way to see the process of motivation is to see it as a stimulus–response mechanism. The individual perceives a particular stimulus, say, interesting work or pay and responds by working harder. Managers manipulate the stimuli in order to change the behaviour. It is not, alas, as simple as this. When we look at the process it is easy to see how needs theories and self theory work together through the medium of perception.

Ask any group of people to do a job for a reward and they all react in a different way. Not only does motivation vary between individuals but they respond differently to the same stimulus. This offers us a clue that the relationship between the content and process may explain the actual differences between people that we see.

Expectancy theory

Expectancy theory attempts to explain how a stimulus is turned into motivation or, put more simply, how a reward produces an enhanced performance. At the heart of the theory is something referred to as 'E'. What 'E' stands for is a wider definition of the drive of motivation. Think of as many words as you can that are similar to 'effort': energy, enthusiasm, expenditure, excitement. They all infer a 'drive' of some kind – motivation. How is the 'E' to be activated?

The theory suggests a number of simultaneous stages?

1. The strength of the need is felt.
2. The expectancy that 'E' will produce a particular result.
3. The result will reduce the need.

What is being said here is that a person has, and recognizes that they have, a particular need. This need will have a certain intensity or strength to it. Management ask for more effort in return for a particular reward. The person then assesses that by expending more 'E' it will produce the reward and that this reward will satisfy their original need. To put it more simply – the outcome is desired and the effort is expected to produce this desired outcome. An example would be helpful. A banquet salesperson is wondering whether or not to make a few more sales calls. The additional sales will lead to a bonus (stimulus). The salesperson is aware that they could do with the money (the need). The expectancy is that by making more calls (effort) more sales will ensue (performance) and that the bonus will be forthcoming. However, everything in this calculus is dependent upon the attractiveness of the bonus. Will the bonus reduce the need? This aspect of attractiveness of the reward is often referred to as the valence of the reward. If the bonus was trivial it would reduce the motivation force considerably.

A query, a question and a useful reminder stem from expectancy theory. The query is over whether people are always conscious of their needs and are as calculating and rational as the theory implies. The question that arises is, where do the expectations themselves come from? On what basis do we estimate that our 'E' will produce the required performance and get the reward? Previous experience of ourselves in similar circumstances and previous management behaviour would seem to be our only guide. This makes consistency in evaluating performance a key area of managerial behaviour. The useful reminder which this theory flags up is that to respond to a stimulus, however subjectively, the individual must perceive it clearly and this puts a premium on unambiguous communication.

So far the process of motivation has been seen entirely in terms of stimulus–response confined within the manager–worker relationship. Yet another powerful influence on our level of effort is our feeling of fairness and equity towards other people. Social comparisons are inevitable in a workplace and it would be unimaginable that they would not influence behaviour.

Adams – equity theory

Possibly the most readily understandable psychological process, equity is about feelings of guilt, anxiety, frustration, envy, psychological discomfort, engendered by comparisons with others. A common enough human process. At work, the focus is on rewards, effort and investment. Adams argues that people will strive to restore a sense of equity when inequity is perceived. It is this restoring process that alters behaviour. He conceived of a ratio between inputs and outputs – the self and the compared other, each having a ratio.

$$\frac{\text{Self-outcomes}}{\text{Inputs}} < \frac{\text{Other outcomes}}{\text{Inputs}}$$

Here the ratio of the other is greater than for the self, therefore a feeling of inequity ensues. Examples of Adams's inputs and outputs could be:

Inputs
- Effort 'E'
- Education
- Training
- Experiences
- Loyalty
- Age

Outputs
- Pay
- Title
- Status symbol
- Benefits
- Time off
- Opportunities for overtime
- Autonomy

Adams, J. S. (1965), 'Inequity in Social Exchange,' in Berkowitz, L. (ed), *Advances in Experimental Psychology*, Academic Press.

What is important here is that this comparison is trading in perceptions only, very little may be visible or factual. Effort is usually fairly conspicuous but other outcomes and inputs, especially for the compared other, are likely to be guessed. Adams argues that when inequity is felt, the person will either take action to achieve equity or alter their perceptions in some way (for a discussion on this particular process, see Chapter 8).

The problem with equity theory is that the only avenue for rectifying inequity is altering effort. This is easy to say but not so easy to do. Ability plays a part here. Everybody has a natural pace to the way they work which is not easily and consistently altered. Try walking abnormally slowly for a while! It may be better seen as an explanatory theory of relationships between people and of grievances rather than as a theory of behaviour modification.

So far, the focus has been on motivation to increase performance and the assumption has been made that motives can be found at work and that management can, within certain limits, influence motivation. Hold on. *People don't come to work as a blank sponge.*

It is all too easy for managers to overlook the fact that what motivates at work may originate outside work and that there may be some limitations on their ability to motivate, yet this must be true. Maslow's need theory, for example, does not specify that need satisfaction can only take place in the workplace. It must be accepted that some of our need and part of our self-identity comes from home, family, social life and other aspects of non-work life. The argument here is that to understand motivation it is necessary to broaden the perspective beyond work.

So far we have looked only at motivation in relation to performance but what makes us perform may be related to other questions about work. There may be a link between:

- Why we work.
- Why we do a particular job.
- Why we work for a particular organization.
- Why we give a certain level of performance.

Job choice and motivation

If, for example, we needed some extra money for the family, we might seek part-time work or seek an organization that offers good pay for part-time work. The basis of our need is for money and convenience. Therefore, motivation stimulation related to these two aspects may be the basis of our performance. The suggestion here is that attachment to the labour market, occupational choice and performance may be related.

The idea that occupational choice and motivation to perform are related must be of interest to hotel and catering managers. For a largely unskilled and low paid workforce, what does this mean for motivation? If the model of the hotel and catering labour markets means anything, it is that the large majority of people who work in the industry are unskilled and therefore have a wide range of unskilled and probably mundane jobs to choose from. Yet the model shows also that people tend to stay in the industry, often moving from place to place, and often in and out of work, but by and large staying inside the wide confines of the industry. If they stay, there must be something in it; some basis of satisfaction.

Ask most people who seek a career in the industry why they want to come into the industry and they usually reply that they like working with people. Not a bad sentiment, but the implication behind it is that people mean variety. The unpredictability of people together with the fluctuating nature of business demand creates a variety in work which is appreciated. Above all, however, is the fact that all jobs, no matter how mundane, are not regimented. Even the dishwasher does not have the iron rigidity of the factory production line. There is a strong 'not factory' theme sitting in this area between job choice and motivation.

Unlike unskilled work in a factory, people have a degree of autonomy in their work and we know that all theories of motivation speak of autonomy and control as a need to be satisfied. The point about mundane work in the hotel and catering industry is that it at least has the potential to be personalized. The attractiveness of unskilled hotel and catering work could be summarized as follows:

- Convenient
- Easy to learn
- Has variety
- Grants autonomy
- It is not a factory
- You meet people

Sometimes it is easy for managers to overlook obvious sources of motivation. In most occupations the reason why we take the job in the first place influences our self-identity and, therefore, the way we see things in the job. In evaluating aspects of the job we are, to an extent, justifying our original good sense in taking the job. The message here is that a few clues as to a person's sense of motivation can be obtained through the selection process.

The way we live and motivation

We have all come across the 'workaholic' who lives only for work, or the person with a vocation who, while not living to work, makes work the driving force of their lives in different ways. These are extreme examples of work values dominating social values. Is there a case for the opposite scenario where it is the way we live in society that gives us our motivation?

We are not talking here about the transfer of habits, for example a painstaking craftsman might well be equally fastidious at home and an accountant might not be able to resist checking the household bills. What is at stake here is whether motivation stems from work or from the way we live.

Goldthorpe – orientations to work

The importance of individual differences has been referred to many times so far, but sometimes a case of similarity can be both revealing and convincing. Goldthorpe found that when interviewing a sample of car workers about their jobs, both the skilled and unskilled workers appeared to have the same mildly satisfied, mildly indifferent attitude towards their work. In other words, those with intrinsically interesting work and those with mundane work had the same attitude. They had something else in common too, a priority for money! To them, work was just a means of earning money – nothing more. This could be anywhere and anybody. Some people are like that. However, the significant finding was that everybody felt like that and that the origin of this attitude was the way they lived in society. These workers led family-centred lives with little sense of community. This isolation produced a need for material advancement which in turn led to an attitude of regarding money as the purpose of work. He argues that as work attitudes are bred outside, work management can only go along with it. What he is saying is that management's attempt to influence motivation counts for nothing because the source is elsewhere!

Goldthorpe suggests that people have general attitudes to work which he calls orientations to work. He suggests there are three broad types:

- Instrumental orientation – work is simply a means to an end.
- Bureaucratic orientation – (a career orientation) where sacrifices are made for future rewards.
- Solidaristic orientation – simply where work and leisure are seamlessly drawn together. Very much a communal orientation.

These motivations stem from outside work in the first case, through family-centred life and a desire for material advancement, in the second case through ambition and the social expectations of getting on and in the third case, through a desire to live in a community. These categories are 'ideal types' and the author acknowledges that they vary by degree. His controversial point is that as this big motivation is brought in with the coat in the morning, management can only go along with it. He is challenging other motivation theories.

Goldthorpe, J. H., Lockwood, D., Bechhoter, and Platt, J. (1968), *The Affluent Worker: Industrial Attitudes and Behaviour*, Cambridge University Press.

This focus on society as the source of motivation rather than work suggests that society and work may be competing not just for the time of the individual but as the source of motivation.

The location factor

Suppose a hotel is located in a geographically isolated outpost. Everyone who works there lives in the local village and the hotel is the major employer in the locality. Now, suppose something bad happens at work. For instance, suppose management makes a bad error which causes a grievance in the workforce. In such circumstances, everyone will take the grumble home with them and discuss it with their coworkers out of work. This will have the effect of crystallizing and magnifying the grievance. Next morning, they go into work with an anti-management attitude which is thus likely to further sour relations and cause more trouble. However, the example here uses something negative but the process would work just as well for something positive.

The principle at stake here is called the integration principle and it emphasizes how such work values can be reinforced or diluted by the degree to which the workforce is integrated in the wider local society. If the workforce is by some means isolated from the wider society, then it is likely that their values of work will be reinforced by life outside work *then brought back to work as an attitude*. The form of isolation may be geographical or related to unsocial hours. The integration argument is that when workers go home and socialize with workers from other industries 'talking shop' is less likely and grumbles are disarmed by comparisons. In these circumstances, what happens at work stays at work.

The relevance to hotel and catering is fairly obvious. Employees in the hotel and catering industry are often physically isolated, work unsocial hours when the rest of the population is at leisure and live in provided accommodation. In these circumstances it would be expected that work values would be fairly dominant values even out of hours, but the message for management is that this reinforcement process can work on both positive and negative raw material.

Motivation and motivating

One of the most common sights in management is to see managers down at heart, blaming themselves when their strategies to motivate their staff appear not to have worked. They attribute the cause to themselves. Yet if there is one message that comes through clearly from the psychologists it is that *motivation is, at best, a game of chance*!

You cannot know another person's needs or how they define themselves. In other words, you don't know what motivates them. You cannot even be sure they have perceived your strategy. If they have and if it works – great. If they haven't or they have and it doesn't – bad luck. The sin in motivation is not getting it wrong but is not trying something else. Motivation is a constant process of trial and error. Criticism should fall on those who duck out not on those who fail.

We have learned recently that the way we attribute the cause of a situation we see gives direction to what action we take. The same is true for motivation. In the absence of firm knowledge managers make assumptions about people in work. Rather like 'orientation to work' these are large-scale manager assumptions about what will get people motivated. A well-known theory:

McGregor

McGregor polarized the assumptions about people in organizations into two extremes, then went further to suggest that managers adopt either of these extremes which then determines their style of management. He coined the much quoted Theory X, Theory Y.

Theory X
1 The average man is by nature indolent.
2 He lacks ambition and prefers to be led.
3 He is inherently self-centred and indifferent to organizational needs.
4 He is resistant to change.
5 He is gullible and not very bright.

Theory Y
1 People are not by nature passive or indifferent to organization needs. If they have become so, it is because of experience.
2 Motivation counts in everybody. Everybody has the potential and capacity to assume responsibility and to strive to meet organizational needs.

Depending which pole you adhere to, you would use different approaches to motivating people.

McGregor, D. (1960), *The Human Side of Enterprise*, McGraw Hill.

This is a 'stick and carrot' approach – coercion versus job satisfaction. Perhaps the real contribution of McGregor is that he makes the point that although motivation is a separate thing for each individual, managers tend to use a broad personalized approach to everyone. They call it their style. Managers cannot be different to each individual, a personal sense of continuity and style is part of being a manager.

In a sense, what matters is not so much what motivates but 'what works for me'. The implication here is that, as a manager, you have to learn from life and experience. We know that some people are better people managers than others, but we also know that people get better at it with experience. That is, providing that they themselves are open to learning. What this means is looking continually at the results of your efforts and being prepared to try different approaches.

This last contention points clearly to one solid fact in the motivation debate – you, the manager, count because as the motivator you will never be neutral in the eyes of those who work for you. In fact, if you ask if there are any certainties, any sure fire bets in the what motivates stakes, the answer is a qualified, yes. We know for one thing that no matter whether you are an X or a Y person, or a pay or job satisfaction advocate, there are four aspects of work to which an employee is never neutral, these are:

- The immediate boss
- The pay
- Their effort
- Their confidence to do the job

While you come to see them as satisfiers or dissatisfiers or whether or not they motivate, they are always salient to the amount of drive being applied in the job.

Notwithstanding the theoretical discussion and the observable fact of individual differences, common sense would suggest that there are a number of actions which may or may not constitute motivation but might register as 'good housekeeping' in this area. These are:

- Clear communication – people cannot respond to a stimulus if they cannot see it clearly, the manager must convince that the rewards and the performance are related.
- Offer valued rewards.
- Do not over control.
- Recognize achievement – recognition appears in every theoretical scheme and it accords with our common sense that to recognize achievement will increase performance.
- Ensure that rewards are equitable.
- Teaching someone something is an excellent basis for being able to motivate them.
- Ensure that all aspects of employment tell a coherent story.

8 Negative behaviour

We have all, at some time, had the experience of being either upset, anxious or angry about something and trying to 'forget it' by immersing ourselves in work. At first it doesn't work, the thoughts that made us anxious keep returning. Sometimes it doesn't work at all. Work and the anxiety compete until the problem goes away or concentration on work eventually triumphs. The point being made here is that we cannot motivate ourselves while we are in any way anxious. If you, as a manager, are trying to motivate a person who is anxious, they simply will not respond because they will not see what you are doing. The message is that anxiety intervenes in the motivation process. This is why any serious consideration of motivation must include a discussion of the role of, for want of a better phrase, negative aspects.

A moment's reflection tells us that we do not always behave in a way which represents the way we feel. If you recall from Chapter 5, our fundamental problem as managers is that we can only deal with the behaviour that presents itself to us. The heart of our problem is whether there is a direct relationship between the way we feel and the way we behave. Can the former be predicted from the latter? While acknowledging that there must be many times when there is such a direct relationship – for example feeling hungry makes us eat – intuition suggests that may not always be so.

The relationship is unreliable and it would be wrong to trust it when you are faced only with behaviour. Either with intent, or unconsciously, an individual may distort the way they behave from the genesis of behaviour; feeling. (Note feeling is not the only source of behaviour, instinct and habit are also salient, but we are only concerned here with feeling.)

In considering how a person responds to a feeling of psychological discomfort two adaption processes are important, these are distortion and dilution.

Distortion

The greatest pressure for us to distort comes from negative feelings. This makes the handling of grievances one of the most difficult aspects of people management.

Festinger

Festinger's theory of cognitive dissonance may suggest a framework for understanding the feeling and behaviour relationship. He argues that if we hold inconsistent beliefs, or are forced into actions we do not believe in, or find the reality of life inconsistent with our expectations, we feel psychological discomfort. He goes on to argue that we cannot walk around forever with such discomfort – it must be 'handled' in some way. The theory does not suggest what we do to render the feeling impotent, only that we must do something.

The obvious resolution is to take the appropriate action, i.e. change your belief or do something else. We could also put it literally out of mind. But we have two other options, we could blame someone or something else for our predicament or we could rationalize it away. The whole point about blame and rationalization processes is that they should be automatic – a pre-prepared response. Think of the time you tried to give up something and the kind of excuses you used to yourself when you failed.

Festinger, L. (1957), *A Theory of Cognitive Dissonance*, Stamford University Press.

This is not a psychological fancy, it is the daily reality where tourism is being developed in economies that are still at a subsistence level. Staff who are living at a subsistence level go to work in a hotel and find themselves in close proximity to rich tourists. This requires some kind of psychological adjustment or adaption on the part of the employees if conflict is to be avoided.

A pre-requisite of feeling psychological discomfort is to be aware of some adverse conditions. That awareness may result from a comparison and may be dispersed by a different, more favourable comparison. What may intervene between the feeling and the need to rationalize it away, or take action to correct it, will be the location of blame and the degree to which action to alleviate the adverse conditions is actually possible. The more extreme the feeling of self blame, the more pressure within to rationalize the condition away or project blame onto someone else, e.g. management, the unions, human nature! Indeed, projection of blame may be a form of rationalization. Furthermore, if you can't see that 'action is possible' then the pressure to rationalize is that much greater.

One possible outcome of this process is the substitution of one grievance for another. Frustrated promotion may come out as a demand for more money. Difficulty with a supervisor may come out as a grumble about the amount of work. Always assuming grievance is voiced at all, the result might be simply leaving employment.

The process of rationalization is encouraged by a number of influences, notably:

1   Your authority
2   The articulacy of the grievant
3   Likely outcome.

Authority is always slightly intimidating. There is always, in authority relationships, a danger that subordinates will not say what they really mean or want to say. Similarly, it is all too easy to overlook the fact that some people may not have the vocabulary to express what they feel.

By far the commonest influence on a grievance is the individual's perception of the likely outcome. Will it be successful and what will it cost? All this adds doubt and makes the actual interpretation that much more difficult. Notwithstanding the problem of distortion, there is yet a further complication.

Dilution

When considering the question of what motivates, we suggested an expanded range of job attributes should be considered. However, it must be obvious that each of these attributes will attract a different *intensity of feeling*. For example, a chef may hate the management, hate the pay, be indifferent to the work group, but love what he actually does. A poor pay rise may produce a mild grumble, but a sudden de-skilling would produce an explosion! In other words, satisfaction and dissatisfaction trade with each other. This is why a small thing can so often trigger a surprisingly hostile reaction.

Conceptual framework

Figure 8.1 attempts to conceptualize the passage of a feeling of psychological discomfort going through the influence of dilution of intensity through an assessment of possible outcome to the individual handling the feeling.

Figure 8.1

It is clear now that the link between dissatisfaction and behaviour may not be direct. Individuals may endure abject deprivation, they may rationalize their grievance away and their resultant behaviour may be more strategic than relevant to their feelings. All this adds doubt. Certainly it would be difficult to predict that a particular form of behaviour would follow from a specific grievance, even if it could be identified! This problem of identifying cause is unfortunately not a simple one of seeking to unravel the processes of rationalization and strategy; there is the serious problem of multiple causation and cumulative causation. There may be many things wrong at the same time and, while they may not all be pressing, accumulation can occur with the result that the behaviour may be only looking to the most salient of the grievances, making life difficult for possible solutions. It is not just a case of 'the pay's rotten, the tools are falling apart and I can't stand the supervisor'. Any one issue can cause a variety of dissatisfactions.

How should we approach grievances?

It is not management's task to solve all the personal problems of the staff, therefore the first question posed is: How far should managers get involved? One obvious answer is to the extent that productivity is being adversely affected by the grievance. That is not so easy to judge and it may be acting too late. If they are out of the door there is no point in intervening. Anyway, this whole area is a bit of a minefield. One man's solution may be another man's grievance – you may unknowingly rob Peter to pay Paul. Is there a way through? Well, there are three considerations here – philosophy, authority and procedure.

A philosophy

If you went to the doctor complaining of a pain in your shoulder, he would examine you and possibly locate the cause of your problem as something wrong with your forearm. He would, therefore, treat the forearm. In other words, look at the symptoms, find the cause and treat the cause. All very logical, scientific and sensible. Yet in the case of management, wrong! Here is a point where management and science part company. Managers must treat the symptoms as well as the causes. If someone says they have a problem with pay, but you have found the cause to be the relations with the supervisor, both the 'real' problem and the worker's own interpretation have to be treated seriously because they are both real to the individual.

Your authority

Your authority is a barrier. Perhaps the sensible way forward here is to conduct your authority in such a way as to be seen as 'being approachable'. One way of solving this is a willingness to come out of 'your territory'. We are not like animals, but we are possessive about bits of space. Listening in another person's space at least helps to break down the barrier of your authority.

Procedure

The importance of having a recognized procedure for grievances is that it introduces an element of justice into the affair, and at the same time sidesteps the problems of authority and inarticulateness. It also has the merit of taking some of the emotion out of the grievance. By going to the procedure, the person has taken some action to alleviate the psychological discomfort. What is left is not the desire for a full settlement of their case, but the desire for justice. The procedure at least offers an outcome, if not the desire outcome. There are a lot of problems associated with grievance procedures, and these will be discussed in Chapter 17, but when they work they are an attribute to labour management and can prevent people settling their grievances with their feet, i.e. walking out.

Good habits

- Avoid promises.
- Take what people say seriously.
- Investigate thoroughly.
- Avoid favours.
- Avoid reciprocal 'deals'.

9 Groups and teams

Go into a restaurant or kitchen or to any behind the scenes area and you will often see some physical similarities between people working in the same area. They might, for example, be roughly the same age or the same sex or both. They might all have little education or all be graduates or all have the same social origin. What you will notice, is that as the similarities pile up the more homogeneous the people become, the more you tend to think of them as a group and the more they may see themselves as having a common identity. It is not that physical similarity causes groups to form, it is just that they may kick the thought process in that direction.

You will become aware that dealing with a group of individuals is not quite the same as dealing with one individual. The approach, the skills – something more is required when you have to manage a group of people. Managers like to talk of teams and teamwork but these words are both difficult to define, let alone achieve. Giving a set of individuals a group task to do won't, of itself, form them into groups. Putting on a coloured shirt and running on to a field with others similarly attired won't make them a team! Yet teamwork can be seen and felt – it is a tangible thing. The real problem is that we organize people into groups, call them teams but don't look to see if they are actually behaving like groups or teams. The words 'group' and 'team' tend to be used coterminously, but one expression is central to both concepts and that is 'common identity'.

It is very easy to fall into the trap of thinking that managing people is an activity involving problems between them (the workers) and us (the management). A few minutes' acquaintance with people management will introduce you to another significant dimension – the relationships between individual workers and between groups of workers. This relationship, if you like, between 'them' and 'them' is just as crucial to the technological process and productivity achievement as the relationship between management and workers.

Management's interest in understanding group behaviour is founded on four premis:

- If people behave differently when they are part of a group than when they are just a set of individuals it is essential for managers to be able to recognize when a set of individuals is a group.
- Because productivity is achieved in different ways by a group as by individuals, it is essential to be able to recognize the features that produce productivity in groups.
- Although managers have the choice of organizing work either on a group basis or an individual basis (subject to technological constraints), in real life the distinction is not always so clear. Often work is organized either in an individualistic mode with group overtones or the other way around. Being able to assess the productivity implications of this is an important managerial skill.
- When is a group a team? If it is either, does it need leadership? If so, are there any special reasons that make the role of the leader more crucial in some circumstances than others? This is a difficult area – leadership and teamwork. What is clear, however, is that managers should at least appreciate their role as leaders and be able to see when the label 'team' might be appropriate.

The two central questions raised here are: When is a set of individuals a group? and on what does group productivity depend? There are two clues to the first question – if they behave like a group and if they display own-group favouritism. At this stage, this is not too helpful. In the case of productivity, if managers are going to organize work on a group basis, that is as a set of interdependent tasks, then there must be something in it for management, that is higher output. If a set of individuals working alone could produce the same or greater output why organize it on a group basis? The implication here is that groups have some special quality that individuals lack – what is it? To understand both these questions the place to start is what psychology calls 'group process'.

Group process

There are four principal components of this process: conformity to 'norms'; cohesiveness in performance; successful image; and attachment. It is described as a process because each component is dependent upon the other three. To understand this relationship it is probably best to begin with what we can actually observe – conformity to norms and cohesion. Not only is it observable but we can feel it ourselves. We are all individuals, we proclaim thus, yet on occasions we dress and behave in the particular way which is expected of us. As long as everybody else does it, it remains a social convention, a group norm. Put on a coloured jersey and run onto a field and we are part of something which is more than just ourselves. Jogging is less boring and less tiring when done with others.

As they are central to the process – what are group norms? They are ideas in the minds of members of what members should do, ought to do and are expected to do in prescribed circumstances. The character of a norm is both that of policeman, in the sense that if we behave in a way that departs from the norm the group will, in some way, punish us back into line, and a secret policeman in that we may prevent ourselves from departing from the norm by feeling guilty. If this is what group norms are, how do they form? It is essentially a social process. Obviously at the very beginning there are no norms, so a simultaneous process of interaction begins in which each member emits a certain behaviour (talking, exhibiting an attitude, expressing an opinion, posture, dress, manner, speech, etc.) which is either accepted or rejected by others. After a while, each member is aware of how far they can go and what is acceptable and unacceptable. There will, of course, be individual differences and varying interaction patterns. In a sense this is the 'mechanics' of norm formation, it doesn't really explain the norms that result. In those stakes there are a number of contenders, notably the majority view, consistency, leadership and consensus.

In practice, groups tend to have a wide range of norms even sometimes covering behaviour away from the group. There are a number of certainties here. You can be sure that there will be norms of performance in relation to quantity and quality, what we think of the management, particular managers, the food, the pay, punctuality and other groups. Norms are one of the defining qualities of groups but they don't actually produce the productivity, what does that is cohesion.

If normative behaviour is 'expected' behaviour, then cohesive behaviour is 'anticipated' behaviour. The productivity of a group depends on its cohesiveness; the ability of its members to work 'like a machine' anticipating each other's behaviour. Without the benefits of cohesion you might as well break it up into a set of individual tasks (assuming that is a possibility).

Normative behaviour and cohesiveness are two tangible outcomes of group formation but there is another such outcome. Over time, a group will create for itself a self image and a reputational image in the outside environment. What seems clear is that this image must be one of success – defined in its own terms. The point here is that the group's way of defining success should be management's way as well. This is not automatic and it is possible for groups to define themselves in an anti-management mode.

So far, it has been suggested that groups have norms, can achieve cohesion and define themselves as successful, but all this depends on members wanting to be part of the group. The glue which binds them is the degree of attachment of each member. Break the attachment and the rest falls apart.

What we have explored here is a *circular* process or dynamic. To be productive the group must be cohesive and to be that it must be successful in achieving its norms, all of which depends on the maintenance of attachment.

A number of consequences appear to be relevant to managers:

- Managers must not expect an individual to give their best personal performance level in a group task.
- Productivity depends on cohesion in a group task.
- To break a group norm is to break cohesion and put productivity at risk.

What you see from the outside is the degree of cohesion. Just a few minutes watching a kitchen brigade can tell you if they are anticipating each other. If that anticipation is not there, then simply calling them a group won't make them anything more than a set of individuals who happen to be all wearing white.

Group identity

At the heart of group process is the idea of attachment. If groups are about conformity why do we do it? Why attach ourselves to a group? Membership is rarely compulsory even at work. In fact, one of the ways by which we might be able to tell, from the outside, if a set of people are a group, comes from a theory of attachment.

Tajfel

He suggests that part of our self-identity comes from affiliations to groups. These attachments may be simply emotion association or real membership, but they become defining qualities – what we are. He goes further to suggest that as group affiliations are part of our identity, we will invest our commitment with a positive character. In other words, we seek something positive through group associations. Crucially, this means that we will favour any group to which we are affiliated. The behavioural effect of this is called own-group bias. Tajfel put forward the idea of own-groups and out-groups. His argument was that as we would favour our own-group, we would define it as different and better than some other identified group – the out-group. The importance of this idea is that first of all it puts onto any group a characteristic that can be seen from the outside, that is favouritism of the own-group, which can thus be used as an identifying characteristic. Second, the concept of own-groups and out-groups suggests a framework for understanding intergroup behaviour.

Tajfel, H. (1978), *Differentiation Between Social Groups*, Academic Press.

What Tajfel is saying, is that attachment carries a positive quality which means that one way of identifying a set of individuals as a real group is if they are clearly favouring themselves and have a clear out-group which they deprecate. Here is a basis for understanding relationships between groups.

Intergroup relations

If we have two groups who are in some way in competition with each other, then we might expect them to see each other in terms of own-groups and out-groups and find ways of defining themselves as better than the others. However, the case of competition is only the obvious one. What is being suggested here is that groups must have some other set of people who they distinguished themselves from 'They are not us and we are not them, thank goodness!' This form of intergroup relations can be kept on purely a perceptual level in which case it is of only mild interest to managers. Alas, it rarely stays at this harmless level and can intrude into operational matters as lack of cooperation, and have serious implications for status and prestige, not to mention pay comparisons. Front office and housekeeping, kitchen and restaurant all have built-in conflicts, but they are all supposed to be on the same side! If each saw the other as an out-group, then operational problems could ensue.

The organization of work – individualistic or group

The real problem with understanding groups is that work itself rarely falls simply into either a group mode of operation or an individual mode. Most work processes have overtones of both. It would be appropriate at this point to differentiate purely individual work from purely group work.

Individual work
- totally autonomous tasks
- Independently resourced
- Only vertical communication required
- Individual differences in status only accepted

Group work
- An interdependent set of tasks
- Uniform standards required
- Shared resources
- Competition for scarce resources

A kitchen would clearly fall towards the group category with independent tasks brought together by interdependence of timing and standard. A restaurant is essentially a set of individual tasks which are surrounded by group overtones, namely the need for uniformity of standards and the distribution of equipment and customers.

A useful way of seeing work groups is as follows:

- *The technical group* To what degree or in what combination is the work organized on a group or individual basis?
- *The social group* A social group may form even when the tasks are individualistic. For example, a group of waiters who are the same age and nationality may form a group which will bring group process to bear on what is essentially individual work.

- *The earnings group* Fundamentally, the pay system should follow the technical system. If the task is a genuine group task, why not use a group incentive scheme? Ideas such as pooled tips are an acknowledgement that in a restaurant individual tasks and effort exist in a group setting.

The important point here is that these formations should not conflict with each other. You cannot do much about social group formation, but certainly the pay system and the work system should be in harmony.

Leadership and groups

It is quite easy to spot sets of individuals who are not yet a group. They meet and someone says 'what shall we do now?' or 'who is going to start first?' or 'who is going to do what?' Eventually someone makes a decision. At work this isn't usually left to simply emerge, it is given to the appointed leader to make. Herein lies a problem. If the leader is appointed, is he or she part of the group – sharing its group process? A common sentiment such as 'you can't be "one of the lads" and expect them to respect you' suggests that the leader is outside the group. What this expression really means is that groups have norms of both a work-orientated and social character and that they are interwoven and tend to be pervasive outside work as well. The basic argument is that too much social closeness undermines authority. The contrary argument would be that the 'distance' between the leader and the led would itself be a group norm. This argument suggests that leaders can be within groups. To see the real problem, it is best to look first at the case of the emergent leader.

The scene is a boat load of shipwrecked souls, cast out on the ocean with not a sailor aboard. They need a leader. Let us suppose one of their number stands up and shouts 'Follow me, I shall lead you to safety.' They might well push him or her overboard, but a challenge has been issued. If everyone in the boat, however conditionally, acquiesces to that person's leadership, they have all simultaneously agreed to be inferior to the leader. This is the group's first norm! Thus, the emergence of a leader and the embryo formation of a group occur causally and simultaneously. This gives the emergent leader a running start.

In the world of work, however, most leaders are appointed. This gives them the disadvantage of not knowing the group norms, but the advantage of having a readymade 'distance' from the led. Sometimes leaders are appointed from the group. They have the advantage of knowing the group's norms, but the disadvantage of having to make more 'distance' and reconcile conflicting interests and loyalties. This is not an arid academic debate because the question of whether or not the leader is part of the group becomes particularly crucial when, as in the hotel and catering industry, quality standards are subjective and require some form of normative agreement as to what is good, proper or expected. No leader can be everywhere checking on everything and if the standards are subjectively measured, then group consensus as to what is good turned into a norm is the maintenance process. This does not excuse the leader from example and vigilance but does embroil them in the group process that sets and maintains the standards.

The role of any leader in any group is always, first and foremost, one of communicating what has to be achieved, then deciding on the distribution of the workload, decision making responsibility and rewards. An integrated approach to this role is presented by Adair.

Adair

Adair developed a concept of leadership he called 'action-centred leadership' which recognized that in any group activity, three things were happening simultaneously. A task was being performed, a set of people were having to act in an interdependent way and each individual was undergoing a process of learning. The great merit of this concept was that it saw the task, the group and the individual as part of one process which it was the leader's responsibility to integrate. In this concept, the leader had three objectives – to achieve the task, to build the team and to develop each individual. Central to the achievement of these objectives is to judge each decision by its effect on the task, on the group and on the individual who has to implement it. Like other good ideas 'action-centred leadership' has a simplicity which is not contradicted by psychological theory. It has the additional merit of becoming a 'good habit' in a wide range of personality types. It gets easier with practice.

Adair, J. (1988), *Action Centred Leadership*, Gower.

Although the role of the leader is always concerned with setting objectives and distributing resources, the task of team building, that is getting the common identity of the group to serve the productive aim of the group, is made harder but perhaps more crucial in particular circumstances. These are:

- Attachment to the group is involuntary and weak.
- The task of the group is actually an individualistic one.
- There is structured competition within the group.
- The group is not socially homogeneous.

10 Feelings about pay

Pay and leisure

In Chapter 7, we briefly touched on the debate over whether pay or job satisfaction motivates people; now it is time to look at pay on its own. It is interesting how easy it is for a legitimate opinion to overlook the obvious. The advocates of pay as the prime motivator are, of course, right and wrong. Pay does motivate in lots of ways, but will people go on increasing this effort endlessly as more and more increments of pay are added?

Common sense tells us that there must be a physical limit, but does it stop before that? Yes, it does. There must come a point when you want to spend your earnings. In other words, at some stage, effort and leisure begin to compete. That is why the labour supply curve eventually bends backwards, so that in the end you get less work for more pay. Figure 10.1 illustrates the relationship between hours of work and pay.

Figure 10.1

The more horizontal the slope, the better is the incentive, but the real test of an incentive scheme is to make it go up to the turnback point, but not beyond it. We cannot have it both ways – if today is a leisure society, then motivating people to work will become harder at any level of pay. We have seen in the model that there is a strong pressure in the system to keep pay low for a majority of workers and that these workers often work unsocial hours. This does not mean that the leisure equation doesn't apply to them – it does. Leisure pursuits can become a priority over effort at any level of income. It is too easy to think of only rich people having leisure – they have more leisure and more expensive leisure – but non-work time can be enjoyed, and therefore valued, no matter what the income. Managers will notice that low-paid staff will sometimes decline a pay stimulus such as overtime. It is worth noting that this whole argument can be turned on its head and leisure used as a stimulus instead of pay. Leisure has its own motivational stimulus as well. This points again at 'convenience' as being the motivational area of the future. The lessons from the relationship between pay and leisure are first, that more pay increases the quality of leisure, but always risks the turnback situation and second, that convenient employment which dovetails into domestic financial needs and leisure pursuits is a genuine motivational strategy.

Grumbles, gripes and more

It has been said earlier that pay is never neutral. There are two reasons for this. On the one hand it is umbilically linked to effort, and on the other it is a language everybody understands. Because of this, you can translate anything about effort into a value that can be communicated. Everybody needs 'more' money, it is a readily understandable sentiment. This gives grievances about pay a special legitimacy that others don't have. Problems about the supervisor or some detail of the work are not translatable currency, people would simply not understand.

All of us tend to take our health for granted except when illness strikes, but even then, at least in the short term, we tend to think in absolute terms ('I'm ill') rather than relative terms ('it's all very well for you, you're not ill'). Pay isn't like that. When people say they are unhappy with their pay, we do not really know what it is they are unhappy with. Pay is related to many things and is interpreted in a number of ways which are not mutually exclusive. One thing is certain, pay has absolute value and a relative value.

Interpretations of pay relationships

My pay compared to:

- Absolute value – 'Cost of living going up. . . .'
- My effort – 'I've worked hard for this. . . .'
- The effort of others – 'He gets the same as me for less. . . .'
- The pay of selected others – 'I should get as much as. . . .'
- Profits – 'They make enough to pay me a bit more. . . .'
- Status – 'Someone of my status should earn. . . .'
- Summing up effect – 'This is your life. . . .'
- Past sacrifices – 'I gave up a lot for this. . . .'

The fourth interpretation 'the pay of selected others' is of particular interest. Who are the selected others and why have they been singled out for comparison? If comparison with others is used as a justification for a pay claim then it certainly matters who people use for comparison purposes. It is easy to make an invidious comparison which will certainly produce psychological discomfort (see Chapter 8). In fact, workers don't do that. The underlying principle of comparisons is usually similarity of skill. In other words, workers compare themselves with workers who have similar skills and who earn more than they do! This gives a pay claim a touch of both common sense and strategy. Tradition also plays a hand here. It is for both these reasons that pay leagues tend to remain fairly stable over time, as do company pay structures.

Hotel and catering workers have no others to compare themselves with if the similar skills principle counts. The hotel and catering industry is an occupational community with a unique set of skills. This, coupled with the phenomenon of occupational rigidity discussed in Chapter 3, means that comparisons that are made are between employers for the same occupation.

Investigators always end up in a maze when seeking the cause of a pay problem. There is, however, an alternative suspect which must not be overlooked – the pay system.

Pay and pay systems

Perhaps one of the strongest findings of pay research has been that people have quite separate feelings about pay and the pay system which produces their earnings. By pay system, is meant the system of overtime, bonus, basic, gratuities etc. used to make up the final pay packet. The model in Chapter 3 talks about the need for flexibility of labour supply and the pay system plays an important role in this, providing earnings flexibility and, at the same time, acting as a grievance handling mechanism in relation to the effort – reward bargain.

By what means is a pay system a grievance procedure? The proposition is based on the function of the pay system as a regulator between effort and reward. The particular grievance referred to here relates to the circumstances where the demands of the job exceed normal expectations. An individual in his job adjusts himself to give a level of effort in return for a certain level of reward. When more effort is demanded, the individual expects greater reward. This is not specially negotiated: the pay system simply comes into action and increases the reward. Two simple examples would be: where extra hours are required overtime is paid; or where more production is demanded the incentive system adjusts the reward. In other words, the pay system is the means by which rewards are adjusted in line with fluctuations in effort. An example of the type of pay system which adjusts in this way is the gratuity system.

The gratuity system rewards this form of extra effort through increased tips or a greater share of the service charge. While it would certainly be wrong to infer that staff increase their effort only in response to incentives, it would be unrealistic to suggest that this has no influence, or that in the absence of an adjustment staff would not feel a sense of grievance.

What the pay system is doing is maintaining a balance between effort and reward under fluctuating conditions. In a sense, the gratuity system settles this type of grievance before it is raised, but not before it is felt. The average size of work group in the industry is small and, therefore, such effects are likely to be felt severely. It is not difficult to see the vicious circle which can follow from this type of situation (see Chapter 4).

11 Organizations and authority

Once anyone takes on the role of manager, they assume authority. Like putting on a coat, they suddenly find they have an additional quality. At first it may not fit too easily, but with experience it becomes more comfortable. If we were to look for some central or pivotal idea which formed the very heart of understanding management we would probably find two things – profit and authority. Our concern here is with authority – the right to give orders and command obedience.

Authority owes its pre-eminence to the fact that first, it is such an intrinsic quality of the 'role' of manager that it becomes part of the psychology of the role incumbrent and second, that it is the very building brick of organization structure.

Perception of authority

It is not unusual for those taking on authority for the first time to find themselves feeling uncomfortable. This feeling is engendered by the presence of a difficult question – how do you know when your authority is working? The answer is by the way your orders are received and carried out by your subordinates. Everything is conditional and a matter of degree and it takes experience to judge when things are going well. Coterminous with the concept of authority is the idea of legitimacy, that is the notion that your right to give orders is regarded as proper and acceptable by those who are on the receiving end. Legitimacy, like authority, simultaneously exists at a general level and rests on specific acts. Thus, in the employee's mind there is a view of management in general and individual managers in particular. To simplify the argument:

1 Employees may accept management's authority in general, but object or withdraw legitimacy on particular acts of authority – 'I'll do anything you ask, but not that. . . .'
2 Some managers will have stronger authority than others in the sense that they will be regarded as more legitimate – 'I'll do that for her, but not for you!'
3 The legitimacy of authority is related to the source of that authority as seen by the employee. Consequently, there will be different ways of legitimizing authority.

It is reasonable to assume that not all orders are perceived as either a reward or a threat; some will simply be obeyed without feeling. It is also not difficult to imagine that within one organization some managers will find it easier than others to command respect and obedience and that any one manager may be perceived in different ways by different individuals.

What really matters is that managers have the respect of their employees. It is still, however, worthwhile considering the various bases of authority. Any manager's authority springs from many sources simultaneously.

Sources of authority

- Responsibility
- Personality
- Right of 'office'
- Type of knowledge or expertise
- Knowledge differential with subordinates
- Age
- Length of service

A manager's authority springs from all these sources simultaneously, but what matters is how the individual manager sees their authority. Part of their self description will include 'why people obey my orders'. It may well be that one of the sources is favoured in this self description. In a similar manner, as authority requires legitimacy, subordinates will have a perception of what that manager's authority is based on and will judge his or her behaviour according to that. In other words, it is the employees' judgement of the manager's competence that causes respect or derision. An example would be appropriate. Suppose a manager defines himself or herself as being highly managerially trained with a set of skills unique to managers. Subordinates, however, see this particular manager's authority as coming from the 'office' backed up by organization rules. Here, the assumptions about authority are not mutual. Does it matter? The answer to this question is yes and no.

Examples can be found to suit both cases. Often assumptions about authority are culturally derived – the hotel and catering industry would be an example where workers assume that managers have technical knowledge of the job workers do. Other industrial workers might be amazed if they found out that managers could do their job, expecting them to know only about management. What is clear is that demonstrated competence can override any difficulties that may arise from lack of mutuality over perceptions of authority.

Five points need to be made about the importance of managers' self perceptions of authority and workers' perceptions of authority.

- Perceptions can change over time.
- Perceptions of authority matter in relationships and form the basis of obedience.
- Demonstrable competence can override any contradictions between managers' perceptions and the workers' view.
- The manager's self perception of anything will change as he or she rises up the organization hierarchy.
- The manager's self perception of authority will be influenced by the form of authority embedded in the organization structure.

Everything so far has been concerned with sources of management authority as if authority only resided in management. This is true only in the legal sense – other sources of authority, legitimate or otherwise, are always at large.

Other sources of authority

- Employee autonomy
- Tradition
- The status quo
- Precedent

You cannot have it both ways. If either the job cannot be totally formally controlled or you deliberately ask a worker to take some responsibility for their work, then you must expect them to grant themselves authority over it. The consequence of granting autonomy to a worker is that you grant authority as well. If, as in the hotel and catering industry, service occupation standards are in the hands of the servers, then conscientiousness is essential. This can only spring from trust on your part and a sense of responsibility on the part of the employee. The formation of an occupational identity and pride in work is based on the individual taking responsibility for their work. Not surprisingly, this can lead to clashes between the authority of managers and that of workers. Two susceptible areas are standard of output and technological substitution. In the first case, it would be more difficult for managers to try to change standards if they did not know how to do the work themselves – an area where perceptions of authority really count.

Not only can workers claim authority over their own work, but situations have authority as well. The status quo – how we have always done things around here – has its own authority, because it has a self-justifying rationale.

People feel comfortable and are not threatened by the status quo. A slightly different case is that of 'tradition'. This implies both a value and an ideal which is worth continuing from the past. The word traditional cannot really be used to justify something except when it is describing some activity which is valued. The authority of tradition lies in the value of whatever it is maintaining. The status quo need not represent a value at all. In a similar manner, precedent is a justification only when it is linked to some value like fairness or equity. In the hotel and catering industry standards can become traditional values; when challenged by economics they can be defended only on the grounds of being appreciated by customers.

The central point here is that these alternative sources of authority present managers with a challenge when they wish to make changes.

Authority and structure

This last point leads us towards the question of the relationship between authority, as a concept, and organizational structure. Organizations consist of sets of 'roles', each with areas of responsibility and authority. These roles are normally arranged in a hierarchy and the whole purpose of the edifice is to exercise control over the activities of the organization. The organizing principle behind the division of labour, both vertically and horizontally, is functional rationality, by which is meant dividing work groups up by clearly different production or service activities, e.g. kitchen is separated from restaurant services which is separated from room cleaning. These activities must be controlled and there are three broad forms of such control. First, the form of control could be technical, based on the control of output or second, bureaucratic, based on rules. The motto of the former would be the 'best way to do things' and the latter would be the 'proper way to do things'. Chapter 6 discussed some limitations on technical and bureaucratic control and therefore the third possibility is normative control which places a greater burden on 'ideals and standards' as the basis of control – 'the way things should be done'.

The point being made here is that different forms of control require different sources of authority. If the form of control is bureaucratic, based on rules, then the form of authority would stem from 'the office' rather than any characteristics of the person holding the office. In such a bureaucratic structure role incumbents are merely administering rules. If the form of control is technical, then this too could form the basis of a bureaucratic structure, but it is more likely to be one in which the authority basis is technical knowledge differentials. The greater the degree of scope and authority granted to a role, the more likely it is that the source of authority will be personality and knowledge. A charismatic leader does not rely on 'position' and 'structure' as the source of their authority but on their own will. There is often a succession problem in roles which use personality as a basis of authority. Rarely does the successor exactly match the outgoing incumbent. Replacing Caesar has always been a problem!

One of the most striking characteristics of the hotel and catering industry is that the rapid turnover of business requires strict formal financial controls but the actual activities that represent that business are very hard to formally control. As long as consumer demand fluctuates, and there are individual differences in performance, this will always be so. For this reason, the industry tends to have a combination of formal control mechanisms and fairly rigid role descriptions which give it the look of a bureaucracy, while at the same time having a structure which copes with all this variation and subjectivity through personal authority and leadership. This appears to the outsider to be very ad hoc.

Power and authority

If authority is a 'right' conferred by a number of sources is that any different from having power? The two concepts are inseparable, but it is important to try to distinguish them. A common classification of types of power would be as shown in Table 11.1.

Table 11.1

Type of power	Applied by
Physical	Force
Resource	Exchange and bargaining
Position	Rules
Expert	Knowledge differential and learning opportunities
Personal	Persuasion

This classification could just as easily be about sources of authority. The way to distinguish between them is to see authority as a 'right to give orders' and power in terms of sanctions and rewards which are a contingent necessity. Rules of discipline and bargaining strength, for example, come from the same knapsack – they are both power 'tools' and can be used as rewards or sanctions.

The difference between power and authority can best be seen by what they share – both require to be legitimized but in different ways. If a manager stopped one hour's pay from someone who was late by half an hour that might be acceptable, but if a day's pay was stopped that would be unacceptable. What is being said here is that the rules of discipline have to be regarded as legitimate, which in the case of power means fair. The difference is that the response to an authority problem would be 'you don't have the right to tell me to do that' while the response to a power problem might be 'that is unfair'.

To go further, authority and power have a different relationship to responsibility. If responsibility confers authority by conferring the right to decide it does not automatically confer the use of any sanctions or rewards. While an area of responsibility justifies authority, power can be justified only 'in usage' and in terms of fairness and necessity. It is the idea that power is judged by how it is used, rather than by its existence, that brings the two concepts back together again. Clearly, if power is seen to be constantly misused, or blatantly unfair, then subordinates will begin to question the authority of the user of power. The less legitimate your authority is, the more you may need to use power, which only undermines your authority still more. It is a cycle which is all too easy to get into.

Authority and communication

It was suggested in Chapter 6 that all management behaviour communicates by sending signals to subordinates. This was particularly so, the argument went, when standards were subjective. If the manager failed to see low standards this might be interpreted by subordinates as the manager not caring. This idea of signals is important, because it reminds us that everything managers do is connected to the perceptions of their authority and that not all communication is written or oral or even deliberate.

It is a universal tenet of management that 'good' communication is a good thing. Like not shooting the cat, it is something hard to disagree with. Good communication is usually seen as clear communication. The merit of clarity is usually seen as giving the recipient of the communication a clear unambiguous understanding of what is required. Exactly, but the argument stops too soon. If we go on, then a connection appears between clarity of communication and perceptions of authority. *Regular* clear communication results in:

- Employees understand what you want and why you want it.
- Employees realize that you know what you want.
- Employees see continuity in your instructions.
- Employees begin to understand your logic and feel more comfortable with your authority, because it cannot spring surprises.
- Employees understand what you stand for.

In other words, the message here is that clarity increases the legitimacy of your authority, and consequently the respect you are given, because regular unambiguous communication encourages the employee to adjust their assumptions of what is expected of them.

12 Attitudes and attitude measurement

Why learn about attitudes?

What should a manager know about attitudes? This is not an easy question to answer except that he or she should know enough psychology to be able to distinguish between attitudes and opinions, to know the limitations on how far a perceived attitude indicates motivation and to understand that if an attitude survey is required it should be designed by professionals. That said, the sensitive manager looking for clues on employee behaviour knows at least that attitudes are often conspicuous to those who wish to listen out for them. This may be helpful in building up a picture of an individual or group.

Introduction

While managing people can be complicated, at least one aspect of human psychology is fairly conspicuous – attitudes. They have entered the daily discourse of managing. You hear references to them every day. A manager reflects on selection: 'Skills are one thing, but give me the person with the right attitude.' A manager senses things are not quite right with the workforce: 'Right now we could do with an attitude survey.' Even American slang has entered the language in the form of '. . . the problem with him is that he's got attitude', meaning of course, a bad attitude. In a sense there is good and bad news here because the fact that attitudes are talked about illustrates their defining quality, that is, that they are positive or negative, but since they are conspicuous it is too easy for others, in this case managers, to generalize the overall personality from the apparent attitude. This is the bad news because attitudes are more complicated and more important than simple guides to employees' personality.

People do not walk around with their attitudes printed on tee-shirts. We can observe behaviour because it is always there, but attitudes appear only from time to time, to be 'spotted' in the manner of 'bird spotting'. This quality of being 'occasionally visible' is shared with another aspect of human behaviour – the opinion. Consequently one leads to judgement of the other and more often than not the two concepts become coterminous. True, people's opinions on matters often betray their attitudes but that does not mean that attitudes and opinions are the same thing. They are two distinguishable concepts. The confusion often leads to confusion in survey work when it is not clear whether the survey is measuring attitudes or opinions. Although close cousins, they are different and must be measured differently. Even though this problem is sometimes awkward, it is reasonably easy to solve. The real problem for attitudes is their relationship to behaviour.

It would not be unreasonable to suppose that, as attitudes have a positive/negative quality, then such a quality might be translated into some form of behaviour. In other words, there should be some consistency between people's verbal expressions of their attitudes towards an object and their behaviour towards it. Although such a connection is notoriously complicated, it is an assumption of the advertising industry that such a relationship exists.

In terms of learning objectives it is essential to separate attitudes from opinions and to accept the complex relationship which attitudes have with behaviour. Demarcation lines between all the concepts involved are of necessity blurred. Clear distinctions rarely occur, therefore the study of attitudes automatically embraces opinions, values, beliefs and behaviour.

What is an attitude?

Of the many definitions of attitudes the one quoted below is perhaps the most famous:

> 'A mental state of readiness, organized through experience, exerting a directive or dynamic influence upon an individual's response to all objects and situations to which it is related.'

The key words here are 'organized', 'experience' and 'influence'. Attitudes are formed by experience and organized in a coherent way within the self. They are also involved in action. Exactly how they got involved in action is complicated, but the connection is nevertheless there. The idea of attitudes as states of readiness is shown by another definition:

> 'A predisposed response to situations, objects, people, other self-defined areas of life. It has both a *perceptual* and an *affective* component. The latter produces a direction in the attitude – positive or negative. This, in turn, can influence the perceptual element – we see what we want to see!'

Unlike the first definition this one draws out the elements of feeling and evaluation attached to attitudes and invests them with the power to influence how we see things; the 'love is blind syndrome'.

Neither of these definitions gets across those characteristics of an attitude that distinguishes it from other aspects of human psychology, particularly opinions. The key characteristics of an attitude are, first, *focus and fixity*. In other words attitudes tend to be focused on an object, a person, groups, specific behaviour, particular ideas. They also tend to be fairly fixed over time. This is not to say that they are permanent or that they cannot be changed – they can. However, evidence suggests that they are fairly stable in the short and medium run. Secondly, they are closely *related to feelings*, whereas opinions may or may not carry connotations of feeling. Thirdly, they live in groups. What this means is that some aspects of being human are organized in a coherent way within the self. To carry positive and negative components which may be contradictory, for example, to be liberal and conservative about a theme issue, is inconsistent and will cause dissonance. The more likely pattern, within the self, would be that someone with, say, a positive attitude towards personal fitness, would also be positive about healthy eating, clean environment, no smoking, etc. In other words, there are rope bridges between specific attitudes which join them together in a coherent way. The sense of wholeness and identity depends on our inner coherence.

If anything is 'fixed' in life, we tend to assume it is anchored to something. This is true of attitudes. The fixity we associate with attitudes comes from anchors and reinforcers. Obviously a person does not go around thinking of a particular object. No object is in constant focus, therefore if the attitude is anchored, the anchor must be broader, deeper and wider than a fleeting focus on an object.

To what is an attitude anchored?

- *To values* – what is desirable and meaningful across a range of life situations and over time.
- *To culture* – shared values, shared norms, shared understanding of symbols.
- *To habitual behaviour.*
- *To approved behaviour.*

If values, culture and behaviour anchor and reinforce attitudes, the question that arises is; where is an attitude anchored? Tied to a tree like a horse? In a way, yes. The clue comes from the second definition quoted. The perceptual element of attitudes suggests that the attitude is anchored in perceptual categories. If, for one moment, the mind can be envisaged as a set of lock-up garages with some we have forgotten we own, some we cannot remember what is in them, but some we find useful, it is likely, then, that we put stuff we like in some lock-ups and stuff we don't like in others.

In other words, our perceptual categories have already been evaluated – things we like and things we don't like. It is this quality of positive–negative within our 'way of seeing' that transfers itself to the attitude and is itself reaffirmed by the positive–negative character of the attitude: 'mutual reinforcement – had to change'. The message from the attitude–perception relationship is that to change an attitude you have to change the way the object is seen, which is the same thing as saying change the way the object is categorized, move it to another lock-up.

The character of attitudes

- They are related to an object, a person, an idea, a piece of behaviour within the individual's environment.
- They influence perception by influencing the way the individual collects information.
- In turn this relationship becomes reciprocal.
- They influence the formation of goals.
- They are learnt and enduring.
- They imply both evaluation and feeling.

Inside an attitude – its components

There are three components within an attitude. These are:

1 Cognitive

This component is concerned with the object in terms of attention to it, awareness of it, learning about it, understanding it, placing it in relation to other things.

The words we associate with this component are concerned with understanding the object's origins, location and consequences. For example:

will lead to	causes
goes with	yields
comes from	produces
results in	costs
	prevents

The flavour is 'the way we see it'.

2 Behavioural

This component is concerned with the action implicit in the perception of the object and sees the object in terms of behaviour, intention and action.

The words we associate with the component are verbs; for example, buy, sell, hit, vote for, kill, rent to, endorse, hire, fire, choose, reject.

The flavour is one of action.

3 Affective

This component is concerned with the object in terms of interest in, evaluation of, feeling towards, belief in, etc.

The words we associate with this component are, for example, like, dislike, love, hate, want, fear, happy, sad, angry, bored.

The flavour is, like it – don't like it.

Clearly, the relationship between these components is not one of constant equal influence. The relative dominance of each will change according to these circumstances:

- How much the person already knows about the object.
- Whether or not the person can clearly identify the object.
- How much interest the person has in the object.

Forming and maintaining attitudes

Attitudes are learnt – babies don't have attitudes! They are learnt by absorbing the culture, through experiences and through our own behaviour. Although they are personal they are not determined entirely by the individual. Not only are attitudes learnt, they are also conditioned by the acceptance or rejection of other people whom the individual regards as important. This may be society itself, a group or simply 'people we like'. This conditioning of attitudes is known as the influence of 'social norm'.

Because they are personal, attitudes perform certain *functions* for the individual such as:

- Direct people; moving from the undesirable to the desirable.
- Help to define who we are.
- Give direction to experience. We have learnt something and our attitudes tell us what to do when the experience is repeated.

Attitudes have two distinct relationships with behaviour. It would be wonderful if we could predict behaviour from attitudes, but alas this is not really possible. However, if the notion of *intention to behave* is placed between attitudes and behaviour, then careful measurement can produce some predictions.

The theory of reasoned action

Through its wide application in the advertising industry this theory carries considerable weight in the world of management. It is used as the basis of studying the relationship between attitudes and behaviour and offers the opportunity to predict the latter from the former. Hence its application in advertising. Theoretically, the theory states the relationship between beliefs, attitudes, intentions and behaviour. At the heart of the theory is the notion of 'intention to behave'. While we do not always act upon our intentions, we often do so when they are focused on some specific piece of behaviour rather than generalized goals or broadly defined areas of behaviour. Note the differences between 'I'd like to be fitter' (generalized goal), 'I should play more sport' (broad category of behaviour), and 'I'm going to play squash' (focused behaviour). The latter is more predictable as a form of behaviour than the others.

The application of this theory is based on measuring two aspects of the attitudes. These are:

- The attitude towards the intention to the behaviour.
- The attitude towards the social norm associated with the behaviour.

By 'social norm' is meant the approval of other people, which may be society as a whole or specific others, on whether the behaviour should or should not be activated. In other words, a person's intention to do something is founded on whether they are positive or negative towards the behaviour and whether or not that behaviour is approved of by people whom the person likes or feels they ought to refer to. This reference to the approval or otherwise of other people has an expectancy-value dimension.

This expectancy-value consists of two dimensions:

- A belief that they will or will not approve the behaviour.
- An evaluation as to how far the person cares about the approval of others.

A degree of predictability can be obtained from measuring attitudes and social norm expectancy-values in relation to the intention to take an action.

Fishbein, M. (1967), *Attitude and the Prediction of Behaviour Readings in Attitude Theory and Measurement*, New York, Wiley, pp. 477–492.

A more intimate bond between attitudes and behaviour can be expressed in the conundrum: do I behave in a certain way because of my attitude or is my attitude after the fact justification for my behaviour? Both are true.

If we habitually perform a certain behaviour, then we take on the appropriate attitude. On the other hand, if we hold an attitude rooted in some personal value and are confronted with the need to respond to some stimulus, then we are likely to follow our attitude and behave accordingly.

Attitudes run in packs

Like wolves, attitudes run in packs. The great advantage of this is that to find and measure an attitude you begin by rounding up 'known associates', rather in the manner of the police. In fact, the idea of 'running in packs' is a rather flippant expression of the psychological conditions of concept organization and of 'consistency'. The need to be consistent within ourselves. It is this need for consistency that is so helpful, because the discovery of one attitude may lead to the discovery of others. Actually this relationship between attitudes is one of ever greater parameters, so that each attitude is subsumed within a larger one.

In other words, each attitude group belongs to a larger attitude group or construct, thus forming a hierarchical basis for 'internal organization'. For example, the attitude 'I hate sport' may be associated with physical laziness, a preference for artistic pursuits, and be subsumed within some larger constraints such as 'a dislike of competition' or 'strong individualism' or 'a dislike of being in teams'. There are many ways in which one attitude can be interpreted and it is the task of attitude measurement to find the attitude under investigation through the manipulation of assumed known associates and assumed larger constructs. A familiar example may help to make the idea clear.

If the object of an attitude study is, 'people's attitudes towards a half bottle of wine', then a sample of wine drinkers would be used in the study. To create a survey the researcher would need to have in mind two *artificial* 'ideal types': characteristics of people who would be in favour of half bottles of wine and characteristics of those who would be negative towards the poor half bottle! The suggested 'ideal type' given in Table 12.1 uses constructs that are far wider than mere 'drinking habits'. Whether these concepts actually represented the attitude to the object can only be proved by testing.

Table 12.1

Positive	*Negative*
Moderate in all consumption	Indulgent
Concern for drink-driving	Thoughtless about drink-driving
Separates business and pleasure	Mixes business and pleasure
Concerned about health	Not very concerned about health

Attitude measurement

The procedure outlined here is a simplified version of what happens in professional attitude measurement. It has been simplified because in real life each stage of the procedure is required to be done several times and the final survey questionnaire piloted several times before it is used. The intention here is merely to get an insight into the process.

The procedure for designing an attitude survey is in four parts:

A   Developing and refining attitude statements.
B   Scaling.

C   Administering the questionnaire.
D   Scoring procedures.

The principle

To put it simply, the objective of an attitude survey is to find this positive–negative tendency towards the object. We do this by developing an equal number of positive and negative statements about the object, then invite the subjects to say to what extent they agree or disagree with the statement. If we are measuring a tendency, then there must be some dividing line between positive and negative. The mid-point in the scale fulfils this function.

The measurement principle is to find a total score and see if the subjects are above or below mid-point score. Above means positive and below negative.

Developing statements

The first task is to develop an equal number of positive and negative statements in relation to the object. First brainstorm as many statements as you can, then refine them into the most likely candidates. To get the imagination going, it is often useful to envisage two 'ideal type' opposites. The sort of person who would be positive about the object and the sort of person who would be negative.

The statements should be carefully worded so as to elicit from the respondent a real feeling towards the object. The statements should create different responses from those who are for the object and those who are against it. In other words, statements should differentiate respondents. Some guidelines are as follows:

- Statements should be expressions of behaviour rather than matters of fact.
- The problem with fact is that both those favourable and those not favourable can agree about facts.
- Avoid ambiguity, but also avoid being obvious: 'Dogs are friendly' and 'Dogs smell' are far too obviously directed statements.

Scaling

A commonly used measurement is the Likert scale. In this method, subjects place themselves for each statement on a scale as follows:

Strongly agree
Agree
Uncertain
Disagree
Strongly disagree

Given these statements, scale the values. In this case we will adopt the usual practice of making Strongly agree = 5, Agree 4, Uncertain 3, Disagree 2, and Strongly disagree 1.

At this point it is worth restating that we have two modes of statement – positive and negative. If we say we *strongly agree* with a *positive* statement, we are saying the same thing as *strongly disagree* with a *negative* statement. If we leave the scale as it is, we would get a score of 5 for the first case and 1 for the second. As the subject would have to answer both the negative and positive statements, the total scores for two subjects responding in this way would be 6 and 6. In other words, they cancel each other out. Therefore, *in scoring* we reverse the values on the negative statements.

Suppose we were trying to find attitudes to dogs. Take two statements: 'positive = Dogs are friendly', 'negative = Dogs are smelly'. If we keep the scale values the same, then a person with a positive attitude to dogs might respond:

	Score
I strongly agree that dogs are friendly	5
I strongly disagree that dogs are smelly	1
total	6

A person with a negative attitude to dogs might respond:

I strongly disagree that dogs are friendly	1
I strongly agree that dogs are smelly	5
	6

They score the same!

If we reverse the scale values of the negative statements, then a person with a positive attitude to dogs might respond:

I strongly agree that dogs are friendly	5
I strongly disagree that dogs are smelly	5
	10

A person with a negative attitude to dogs might respond:

I strongly disagree that dogs are friendly	1
I strongly agree that dogs smell	1
	2

By reversing the negative values we have shown a clear difference in the scores. Enough of dogs and scales. When the questionnaire has been completed by the appropriate sample, it is then a case of scoring the whole test.

Scoring

If, for example, the questionnaire had 10 statements, the maximum score would be 50 and the minimum would be 10. The mid-point is 10 × 3 = 30 (3 is the mid-point of the scale). A score of say 35 is just above the mid-point and is therefore a measure of a mildly positive attitude. A score of 40 would be strongly positive.

Scoring a sample

If you have 30 questionnaires with 20 statements (10 +, 10 −), the procedure is to create a matrix of 30 subjects × 20 statements:

Subject	Statement						
	1	2	3	4	5	n ...	Total score
01							
02							
03							
04							
05							
06							
07							
08							
n							

Average per statement

The important column is the total score for each subject – you will have 30 such scores. Now as you have 20 items, the maximum score would be 100 (20 × 5) and the minimum score would be 20 (20 × 1). The important figure is the mid-point which would be 60 (20 × 3). You then *count* the number of subject total scores that exceed 60 and the number that score below 60. If, for example, the result is 25 positive scores and 5 negative you might conclude that the sample was positive towards your object.

You have now completed an Attitude Survey and you've got a result. *Alas, this is not so!*

How do we know that the statements are really measuring what you think they are? The answer is we do not. Not unless we do an item analysis. How can we judge if any statement is really measuring just one thing and the one thing we want? It is a complicated process. The principle is that a statement is likely to be valid if it is strongly related to all the other statements (remember the idea of running in packs). Therefore, the process is one of correlation of each statement score with the total score minus the statement score itself.

An example is given in Table 12.2. This example correlated at $r = +0.96$. This is a very high level of correlation, therefore the item is retained. If items do not reach a level of $r = +0.3$, then they are normally rejected from the pool.

Table 12.2

Subjects	Total score	Score on item 5	Total − item 5
1	45	5	40
2	42	5	37
3	35	4	31
4	35	4	31
5	20	1	19
6	39	4	35
7	33	3	30
8	40	4	36
9	22	1	21
0	27	2	25

Doing an item analysis test

Take the matrix, then correlate each item column with the total score minus the score on that item.

See how many scores are above +0.3. This test may well devastate your original results. Those which make the +0.3 re-enter the survey. If sufficient items pass the test, then an attitude may be measured from this remaining data. However, it is more likely that a new questionnaire will emerge using the validated item with more statements and the process run again. This is why professionals are needed.

13 Understanding customer–staff relations

Introduction

In a direct service industry where a proportion of employees deal face to face with customers, the human resource strategy is often simply 'get the right people' and everything will be fine. While it is undoubtedly true that not everyone can take on a role of this type, it is also true that sometimes there are those who can find performance difficult to sustain. In other words, there are inherent problems in the customer–staff relationship that have to be faced by those who are suited to the work and by those who are not. It is not just a case of recruiting the right people.

Initial observation of the relationship suggests that the problems lie in the subjectivity of evaluation and that there are degrees of success and failure which are hard to define. What are 'good' interactions and what are 'bad' interactions? In a sense, only the customer can say. However, observation shows that extremes are fairly conspicuous; for example, a row in a hotel lobby or a taxi rank tends to attract attention. Similarly, familiar, friendly encounters, while less conspicuous, are nevertheless visible. Between the happy stimulating encounter and the row lies a range of behaviour which is visible only to those taking part. Management only learns of how customers evaluate such encounters through feedback systems. Although it is quite obvious that extremes of behaviour are conspicuous, there is another form of behaviour which is not extreme but equally visible, that is, the icy, standoffish, legalistic type of encounter where the minimum is exchanged. Observers of the guest–host relationships in tourism often point to this type of encounter.

What this type of behaviour teaches us is that the nature of any encounter is not just a matter of the interaction itself, that is, what was said and done, but what both parties *brought to* the encounter. A frosty, indifferent encounter is the result of antecedents. Among other possibilities, this suggests that previous experience of encounters are brought to the current encounter. If this is so, then an indifferent encounter engendered by antecedents produces negative consequences which then enter the next encounter. All encounters are connected! Presumably, the influence of one encounter on another depends on the time gap. If a member of staff is constantly dealing with people, then this rate of interaction itself ensures that the mood of one encounter invades the others. What this means for management is that 'good' customer–staff relations have to have a 'sustainable' quality.

Some inherent problems in customer–staff relations

The following paragraphs describe factors which influence the characters of social interaction between customers and service staff.

1 *It is essentially a demand and supply relationship.* Although there is an exchange taking place, the direction of control lies with demand rather than supply. The customer wants something.
2 *Wide range of demands.* It is not uncommon to find customer service staff interacting with customers on a wide range of topics and purposes.
3 *The fleeting nature of the exchange.* Most encounters are short fleeting affairs where the parties do not interact for a second time. This is *not* true of all exchanges; for example, staying in a hotel implies repeated social encounters with the same staff.
4 *The knowledge differential.* Both customers and staff have different knowledge. This can be helpful but it can also be problematic. At one level, a tourist wants to go to a particular street. The taxi driver knows where it is. In this case, information is part of the exchange. However, demands have a qualitative element which is open to interpretation. It is when each person interprets matters differently that problems ensue. What the customer thinks is 'good service' and what the employee thinks is 'good service' may not coincide. This is the basis of the 'co-orientation' model.
5 *The intersection of production conflicts.* Some customer service staff inhabit roles which are at the intersection of work processes which have built-in conflicts. For example, the waiter wants the dish now! The chef wants it to be 'just right'. This is a speed versus quality conflict where the pressure is on the party which has to face the guest, who of course wants the dish perfect and quickly!
6 *The rate of throughput.* The quality of each encounter is influenced by the rate and quality of previous encounters. The customer at the end of the queue brings that fact to the encounter, while the server brings to it the fatigue of all the previous encounters.
7 *The 'natural' ignominy of service.* This is controversial, but what is undoubtedly true is that in some countries service is seen as demeaning work. There are often historical reasons for the value placed on occupations.
8 *Economic difference between customer and staff.* This is an immensely important consideration for the tourism industry. When two people of widely different economic status meet, there is the likelihood of the employee feeling deprived. The behaviour responses to this can be both negative and positive.
9 *Cultural difference between customers and staff.* In a sense, this is a special case of paragraph 4, where differences in cultural background increase the chances of misunderstanding. These differences are often engendered by group membership.

These 'inherent' problems could be viewed as potential problems, as it is certainly not the case that they are automatically and universally influential on social interaction. Some of the problems are in close proximity to interaction, but some are background elements. For example, a useful classification would be:

Behavioural influences: paragraphs 1–3, 6.
Situational influences: paragraphs 4, 5.
Background influences: paragraphs 4, 7–9.

Note that the knowledge differential can be both a situational influence and a background influence. Perhaps the most important theme to emerge from this list of inherent problems is the significance of what both parties bring to the encounter – the antecedents. Expectations of what might happen or 'ought' to happen are there before the parties actually meet.

Understanding encounters

Antecedents collide!

The importance of what each person brings to the encounter is that their status, their experience, their mood of the moment, all influence their *expectations of the encounter and their perceptions of the purpose or subject of the encounter*. For both parties, how they 'see it' and what they anticipate is decided before they get to the encounter – even if they are not conscious of it! To go even further, precisely because people are not 'aware' of what they are bringing to an encounter, their responses within the encounter will, in part, be conditioned by antecedents.

Exchange theory and the nature of interaction

Put simply, Homan's exchange paradigm assumes that all social action *simultaneously* involves cost and benefit for the individuals. Furthermore, an individual behaves in the expectation of maximizing benefits and minimizing costs. In terms of interaction with others, the realization of benefits will depend on the response the individual's behaviour elicits. If the behaviour is not recognized, rewarded or is in some way rejected, then three things happen *simultaneously*:

- The benefit of that behaviour recedes.
- The costs of that behaviour also recede; and most importantly
- The benefits of some other behaviour rise as well.

An example would be helpful. In the context of group membership, an individual is enjoying benefits of membership for which the cost of having to conform is to lose some of his or her individuality. Suddenly the individual's behaviour is rejected by other members, so the benefits of membership decline, but as they do the costs decline because the individual is no longer paying the price of conformity and thus the benefits of being an individual return. In other words, behaviour is altered because of a negative response from another person.

Homan, G. (1962), *Sentiments and Activities*, London, Routledge, Kegan Paul.

What exchange theory teaches us is that the currency of exchange is individual expectations and that behaviour is essentially a set of responses in which expectations become manifest and are either realized or not. What is especially interesting about exchange is that it shows that when expectations are frustrated the result is not automatically conflict, because there is room in the encounter for both parties to retreat into what is termed *second position behaviour*.

Second position behaviour is a 'bolt hole' where expectations are lowered to the minimum and the exchange becomes 'legalistic' and 'standoffish'. It is to be contrasted with 'desired behaviour' which is first position behaviour.

To understand how benefits and costs operate in an encounter it is useful to speculate on what they might be in a particular encounter between a service worker and a guest. Taking the server first, there would appear to be a range of benefits, e.g. the chance to receive gratitude, to display resourcefulness and ingenuity, to satisfy altruistic tendencies, to have skill admired, and to have some aspect of personality recognized. The costs of these benefits might be – the detachment of effort from reward, the insecurity of stepping out of a prescribed role, a possible conflict of interests between guests' wants and supervisors' wants, and a possible loss of dignity. For the guest, the benefits might be – a chance to enhance the ego, feel important, display knowledge, place the self in relation to others in an advantageous way, and be recognized as an individual. Possible costs are having to present the self to match the project image, the effort of communication, and the effort of recognizing the server's behaviour.

If it goes wrong, for whatever reason, both parties might retreat; the server might give up being helpful and hide behind 'rules' and 'I only work here' attitudes. The guest might abandon politeness and become more cryptic and demanding. There is a positive outcome, but with the minimum of 'good grace' on either side.

Social distance

A very common occurrence in tourism is a status and economic difference between tourists and tourism workers. This is often accompanied by cultural and ethnic differences. The concern here is that social distance of this kind can lead to feelings of deprivation and feelings of cultural degradation. In this situation, encounters can be influenced by envy and by communication breakdown based on cultural misunderstanding. However, it is also the case that the differential can be a motive for a desire to serve. A gap can be both negative and positive. Evidence of the positive incentive of status differences can be seen in the problems of service in societies with equality. Nevertheless on balance, the evidence points to subordinate status and invidious comparison as being the prime cause of employee stress.

Employee reactions to the problems of customer staff interaction

Anyone dealing with the general public for just a few moments will recognize that such work can be stressful and cause anxiety. Yet job satisfaction is very common in direct service workers. Even when under pressure from a heavy throughput or from a hostile customer, staff often express satisfaction. There are obviously coping strategies around.

For service workers, coping means finding psychological ways of doing their job in a way that satisfies their employers and a sequence of strangers while simultaneously protecting their ego from the assaults of servility. The conventional wisdom based on empirical evidence suggests that serving staff adopt a range of strategies of which examples would be:

- A coherent communication style.
- Emotional labour.
- Social emulation.
- Stereotying.

Communication style

Communication, even when it appears to be spontaneous, is actually well-formed and based on a conditioned style. Through experience and habits, skills can be developed which form a basic style of communicating. Often people are unaware of their own style or that they have one. Always operating in the same style, no matter what the problem, is an aid to combating stress in social interaction. It connects social interaction with personality.

Emotional labour

The concept of emotional labour is concerned with emotional reactions in continuous service situations. These reactions are based on expectations which give rise to 'feeling rules' that express the range of intensity, duration and object of emotions. Funeral directors are expected to feel sombre, receptionists are expected to be friendly and nurses are expected to feel empathy with their patients. These expectations can be accomplished by 'surface acting' in which the employee attempts to achieve the required performance by careful presentation, or by 'deep acting' in which the employee actively attempts to exhort the appropriate feeling.

Hochschild, A. R. (1983), *The Managed Heart: Commercialization of Human Feeling*, Berkeley CA, University of California Press.

Social emulation

Perhaps one of the hardest concepts to understand is the behaviour of a person in a subordinate position who emulates his or her supervisor. It is not just a case of ambition, that is, wanting to join them, but actually to live in the present tense as if the person already was 'one of them'. Admiration of a 'better style of life' can lead to its adoption by people who are, in effect, its servants. Social emulation is a process which gets rid of objective social distance and invidious comparison by simply 'changing sides'. This phenomenon can be seen in imitation and hero worship and is often associated with 'growing up', but it is in fact a coping strategy at any time of life and is particularly relevant to the understanding of tourism relationship where differentials are often conspicuously wide.

Stereotyping

Perception is a process whereby what we see is recognized through its similarity and reference to categories which exist in our minds. We live in a world where we have seen almost everything. Nothing is new, nothing can surprise or frighten us. We need to be able to handle information from the environment and in this respect having already formed groups of items or categories is very useful. We categorize people in the same way, by putting them into groups and giving them group characteristics – *this is stereotyping and it is natural*. However, it is not necessary for behaviour to actually follow the stereotype – it can be overridden. The problem for service staff is to make the hard route of overriding in stereotype instead of the easier one of using it.

No matter what the strategy actually is, the maintenance of a coping strategy depends on the degree of organizational support. An individual cannot maintain a particular behaviour without the conscious support, tacit or by implication, of the organization. Organization cultures have been described as being either supportive or defensive. The supportive culture encourages the appropriate response and an openness to communication. The defensive culture is closed and gives minimal information. It is not difficult to see that these climate variations influence behaviour.

Managing the customer–staff relationship

Management approaches to influencing this important relationship fall into three types:

- Selecting the right people.
- Social skills training.
- Information and environmental design.

Selecting the right people

Many people express the desire 'to work with people'. They see that dealing with people will fit their personal needs. This motive is very complicated. In one respect, it could represent merely a retreat from producing something, from working with data, or even from making decisions. One deals with people because one doesn't want to deal with figures or machines! In another respect, the motive could represent a wide range of personal needs from altruism through to the need for applause! No matter how many ways it can be construed, there always lies within one specific the motive – to avoid 'routine'. People are seen as variety.

It is one thing to want a job dealing with people and quite another to be good at it. Among the many attributes that support selection criteria, two emerge as being central. These are, having good verbal communication skills and giving the appearance of calmness and confidence under stress, which indicates the need for a developed coping strategy.

Social skills training

The dilemma for social skills training is one of choice and emphasis:

1 To train employees in cultural awareness which increases their understanding of how customers will perceive their services.
2 To train employees to be more self-aware of the psychological process and coping strategies which they use.
3 To develop a 'communication style' based on verbal skills and self-confidence.

In a practical sense, these items are mutually exclusive. The first aims to expand consciousness and knowledge, the second to expand self-awareness and the third to improve behaviour. 'Cultural understanding' courses for tourism workers would be an example of the first case; 'transactional analysis' would be an example of the second; and anything from media-based training to 'fully scripted performances' in the manner of Disneyworld would be illustrative of the third case.

In the long run, the second option probably provides the best sustainable results. Some objectives of this approach include:

- Awareness of what personal needs are being fulfilled in the role.
- Awareness of how and why they defend their ego.
- Recognition that retreating into a minimum obligation position leads to a similar response.
- Awareness of the dangers of stereotyping.
- Understanding why inexperienced customers behave differently from familiar ones.
- Understand the paradox that treating a person as an individual means recognizing the group to which the customer affiliates.

You do not have to have a degree in psychology to be aware of the relationship between personality and role.

Information and environmental design

Although it has been suggested that the outcome of interaction is a result of what the parties, as people, bring to it, the context cannot be ignored. Furthermore, management has a way to influence interaction by influencing the information within the situation or context of the interaction.

The problem is easy to understand because it is within everyone's experience. Anxiety and frustration of varying degrees of intensity are experienced when:

- A person is unable to make sense of information.
- A person feels they have no choice.
- A person feels too dependent on another person.

A tourist is faced with unfamiliar territory, possibly linguistic isolation, strange uniforms, vague obligation (how much should you tip!) and unusual symbols. This strangeness is in fact a motivation, and a curiosity to learn is part of the tourist experience. However, if it does not work, that is, the individual cannot orientate themselves to the environment, then frustration follows. This problem can impact on the person-to-person relationship between tourist and tourism workers.

The approach of management to what is, in its most clinical terms, an information problem is to provide clear information and to reduce the amount of information needed by the customer. One approach is to make employees good communicators. However, the environment can be more complex than any one individual can express. Furthermore, the product is partially intangible which makes it even harder to express. In a very real sense, the staff are part of the product. An alternative is if management simplify the environment by reducing choice to a small number of clear alternatives, reduce services, cut out rituals and generally make everything more tangible – then the customer has an easier task and the risk of frustration is reduced. There are, however, two possible dangers here: firstly, the chance of making something special into something mundane and, secondly, if everything is specified then the social interaction between customers and staff is similarly likely to be simplified into a businesslike exchange.

Part Three

Some Useful Techniques

14 Labour utilization and productivity

It is not at all uncommon to find some very sophisticated arguments surrounding the concept of productivity – what it is and how it should be measured can get very complicated sometimes. At least in the conceptual sense, labour-intensive service industries have it rather easy for the simple reason that the demand for labour is direct. Not for them the productivity of a machine. Instead, labour is demanded for what it can produce directly – clean a room, serve a drink, escort a tour etc. There are two very important implications of this, which are:

- That productivity is essentially about physical productivity and human capacity with all the scope for variation that that implies.
- That the origin of demand for labour is sales. A pattern of sales or forecast pattern of sales *is simultaneously* a pattern of demand for labour.

It follows from this, that productivity in labour-intensive service industries is essentially about the utilization of labour and in this respect there are two essential management tasks, which are:

- To manage the physical output by designing jobs in such a way as to ensure efficient working practices and best technological methods while at the same time setting a hiring standard in terms of personal capacity to suit the job.
- To manage the relationship between a forecast demand for labour and the actual supply of labour. *Above all else, productivity is about efficiently matching labour supply to demand.*

The two tasks share different problems but one solution. On the one hand, how is physical efficiency or personal capacity on the job to be defined and judged? On the other hand, how is a sales forecast to be translated into a forecast demand for labour? In fact, the solution to the first question becomes the solution to the second as well, and is to apply a *set performance standard*. A performance standard is an expression of output measured by a time period, for example if the unit of time is the man-day, then performance standard for room maids might be sixteen rooms per man-day or for cooks 120 covers per man-day.

Setting a performance standard

Two things need to be said about setting performance standards straight away. First, for every occupation they are personal to a particular operation and therefore not transferable between operations, and second, they are easier to set for some jobs than others. That said, the setting of a performance standard requires a full work study analysis using all appropriate techniques. The testings and timings must be done on the basis that:

- The best possible methods are being used.
- All possible technological substitutions have taken place.
- The final timings must be based not on the best or the worst or the average workers, but on an above average worker who represents a standard that can be sustained by the training and supervision functions.

The choice of measuring unit and time span should be appropriate to the job in question. For maids the choice is obvious – the number of rooms cleaned, as is the number of journeys for a room service waiter and the number of covers for a waiter. The choice of time period depends on the problem you suspect you have. If you suspect a part of the workforce is at some time overstretched and at another underused, use a unit which splits these periods, for example journeys per hour might well reveal large variations through the day of a room service department.

A performance standard has four direct functions:

- It allows a sales forecast to be translated into a demand for labour.
- It provides a guide to the hiring standard.
- It is an objective for the training function.
- It allows actual productivity to be compared with forecast productivity.

It is worth making the point that it is not necessary to measure the productivity of every job, but it is important to do so where numbers employed vary directly with the level of business.

Translating sales into a demand forecast for labour

Once a performance standard is in place, its key function is to allow management to translate a sales forecast into a forecast demand for labour. This function is crucial to productivity. To illustrate just how crucial it is, it is appropriate to return to that central characteristic of life in the hotel and catering industry – short-term sales instability.

Figure 14.1

Figure 14.1 shows the annual pattern of room business for a hotel. It is fairly clear that there is some seasonal variation.

However, while such forecasts are important, this time span hides the minute variations which determine the hotel's actual productivity. Figure 14.2 shows two identical patterns of variation and one that strays. Line SF is a forecast of sales on a daily basis and shows enormous variations from day to day.

Figure 14.2

If the demand for labour is direct, then a line representing the labour demand LD would exactly shadow line SF. Now, *in a perfect world*, the actual supply of labour (LS) would follow the pattern of the other two lines exactly. Alas, we don't live in a perfect world and the actual productivity task of management is to *make* labour supply match labour demand. It is not an exact science, because the starting point is a sale forecast which could be wrong, but you have to work from something. Having a performance standard allows the manager to translate line SF into line LD.

In conditions of fluctuating business the manager has two objectives, which are:

- To regulate labour supply to match demand.
- To determine the proportion of fixed labour supply to variable labour supply.

The principles of *workload analysis* address both these questions.

Workload analysis

The objective of workload analysis is to produce an estimate of what labour supply should be so that managers can adjust labour supply to meet the forecast targets. Six activities are necessary before reaching the final stage of adjusting labour supply.

1 *Determine a system of forecasting demand (sales forecast)* – operations should have a sales forecast for several reasons besides workload analysis. However, for whatever reason a forecast exists, the frequency of the forecast, i.e. monthly, weekly, daily or hourly, will depend to an extent on how much scope management actually have to adjust labour supply. If you can only adjust monthly, then it is pointless measuring the workload daily!

2 *The classification of the job* – the jobs which really require analysis are those which 'vary directly with the level of business'. However, in practice it is not so easy to classify jobs into direct 'sales related' and 'non-related' – there are many grey areas.
3 *Determine an appropriate unit of measure for each direct job.*
4 *Turn the unit of measure into a performance standard* – for example:

Job group	Performance standard	Time unit (hours)
Waiter/ess	20 covers	4
Cooks	90 covers	8
Maids	15 rooms	8
Bar staff	£200	8

5 *Translate the sales forecast into a forecast for the demand for labour by using the performance standards.*
6 *Compare forecast labour demand with forecast labour supply.*
• *Adjust*

An example for maids

Sales forecast	390 rooms
Performance standard	15 per man day
Demand for labour	26 man days (390 ÷ 15)
Estimated labour supply	24 man days
Adjustment	+ 2 man-days

It is worth emphasizing that as workload analysis works from a forecast and ends with some kind of adjustment to labour supply, the possibility exists that the forecast may not match what actually happens. So it is not an exact science and adjustments may over- or undercompensate.

Earlier, it was stated that there were two objectives in the task of utilizing labour efficiently in conditions of fluctuating demand. The following examples show how these two objectives are addressed by the technique.

Objective 1 Matching labour supply and demand

Table 14.1 is an example of a workload analysis for a seven day forecast of room sales for a hotel. The occupation under measurement is room maid and there are thirty-two maids employed.

Table 14.1

1 Room sales	2 PS	3 Requirement	4 FT staff	5 Staff dist	6 Room dist
375	15	25	23	−2	−30
420	15	28	23	−5	−75
480	15	32	23	−9	−135
210	15	14	23	+9	+135

480	15	32	23	−9	−135
360	15	24	23	−1	−15
300	15	20	23	+3	+45

Column 1 = Daily estimate of room sales produced by rolling forecast technique.
Column 2 = Performance standard.
Column 3 = Man/day requirement or demand for labour (Column 1 ÷ Column 2)
Column 4 = Number of full-time staff on duty or estimated labour supply (the estimate of labour supply should be expressed in terms of numbers on duty which will differ from total numbers employed. To get the figure, total number employed should be adjusted to their actual daily hours, e.g. if maid works a five day, forty hour week and you employ thirty-two maids, the daily supply of labour is:
32 × 40 = 1280 total LS per week
to get total LS per day ÷ 7 × 5 = 914 hours/day
to get the LS per day ÷ 40 = 23 maids
Column 5 = Difference between requirement (Column 3) and estimated labour supply (Column 4). A minus means a shortage and a plus means an excess.
Column 6 = The differences in Column 5 are expressed as room differences simply by multiplying Column 5 by Column 2. This column can be seen as representing under or overcapacity.

The purpose of Table 14.1 is to show the manager where oversupply or undersupply will occur. In this example, on five days there is a projected shortage and on two of those days it is sizable. The argument is that the situation is manageable in advance once the position is clear.

Objective 2 Estimating the optimum level of full-time employment

There is no exact way of measuring the optimum level of full-time employment, but the same productivity analysis that helps to match supply with demand also contributes to this problem. The principle is: given any forecast of sales, what estimate of mismatch is produced by every possible range of full-time employment. Table 14.1 uses the same room forecast as Table 14.2, but this time the room difference calculation is carried out for a range of employment levels from twenty-eight to thirty-six.

Table 14.2

Room forecast	28	29	30	31	32	33	34	35	36
375	−75	−60	−52	−45	−30	−22	−15	–	+15
420	−120	−105	−97	−90	−75	−67	−60	−45	−30
480	−180	−165	−157	−150	−135	−127	−120	−105	−90
210	+90	+105	+112	+120	+135	+142	+150	+165	+180
480	−180	−165	−157	−150	−135	−127	−120	−105	−90
360	−60	−45	−37	−30	−15	−7	–	+15	+30
300	–	+15	+22	+30	+45	+52	+60	+75	+90

Clearly, how these figures are interpreted will depend on the ease or difficulty the hotel has in adjusting labour supply. Here, 34–35 looks manageable.

What has to be emphasized is that because the problem is fluctuations in business the measurement technique is by necessity 'trial and error' and strongly dependent on the conditions of adjustment.

The comparison of actual productivity with forecast productivity

In addition to being an aid to forecasting, the performance standard also allows management to reverse the process and ask: 'How productive were we?' After all the forecasting and adjusting has been done, an actual amount of business occurs in a particular period and it is then possible to use the performance standard to examine exactly what did happen: How accurate was the forecast? How accurate was the adjustment? The example shown in Figure 14.3 simplifies the process by using only room sales on one day.

Forecast sales	390 rooms	Actual sales	360 rooms
• Performance standard	15	• Performance standard	15
Forecast demand for labour	26 man-days	Actual demand for labour	24 man-days
Forecast labour supply	24 man-days	Actual supply	26.5 man-days
Adjustment	+ 2 man-days	Surplus/deficit	+ 2.5 man-days
		Actual productivity	13.6 rooms

Figure 14.3

In this simple example the hotel was overstaffed which produced an actual performance standard of 13.6 rooms per maid (actual sales divided by actual supply).

This concept of using the performance standard to analyse actual business brings labour management directly into the budgeting and accounting systems. The figure for actual labour supply can always be obtained through timesheets or wage documentation. This means that, once broken down by appropriate activities, the various performance standards can be used to compare the performance of these activities in different periods in the past. An example would be useful. Take a restaurant at lunchtime, with a performance standard of twenty covers per waiter (Table 14.3).

What this means is that in Day 1, the restaurant was overstaffed and that they really needed only seven waiters to serve that number of guests. In Day 2, the waiters produced over the required standard.

Table 14.3

		Day 1	Day 2
a	Actual lunch cover	133	354
b	Actual labour supply	12	16
c	Performance standard	20	20
d	Productivity standard	7	18 (a ÷ c)
e	Actual productivity	11	22 (a ÷ b)

Managing labour supply

The key to efficient labour utility is not the measurement of productivity, but the flexibility of labour supply which follows from that measurement. It is through the actual adjustment that productivity is achieved. The extent to which management can adjust is very much subject to prevailing conditions in both the external and internal labour markets and, where applicable, the conditions of the union agreement. That said, the range of options given to management is as shown in Table 14.4.

Table 14.4

Reduce demand	Adjustment mechanism for labour supply
Reduce services	Increase personal productivity
Substitute technology	Recruitment
	Labour turnover
	Absenteeism
	Overtime
	Staff adjustment
	Shift realignment
	Flexible hours
	Increase part-time work
	Casualization
	Days off
	Holidays
	Contract work
	Increase internal mobility
	Retirement
	Redundancy
	Natural wastage
	Lay off
	Pay

On a day-to-day basis, not all these options are open; technological substitution, for example, requires considerable planning. Given the short time span in which adjustments have to be made, the most common methods of extending labour supply are: overtime, some form of bonus system, casual labour and part-time employment. At the very least, management should be aware of, and have compared, the cost of these alternatives.

Productivity and work scheduling

Perhaps the most basic rule of labour management is that as the work ebbs and flows management should be constantly monitoring those flows and scheduling workers in line with the peaks and troughs. The example of the maids was based on a time period of a day but in other forms of work the production is best measured by the hour – most food and beverage work and reception come into this category.

To do this it is not necessary to have someone standing around all day recording the number of guests handled each hour. A quicker method is to time stamp every bill or check and use that as the collection base. If there is a night audit function they can be delegated to sort the bills into an hourly timeframe. The whole process has five stages:

- Create a chart displaying 24 hourly periods.
- Time stamp all checks or bills.
- Record each check into the relevant time period.
- Produce a histogram.
- Adjust staff schedules to suit the pattern of demand.

Note the overall time chart need not be twenty-four hours and that any period can be brought into focus.

Work study

Work study is the practical tool of the scientific management movement. Its aim is simple: to produce the most efficient method of doing a task. The techniques of work study are rooted in the man–machine relationship in manufacturing industry and the image is of a man with a stopwatch. The stopwatch is still relevant but the techniques have spread to all areas of work.

The primary role of work study is actually at the planning stage in the design of the workplace. Rarely, except through specialized consultants, is operational knowledge incorporated into design. Not unnaturally, the priority is always the guest. Notwithstanding design considerations, managers have to work with what they have got and make it work efficiently. Work study can help.

We know already that the main productivity problem is matching labour supply to demand. Workload analysis can contribute, but its contribution depends on the creation of performance standards. It is here that work study can play an important role. Just a few minutes' observation in any area will show how significant to performance is the number of journeys made by the worker – most jobs are not static. Here is an obvious area where work study can contribute. Work study is not just standing around with a stopwatch and timing every task, it is a range of techniques to solve particular problems. Some applications are as follows:

Problem 1   The efficiency of group work

Two of the factors which contribute to the efficiency of group work are the distribution of the tasks amongst the group members and the order in which those tasks are done by each individual. One way to check this is simply to observe everyone all the time and record everything that they do. This is an onerous task and the technique of work sampling makes it a great deal easier. The basic idea of work sampling is to take a type of photograph of the work group at regular intervals during the day. The procedure is as follows:

- Draw up a matrix sheet with employees along the top and time period along the side.
- Choose a time period; basically the larger the number of tasks being undertaken the smaller the time period. A common practice is to use one-hour periods.
- At set intervals record what each member of the group is doing. It is essential to keep the intervals exactly the same. Do this throughout the day.
- Total the proportion of time spent on each activity. Note that each sample represents the whole of that time period.

Care must be taken in interpreting the results because one activity is unlikely to represent everything that worker did in the period but with this technique it does. For this reason the first three steps of the procedure must be repeated many times before being totalled. What the technique shows is:

- The loading on workers (distribution of tasks).
- The amount of wasted time.
- The order of tasks.

Two extra benefits follow from this technique. First, a model can be built showing how the work tasks should be distributed and priorities attached. Second, more detailed work can be done on those tasks that appear to be taking a disproportionate amount of time. A simplified example illustrates the procedure.

We are looking at a group of waiters and porters preparing a large banquet. In this kind of exercise coverage must be comprehensive, it is no good looking at part of the group. Here we are reproducing an extract of only four staff (Table 14.5).

Table 14.5

	Waiter 1	Waiter 2	Waiter 3	Waiter 4
3 pm	Polishing silver	Moving chairs	Cleaning glasses	Folding napkins
4 pm	Standing talking	Laying tables	Standing talking	Folding napkins
5 pm	Folding napkins	Laying tables	Distributing condiments	Standing talking
6 pm	Laying tables	Laying tables	Standing talking	Laying tables

The time span is four, one-hour periods leading to service at 7.00 pm. All the staff are surveyed and a proportion expressed as a histogram (Figure 14.4). As banquet preparation is not a continuous task, to get a proper analysis several banquets would have to be surveyed in this manner.

Remember that these are only estimated proportions.

```
┌─────────┐
│ Laying  │
│ tables  │
│         │┌─────────┐
│         ││ Folding │
│         ││ napkins │
│         ││         │┌──────────┐
│         ││         ││ Standing │
│         ││         ││ talking  │
│         ││         ││          │┌───────────┐
│         ││         ││          ││ Polishing │
│         ││         ││          ││  silver   │
│         ││         ││          ││           │┌─────────┐
│         ││         ││          ││           ││ Moving  │
│         ││         ││          ││           ││ chairs  │
└─────────┘└─────────┘└──────────┘└───────────┘└─────────┘
```

Figure 14.4

Problem 2 The best way to clean a room

In a hotel, room cleaning is the central work activity of the organization and as such getting it done efficiently contributes greatly to profitability. Comparative studies of productivity in this area always show a wide variation. Alas, the reason for this variation is often not efficiency but differences in the factors which create the productivity. For this reason productivity studies and pay surveys have to be very carefully scrutinized.

Factors affecting productivity

1 *Time taken to clear a room*
   - Personal ability of cleaner.
   - Personal motivation of cleaner.
   - Size of the room.
   - Design, layout or decor of the room.
   - Standard of cleanliness required.
   - Order of work.
   - Number of items to be placed in the room.
   - Quality and appropriateness of the equipment.
2 *Number of rooms cleaned in a specified period*
   - Pattern of demand from guests.
   - Proximity of rooms to be cleaned.
   - Quality and appropriateness of the equipment.

The process of cleaning a room contains four elements which are:

- Time to accomplish each separate task.
- The standard to be achieved.
- The order of work.
- The number of journeys.

The objective of work study would be to get the best methods of accomplishing each task which is mainly a matter of the right equipment, and to get the best sequence of work. Practice shows that the overall time is greatly reduced if the number of journeys is reduced and this is a function of the sequence or order of work.

The approach is in two stages: first, to observe and measure the performance of a worker who is considered to be a good performer and to compare the results with observations of slower workers who produce the same quality. Second, to examine closely the observations of the good performer. A quick way into this work is to examine journeys, because that automatically gives you the work order. The technique for this is the 'string diagram'. Here a peg board is used with a peg representing each place where the cleaner stands and works, e.g. bathroom, RHS bed, LHS bed, trolley etc. A piece of string is tied to the trolley peg and the observer simply simulates the worker's journeys on the board. The length of the string measures the total journey length and is compared between cleaners.

If this does not show substantial differences between good and poor performers then the difference must be in the time taken to undertake particular tasks. The next step, therefore, is to time particular tasks such as bathroom cleaning and bedmaking. If this doesn't produce differences then the poor performance must be wasting time which is a problem for supervision.

15 The measurement of labour turnover and labour stability

Given that labour mobility is a conspicuous feature of hotel and catering industries, the question of measurement needs to be addressed. There are four principal reasons for measurement.

- As has been shown in Chapter 2, labour turnover determines the rate of recruitment.
- It is an indication of the state of the external labour market.
- High instances of labour turnover are usually seen as being bad for the organization, although skill accumulation does require a degree of mobility.
- If a rate is measured, then performance can be compared between defined categories such as organizations, individual units, departments, occupations, age groups etc.

The commonest way of measuring labour turnover is the straightforward percentage. The calculation is:

$$\frac{\text{Number of leavers in a specific period}}{\text{Average number of employees during the period}} \times 100$$

The average number of employees during a period is simply calculated by taking the number employed at the beginning of the period and the number at the end of the period and finding the average, for example:

Number of leavers during the year	200
Total number of employed at the beginning of year	400
Total number employed at the end of the year	430

$$\frac{200}{415} \times 100 = 48\%$$

The merits of this measure are obvious, particularly in comparisons. The rate of labour turnover in different departments or in different establishments can be compared. There are, however, two important drawbacks. These are:

- If one of the pairs in a comparison has, during the period, undergone a major change in employment level (up or down) then you are not comparing like with like, because the percentage figure doesn't capture the essential relationship between recruitment and labour turnover described in Chapter 2. When reviewing

a set of percentages this possibility must be borne in mind. It would be wrong, for example, to compare a unit that had just opened with ones that have been running for some time, on the basis of this measurement.
- The percentage figure of labour turnover can hide areas of stability within the target population. A figure of 100 per cent labour turnover may be produced by the 400 per cent turnover of a quarter of the target population, thus hiding both a more serious problem and an important characteristic of the majority.

Measuring stability in a workplace

If there are many reasons for labour turnover there is one very sound reason for having a measure of stability, and that is that such a measure would be a good indication of the effects of policy change on the conditions in the external labour market. What stability means is the capacity for a firm to retain its labour force. In order for a measure to be useful, it must express this capacity over time and allow for comparisons in the same way as the labour turnover percentage. The stability index fits these conditions well.

Stability index

This index simply expresses the total length of service of all *present* employees in the time frame as a proportion of the maximum possible stability. This notion of the maximum possible stability simply means: the total length of service if nobody left in the time frame. For example, if a firm employing ten workers was ten years old and everyone who started ten years ago was still with the firm, then the maximum possible stability would be 100 years. If, as in this example, the length of service of present employees is also 100 years, the stability index = 1, which is maximum stability. The stability index goes from 0.0 to 1 and can be turned into a percentage by multiplying by 100. Two examples would be useful.

Example 1

A hotel employs 400 people. Let us say that 200 employees have one year's service, 100 have two years' service, fifty have four years' service and fifty have five years' service. The total length of service of all present employees is 850 years.

The period under measurement is five years. The maximum stability is, therefore, 400 × 5 years = 2000 years.

$$\text{Stability index} = \frac{850}{2000} = 0.42 \text{ or } 42 \text{ percent}$$

In normal usage the stability measure looks backwards over time and often the size of the firm will have changed over time. This is purely a technical problem for the index and it is resolved as shown in Example 2.

Example 2

As in Example 1, we take a hotel with 400 employees who have a combined length of service of 850 years, only this time the size of the workforce has fluctuated.

Size of workforce
$$2 \text{ years} \times 400 = 800$$
$$2 \text{ years} \times 450 = 900$$
$$1 \text{ year} \times 410 = 410$$

Maximum service possible = 2110

Stability index = $\dfrac{850}{2110}$ = 0.4 or 40 per cent

Comparing the two examples shows that size changes do make a difference. It would be completely wrong to work from the current size of the firm if it were known that, in the period under examination, changes had occurred in size. The beauty of this measure is that it is possible to make genuine comparisons between organizations of different sizes.

One word of caution – great care must be taken with the interpretation of comparative data using the labour turnover percentage or the stability index when it is suspected that some of the firms in the sample have experienced considerable changes of size. Where the change is an increase the labour turnover measure becomes suspect, and where it is decreased the stability index loses its power.

An example of how these two measures can tell a different story is illustrated below.

Table 15.1 *Labour turnover and stability indices for nine hotels*

Labour turnover rate	Stability index
55.2	77.0
62.8	96.5
89.2	75.4
55.0	75.5
92.0	71.2
119.1	71.6
70.8	76.9
69.6	76.6
32.9	71.7

Source: Simms, J. (1987), *A Study of the Extent and Nature of Labour Turnover in Hotels*, MPhil, University of Surrey.

The nine hotels illustrated in Table 15.1 display a similar level of stability, yet at the same time a wide dispersion of labour turnover percentages. What this suggests is that a hotel gets a similar level of service from those who stay, while an unstable element creates turnover percentages very much larger than the overall indicates.

16 Recruitment and selection

Recruitment is at heart a 'search' process. This process contains four main elements: the hiring standard (what you want); the target market (where you think you will find it); the sources of recruitment (by what means you intend to get it); and the cost (how much you are prepared to invest in the search). Clearly these elements are interrelated with performance in one determining performance in another. For example, if you are vague about what you want, you will probably misread the market, which in turn might make you choose an inappropriate source or channel and it will end up costing you more than you thought.

Surprisingly, there are only really three recruitment strategies:

- *Ring the bell* – make your organization visible in the market by spending money on the search process.
- *Pump up the balloon* – extend the size of the labour market by paying more.
- *Do-it-yourself* – Extend the size of the labour market by lowering the hiring standard and offering more training.

Obviously, there are many variations but what will determine your recruitment strategy will be your approach to the four elements of the search process. Recruitment is not an exact science but if you get the first element wrong, you may get the next wrong as well. In other words, the key to recruitment is *defining what you want in the first place*.

This is never easy because you need to translate a job into a person! Or do you? Eventually, yes, but that is not the first stage. You start with the job because a great deal of the labour market possibilities can be estimated from the nature of the job you are recruiting for.

First look at the job

There are five broad characteristics of labour markets. These are:

1 Size (large/small)

Labour markets vary in the number of people they contain. Clearly the principle cause of this would be the level of skill. The more unskilled the work, the larger the market would be.

2 Status (primary/secondary)

Strongly related to size, markets are classified into *primary* and *secondary*. Primary markets contain good jobs with careers attached and require qualifications to enter. As a consequence, they are more stable. By contrast, secondary markets contain largely unskilled jobs requiring no training. Consequently, such markets are characterized by mobility and variable attachment to the market.

3 Response to supply and demand changes (fast/slow)

The speed of response to changes in supply and demand varies with the level of skill involved. A shortage of highly-skilled chefs cannot be made up quickly simply by raising the pay because it takes time to train people. On the other hand, a shortage of room maids could be made up quickly by a pay adjustment.

4 Pay level (high/low)

Markets can vary by level of pay, usually determined by level of skill.

5 Pay distribution (wide/narrow)

For any given occupation is the range of pay wide or narrow?

It is not difficult to see that if you are looking for someone in a small primary market with a wide distribution of high pay, it is a totally different problem from looking for someone in a large secondary market with a narrow distribution of low pay. The strategy will certainly be different.

How, though, can these market characteristics be anticipated from job characteristics? In this respect, there are four key indicators:

1 The level of skill.
2 The degree of specificity (how specific the skills are to an organization).
3 Whether or not performance standard can be measured.
4 The extent to which personal qualities play a part in the job.

The effects of 1 and 2 are fairly obvious – they will change the size of the labour market, but 3 and 4 have an interesting effect. They both represent the possibility of greater individual differences in performance. If standards cannot be formally specified you are going to get a variety of performances. Similarly, if the jobs require personal characteristics, they are going to get a variety of personal differences. Both have the effect of producing a wider distribution of pay in the market.

To see how jobs can foretell market characteristics, it is helpful to give job characteristics a direction, for example as shown in Table 16.1.

Table 16.1

Job characteristics	Direction	Labour markets
Level of skill	The higher	Produces a primary market of small size, slow to react to supply and demand changes, with high pay narrowly distributed
Degree of specificity	The greater	Produces a small market, slow to react to supply and demand change, with high pay narrowly distributed
Measured performance	The greater	Will produce a wider distribution of pay
Personal qualities	The greater	Produces a larger market which responds quickly to supply and demand changes and has a wide distribution of pay

The reverse direction would indicate opposite market characteristics. The model of hotel labour markets suggests that, with the exception of the skilled levels, most hotel and catering recruitment takes place in a market which is *secondary in status, large, quick to respond to supply and demand changes, and has low pay with wide differentials.*

There is an 'active principle' at work in the area where job characteristics meet labour market characteristics – it is a 'substitution effect'. If, for a moment, it is assumed that the larger the labour market the better chance you have of finding what you want cheaply, then it is in the interests of the employer to design jobs in ways that increase the ability of the organization to substitute one person for another in the same job. The substitution effect becomes easier when:

- The more unskilled the job.
- The more training is offered by the company.
- The more personal attributes count in the job.
- The less dependent the job is on previous education.
- The more knowledge can be substituted by information.
- The less the degree of specificity.

A football manager is only allowed two substitutes in a game. Normally it is one defender or one attacker, but eleven substitutes would be more efficient and would bring down the price of the first eleven!

Now look at the person

Nothing helps the recruitment campaign more than knowing exactly what you are looking for. A word of caution is necessary here, because the labour market will not pass up someone who exactly meets an exacting specification. It is always a case of approximation, therefore the specification must be focused but at the same time couched in terms which allow a range of quality across desired attributes to be accepted. This will allow the selection process to be more efficient.

The device for focusing jobs and people is the hiring standard or hiring specification.

The purpose of this device is to specify the desired attributes of the person required for the job. Three central features of a hiring specification are: essential attainments, preferred experience and preferred education and training. It is also useful to specify aspects you don't want. In the hotel and catering industry, hiring specifications try to express a balance between technical aspects of the job and personality traits deemed essential. An example of a hiring specification for a receptionist would be as shown in Figure 16.1.

Hiring specification

Job: Receptionist   Department: Front office

Specification

Age range: 18–30

Physical qualifications: Clear speech

Education and training

Good general education
A modern language preferred
Office skills training

Preferred experience

Occupation:	Reservationist, receptionist, secretary, telephonist
Length:	One year minimum – three years preferred
Type of establishment:	Hotel, hospital or professional office
Size of work group:	Prefer small work groups
Quality of work:	Able to demonstrate experience of dealing with people, preferably on the telephone. Should have good on-line computer experience particularly with booking systems

Essential attainments

30 wpm typing
Good telephone manner
Computer experience

Disposition

Able to work under pressure – not panic, not easily bored, flexible, dependable

Circumstances

Stable domestic life

Contra-specifications

The job has limited promotion prospects and would not suit the eagerly ambitious

---

Figure 16.1

Recruitment strategy

It might be thought that recruiting in a large market is easier than recruiting in a small one. This is a matter of conjecture. They are two different problems. Having defined what you want, the strategy adopted will be directed by the answers to the questions:

- What is the size and character of the labour market?
- Who are the competition?
  - Other companies
  - Leisure
- What information will attract candidates?

The next step is to ask two more questions:

- What information should be given out?
- What source of recruitment would be appropriate for the vacancy?

The first question depends on the size of the market. Basically, the smaller the market the more specific and revealing the information should be. The second question is a matter of selecting an appropriate source or channel. Again, the size of the market is influential. Trawling through a large market may require a number of sources used simultaneously but fishing with a fine net in a small market may require something very specific and limited. The sources of recruitment are:

- Advertising
- Employment agencies
- Job centres or job points
- Consultants
- Headhunters
- Outplacement consultants
- Existing staff
- Waiting list
- Previous applicants
- Casual callers
- Education systems
- Casual correspondence

If the vacancy is to be advertised you have to consider:

1. Choice of journal – circulation figures, readership dates, publication dates and comparative cost.
2. Timing of advertisement – when published, best day and resource of personnel department.
3. Cost effectiveness – display, semi-display and lineage.
4. Classified sector.
5. Cost effectiveness of repeats.
6. Use of logo.

Cost and speed are always a factor. The hotel and catering industry has a time pressure built into its recruitment functions, therefore recruitment means fast recruitment. For this reason, the processing of applicants who apply without vacancies, becomes a prime source of recruitment. Waiting lists are cheap to maintain.

The employment interview

By far the commonest method of selection is the employment interview. Its popularity persists, despite constant criticism of its effectiveness. Such effectiveness is usually measured in terms of the ability of the method to predict job acceptances by candidates and their performance in the job. Critics cite the case for psychological testing and biodata methods as more valid alternatives, because they are based on more solid measurements. Thus the interview is labelled highly subjective and unsuccessful. While this is true, and, without denying the merits of alternative methods, the whole of people management could be said to be subjective. Of course, interviews are subjective and require judgement just like most of management. The real problems with the interview are that too much is expected of it and that it is often done badly. Fallible though it is, the method is quick, convenient and, when done well, an effective method is selection.

The objectives of the employment interview

An interview is a conversation with a purpose, in fact it has several purposes all pursued simultaneously. These objectives can be stated quite simply, and are:

- To decide if the applicant is suitable for the job, or, to put it another way, to decide how suitable the job is for the applicant.
- To decide if the applicant will fit into the existing work group and fit into the organization as a whole.
- To attract the applicant to the job (the interview is part of the recruitment process).
- To communicate the essential expectations and requirements of the job (the interview is part of the induction process).

The structure of the employment interview

Looked at clinically, an interview is an information-gathering, information-distributing, information-evaluating and judgement-forming activity! That makes it sound mechanical, but it does emphasize that judgement is based on information; not pre-conceived ideas, but gathered information. Good interviewing is often described as a skill implying that there is some set technique which is universally good. This is true, but only up to a point. Good interviewing technique is simply *some good habits and the skill of asking questions*. Be wary of formulas and set plans! There are dangers in overstructuring an interview. There is, however, a format which combines activities with thought and which constitutes a good habit.

Interview format

```
Pre-interview  →  Gather      →  Evaluate  →  Earmark key
material          information                 questions
                                    ↓
The           →  Gather       →  Evaluate
interview        information
                                    ↓
                                Evaluation
                                and
                                judgement
```

Figure 16.2

The message of the format shown in Figure 16.2 is that the pre-interview stage and the interview itself are two separate sources of information which should be *evaluated at first separately, then together*, to form the judgement. Each will tell its own story. Are they telling the same story or different ones? The point here is not to come to judgement on the pre-interview material. Just evaluate it, then combine it with the interview information.

Should you know the job?

The answer is yes, but it's not an absolute pre-requisite for good interviewing. It all depends on what we mean by 'know' the job. Actual experience of the job or supervising the job brings a certain bias with it, but is, nevertheless, enormously helpful. The task of the employment interview is to bring the character, experience and skills of the applicant and the requirements of the job together in a judgement. To have no knowledge of the job is to render the interview ineffective. Why is job knowledge so necessary? There are three main reasons, which are:

- It tells the interviewer what questions to ask.
- It enables the interviewer to assess the relevance of the applicant's career to the job in question.
- It enables the interviewer to discuss the job with the applicant.

This does not imply that interviewers must have experience of the job. There are other ways of obtaining job knowledge, the most common of which is job analysis. A detailed description of all the duties and responsibilities of a job can be obtained through analysis of the job and laid down in a job description. The job description can then be given to the applicant. The problem with a written job description is that it may mean more to the applicant than it does to the interviewer, and is thus not too helpful to the latter in forming questions. However, from a good job description a set of required knowledge, skills and abilities (KSA) can be derived for each duty or responsibility.

- *Knowledge* – a recognized body of information that is required for successful performance in the job.
- *Skill* – a competence with a measurable level of performance that is essential to the job.
- *Ability* – A more general capability.

There are four stages in transferring a job description into an aide for interviewing, which are:

1. Job analysis produces a list of tasks.
2. Rate the tasks in order of importance.
3. Apply KSA to each task.
4. Decide which KSAs will influence selection.

Thus, the interviewer has a set of key KSAs at his or her disposal, but this approach does not directly translate into questions which will help distinguish good from poor.

Perhaps a more direct approach is to combine KSAs with a form of job analysis known as *critical incident technique*. The essence of critical incident technique is that people with experience of a job identify 'incidents' and attach to them examples of good behaviour and poor behaviour. These incidents are more explicit descriptions of behaviour than the simple description of the task. A number of incidents can reflect one task. The key requirement here is a panel of expert people, who know the job through experience or supervision, to judge important incidents and justify good and bad examples.

An example might be useful here. Suppose the job in question is a Hotel Assistant Manager and you have already obtained a list of tasks and ranked them. One particular task has been identified, among others, as being a useful selector. The task is handling individual guests in respect of personal credit and settling accounts. You now need to identify KSAs.

A critical incident exercise throws up an apposite incident: A maid reports to her supervisor that a room has been severely damaged with mirrors and furniture broken. The supervisor verifies this and reports it to the Assistant Manager. The guest is not due to check out for another day.

The first task of the team is to identify what the knowledge skill and ability are in respect of this incident. They would come up with something like:

- Knowledge:
  - The legal position.
  - The insurance position, including assessment rules.
  - Rules on credit and procedures.
  - Current reservation situation.
- Skill:
  - To analyse situations into information collection area.
  - To be able to devise a set of alternative strategies based on the information collected.
  - To be able to think through and anticipate client reactions.
  - Personal assertiveness.

– Recording formally what is required.
- Ability:
  – A general ability to confront difficult social situations.

Clearly this situation will revolve around information on client status, booking situation and damage assessment. The team should then be able to produce a range of examples of what would be good practice and bad practice. The final stage would be to translate this into a situational interview question. This might be either a straightforward 'What would you do?' or the more detailed 'What information would you need to handle this incident?' or 'Would you confront the client?'

Given a set of tasks with KSAs attached to them, there are five stages to the procedure of developing something useful to the interviewer:

- Through the experts, get examples of good and bad practice associated with each critical incident.
- Allocate incidents to just one KSA that each best illustrates. The process collects the incidents that are selected and rejects those that are not.
- Translate the salient critical incidents into 'situations' which form the basis of a situational interview. These situations describe an important piece of behaviour in the job.
- Divide situations into those that would require experience to deal with them and those that would not. In the case of the latter, additional information has to be added to the situation.
- The question attached to the situation is: 'How would you handle this situation?' It follows, therefore, that some guidance as to what might constitute good and bad performance is required. To do this, the panel of experts has to create a range of answers.

The application of critical incident technique brings the dull job content list to life. By creating situations which illustrate the degree to which an applicant has the relevant KSA, the interviewer gives him or herself something concrete to assess. One way or another, some knowledge of the job is required by the interviewee. The more realistic and 'alive' the knowledge, the more likely it is that the evaluation of the answers will move from 'yes, they can do it' to 'yes, they will probably do it well'.

Forming questions, question types and strategies

Time is always a constraint in an interview, therefore it is not to be wasted. The technical goal of the interview is to get yourself into a position to answer four basic questions:

- Can they do the job?
- Would they do it well?
- Will they fit in?
- Are they motivated?

The situational interview places the emphasis on the job and asks: Can the applicant match up to good practice in this job? The drawback is that the applicants are being invited to speculate in a way which will make them look good on the basis of what they think the interviewer considers good practice. An alternative strategy is to work solely from the reality of the applicant's past. In other words, the strategy is to probe their previous employment in order to ascertain what the applicant *did*. This approach is applicant centred rather than prospective job centred.

If probing the past is the strategy and there is the usual time constraint, then the style of question must be incisive without being intimidating.

Episodic questions

Episodic questions ask the applicant to recall some specific aspect of the past. Table 16.2 contrasts episodic questions with more generalized questions:

Table 16.2

General	*Episodic*
Do you like your present job?	What has been the best moment so far in your present job?
Why do you want to work for us?	Where were you when you made the decision to apply to us?
How do you feel about moving to this part of the country?	What happened in your domestic life when you last relocated?
Do you find dealing with the staff easy?	What happened last time you had to deal with an openly uncooperative employee?

The answers to the episodic questions in Table 16.2 will be more revealing, because they produce more precise information. As they say in detective stories: 'We got the facts, but no motive.' Episodic questions must invite the obvious rejoiner – why did you do that? or, what alternative did you consider?

However, an interview consisting solely of these types of questions would eventually intimidate and would leave the interviewer with a lot of small 'bits' of information to piece together.

General and open questions

A severe limitation of episodic questions is that they can easily miss the big picture. Motivation is part of that big picture. No one question will give you a clue, an impression has to be formed from a multitude of stimuli. One clue to motivation is the applicant's references and priorities. Here, the general open-ended question can be useful.

- 'Did you enjoy college?'
- 'Tell me about your present job.'

Moving from the general to the episodic, a good strategy is to open with a general question which simply defines the area to think about, then follow it with an episodic question with the appropriate follow-up. The technique is called funnelling. An example:

- 'Tell me about your present job.'
- 'What aspect do you most enjoy?'
- 'Can you give me an example of when that aspect went particularly well?'
- 'Why do you think it worked well on that occasion?'

Here, the questioner has gone from the general and, working from the responses, funnelled down to a specific piece of behaviour.

Closed questions

These can be useful to clarify what is already known: 'How long did you spend in sales during your training?', 'You left college at 21?'

Does the job make a difference to the strategy?

Clearly it should! Interviewing a prospective assistant manager and interviewing a prospective chef cannot be the same task. Similarly, interviewing someone for a job to which they aspire, but of which they have no actual experience, must be different from interviewing someone who has done a similar job before. In this case the main thrust of the task is different. First, you are looking for managerial ability, second, to verify qualifications and skill, third, to assess potential and ability to learn, and finally, to verify experience.

Perhaps the key difference is whether the job is one requiring managerial skills or manual skills. Clearly, as management is action orientated the situational interview or questioning based on action taken in the past might be appropriate. This type of behaviourally-orientated questioning is not too appropriate when the job involves manual skills.

For manual skills, it is advisable to have checklists of skills you require and ask the applicant to record this level of competence before the interview. Figure 16.3 is an example of a culinary questionnaire.

Pre-interview material – do leopards change their spots?

The longer you spend with this material the better. Normally, the kind of pre-interview information available to an interviewer falls into four categories: personal circumstances; employment experience or career; education; and references. They should be addressed separately then judged for coherence. Do they tell a story? What information is missing?

Culinary interview checklist

What is your strongest area?

Do you have any banqueting experience?

Any insecure fields?

	Which of the following can you cook?	Which have you cooked in your last job?
Preparation of paté	☐	☐
Galantine	☐	☐
Mousseline de sole	☐	☐
Chaudfroid sauce	☐	☐
Lobster mousse	☐	☐
Bouillabaisse	☐	☐
Consommé	☐	☐
Brioche	☐	☐
Praline	☐	☐
Butter sculpture	☐	☐
Ice sculpture	☐	☐
Chocolate modelling	☐	☐

Figure 16.3

In reviewing the material on personal circumstances, the key question would be: 'How do the personal circumstances fit with the demands of the job?' Also: 'What might be the effect of the job on these personal circumstances?', 'What change, if any, is implied?'

In reviewing education and formal qualifications, the obvious question is: 'Are they appropriate and sufficient?' References are more difficult to handle. More than any other aspect of the process they carry the assumption that the past indicates the future, that performance in one job has some continuity with the next.

Do leopards change their spots? This is the usual unspoken question which passes through the interviewer's mind while scanning a career history. Indications of work stability, skill accumulation, can be obtained from a career history. The important point is that judgements are not made at this point, but questions arise to be covered in the interview.

Evaluating between applicants

There is one safe rule when several applicants are being considered, which is evaluate each one separately before you begin to compare their relative merits. This maxim is true whether or not you've used a structured interview.

For each applicant you will have four sets of information to evaluate:

- Domestic circumstances
- Previous career

- Organizational compatibility
- Suitability for the job

The advantage of using a structured interview technique based on KSAs, or KSA attached to situations, is that you can compare the performance and response of each candidate against each KSA and situation. However, a holistic evaluation of each candidate must precede any comparisons.

Biases and traps

Perhaps the most helpful hint that can be given to anyone attempting to develop and improve their skill at interviewing is to be aware of the natural biases and common traps associated with this activity. Here are some:

- Favouring negative information over positive information. Selecting a poor performer will be noticed, but missing a good one will go undetected, therefore screening for negatives tends to be given more emphasis than looking for positives.
- Exaggerating the importance of aspects of the job that you have no knowledge of.
- Letting an impressive attitude make you forget to ask some essential questions about skills and knowledge.
- It is easy to become too systematic and overstructured. Applicants can sense this and anticipate your questions. When this happens you both begin to tango.
- Letting first impressions (good or bad) overrule the evaluation of evidence from the interview.
- Making a judgement on the basis of the pre-interview material, which either the interviewer spends the whole time trying to verify or which simply renders the interview pointless.
- Perhaps the most common and damaging fault is simply to make a decision too soon, often during the interview itself. It needs an effort to train oneself into the habit of always reserving judgement until all the information has been gathered and evaluated.

Some good habits

Often the obvious is taken for granted and thus overlooked. It goes without saying that applicants should be put at their ease. Anxiety, however mild, is a barrier to communication. Space can be intimidating. Thus, inappropriately large rooms and placing the applicant and interviewer wide apart all tend to intimidate. Some writers argue that the interviewer's desk is a barrier and that both parties should sit side by side. The problem with this solution is that it is harder to take notes on your lap and, of course, notes must be taken. Here is the interviewer's main physical problem – how to concentrate and take notes at the same time. The worst position to be in is finding yourself unable to recall an answer to a key question when you are evaluating at the end. Last, but not least, allow yourself time. Not just for the interview, but time to appraise the pre-interview data and time to contemplate your decision.

Some bad habits

Two habits that commonly undo good intentions are first, trying to see too many people in too short a time. In such circumstances, the squeeze comes on time for evaluation and judgement. Second, interruptions are preventable, and if they occur unforgivable, and that includes during the time you have set aside to think over the applicant.

17 Appraisal

Everyone wants to know how they are getting on – it's natural. Therefore, feedback becomes part of the interaction between the subordinate and the superior. Knowing 'where you stand' and 'if you are on the right lines' are part of everyday work and, as such, informal appraisal is continuous and part of daily life. That an organization would want to turn this process into a formal system is quite rational. Each part might be 'on the right lines' but is the whole? An appraisal system attempts to ensure some continuity of purpose by checking the validity of individual goals in terms of organization goals. However, everyone not only wants to know how they are getting on, but to know this in relation to others. Again, perfectly natural, but potentially problematic for a system. It would be obvious to use an appraisal system to rate employees for promotion, but in doing so it may introduce a note of ambiguity in the way the system is perceived by both managers and workers. To illustrate the point, if a worker comes to an interview thinking that its purpose is to discuss the development of skills, he or she might tell of personal weaknesses. This would not be in their interests if the appraiser considered the purpose of the interview to be to decide on pay in relation to others! All appraisal systems have the potential to disrupt in this way.

An appraisal system can promote effectiveness, job satisfaction and better manpower utilization. It can also promote organizational inefficiency, personal insecurity, distrust and conflict; which way it goes depends on how it is done. Doing it well means, at a personal level, the interviews being conducted professionally, and at an organizational level, by the purposes of the system being clearly defined with natural contradictions resolved. To a large extent, the performance of appraisers is dependent upon the integrity of the system.

Purposes: a case of potential ambiguity

Possibly the best way to understand the purposes associated with appraisal systems is to ask why an organization would have a formal system. There are a number of reasons.

1. To ensure that each job is being done in the way which the organization wants it to be done, e.g. output standards, the right method and the right priorities.
2. To stimulate better performance.
3. To assess performance and inform those assessed about how their performance is seen.
4. To collate aggregate information on manpower capacity. Literally a skills audit.
5. To measure the strengths and weaknesses of the selection procedure.
6. To measure the relative performance of employees.
7. To highlight promotable empoyees.
8. To indicate where skills need to be developed and improved.

Looked at objectively, these purposes seem perfectly reasonable. The problem occurs when they are telescoped down into an interview. 'Why are we here? Is it to fulfil all these purposes?'

Is the character of the interview:

1. Counselling – to help the employees to overcome some difficulty?
2. Promotion – assessing the potential for another job?
3. Training and development – assessing future needs?
4. Pay – deciding of how much performance deserves?

An appraisal interview cannot accomplish all these objectives, therefore to ask it to do so simply renders it ambiguous and ineffective at achieving anything. If ambiguity exists in the system, people will become defensive at interviews and managers will become cynical about the system itself. This is self-defeating.

At the heart of the dilemma lies the absolute nature of a development need. If an employee is not performing properly in a particular area of the work, it matters not a jot whether he or she is better or worse than someone else. When it comes to development, relative judgement doesn't count. To remedy a deficiency you have to look at it in absolute terms. This is why appraisal for development and appraisal for promotion don't sit comfortably together.

Resolving the ambiguity

An organization has to ask certain questions in order to reduce the ambiguity of a system.

- Is the appraisal system part of the control process?
- Is the appraisal system there to allocate rewards?
- Is the appraisal system for developing the needs of employees?

The answer may be yes to all three. It is a question of balance and emphasis. What has to be remembered is that overemphasis on the first two will negate the third almost completely. One approach is to let the control system do its job and let the appraisal system address development issues.

Job alignment

Perhaps one of the most fruitful returns which an appraisal system can give is to regularly realign people with their jobs. This is particularly important where the quality of work is both crucial and difficult to measure.

People become comfortable with their jobs over time. A natural bias creeps in which is to give priority to:

1. The visible results of the employee's work which the control system measures.
2. What the employee is good at.
3. What the employee likes doing.

Thus, important points of the work which aren't measured, the incumbent is not good at or doesn't enjoy are neglected. An appraisal interview can find this bias and reintroduce the incumbent to the priorities as seen by higher management. A receptionist may enjoy working with the computer and find it easy, what is more, the control system demands regular reports but no attention is given to guest relations. What does management want? Usually it is everything, so it is a matter of realigning priorities. An appraisal system is good at this.

The type of work and the systems

It could be argued that if the output of the job can be measured accurately, then all you need is a control system rather than an appraisal system. This is true only if you ignore the personal needs of the operator. What is also true, however, is that in certain circumstances appraisal systems become more important. These are:

1. When the job requires a good deal of employee discretion.
2. When personal character plays a large part in the success of the job.
3. When the job has wide scope.
4. When it is difficult to measure the output of a job.
5. When quality is difficult to measure and requires some consensus as to what is 'good'.
6. When there is a high rate of technological change.

In other words, where standards cannot be easily measured and where jobs are under pressure to change that is when 'talking a job through' can play a significant role.

Common faults of the system

- That any ambiguity in the system is allowed to enter the interview. There may be confusion over the purpose and meaning of the exchange.
- Setting artificial performance measures to please the system, for example asking people to affect things over which they have little control.
- The Mr Average syndrome. Appraising employees in relation to some idealized 'benchmark' standard. Using only relative comparisons makes a mockery of absolute performance. If the 'benchmark' person were to leave, everyone's 'performance' would change without any actual change taking place. This syndrome distorts the whole process and leads to complacency.
- Letting relative values dominate objective performance values to the extent that everyone is doing relatively well, but everyone's standards are not good enough.

The appraisal interview

What skills are required

Two skills are essential to the appraisal interview:

- *Being able to give feedback.* The ability to give 'good news' and 'bad news' without causing exaggeration, overconfidence or resentment.
- *Being able to elicit facts and feelings.* The ability to draw out how the individual sees their job and to distinguish between facts and feelings.

Preparation and strategy

In a very real sense, the skills mentioned above stem from preparation and from strategy. Assuming that the interview will be based on some performance measures and conduct reports, the interviewer must be prepared to support comments with facts. Support for comments is best achieved by looking at performance from a variety of perspectives – behaviour towards supervisor, behaviour towards colleagues, achievements, quality, quantity etc.

Again, working from the reported performance it is useful to make a list of good and bad performance indicators. Using this as a guide, the interview should elicit feelings about these aspects of the job. People have priorities, and by seeking their priorities the interviewer may also be finding out what they like and what they don't like. This strategy follows the job alignment principle. How far do the good performance indicators relate to priorities and likes and the bad indicators to priorities and dislikes?

The assumption of the above approach is that disliking something leads to poor performance. While this is true in general, there may be barriers which intervene and cause the dislike or simply prevent achievement of anything. When the interviewer comes across a barrier he or she must check that it is real and not just an invented excuse. The outcome of an appraisal interview should be:

- An assessment of performance.
- An assessment of priorities.
- An assessment of barriers to performance.
- An agreed plan of action for the future.

Common faults in the interview

- Saying to the appraisee, 'Overall you were fine, but. . . .' and continuing with a string of negatives.
- Saying, 'Let's start with the bad news – leaving the good to the end.' Always start on a positive note.
- Too much criticism – there is a limit.
- Saying, 'You and I know each other – let's get this form off to Personnel!'
- Entering into negotiation – bargaining and contesting the evidence.

18 Pay administration

An earlier chapter discussed the potency of pay as a motivator, but whether that is true or not, what is certain is that pay is always philosophical! You are what you pay. This might seem strange at first, but the way an organization pays its employees contains a philosophy about how they are motivated. An organization which wishes to retain staff and motivate them through loyalty might adopt a paternalistic pay philosophy whereby all new employees receive all benefits from their first day – nothing is conditional. Such an organization might feel that they can best utilize labour and develop flexibility when the labour force is stable. Alternatively, another organization may have a philosophy of conditional merit, whereby nothing beyond the basic is earned except by merit criteria. This assumes a calculative and competitive motivation in staff. What is being said here is that the way an organization administers rewards tells a story to its employees about what it assumes is their motivation.

In any organization different occupations have a different value to the organization, have different training periods, and have different labour market characteristics. Consequently, there are different levels of reward. The structure of pay differentials is an intimate part of the structure and functioning of the organization. That the structure is acceptable to those who live it is crucial to the health of the organization. One thing is certain and that is that the greater the differentials the more salient pay is in the relationship between workers. Simply because pay is distributed differentially by management it follows: first, that there has to be some overall justification for the differentials, second, that this rationale has to be acceptable to the staff and third, that questioning the structure is questioning management's authority and judgement. It is suggested in the model described in Chapter 3 that units in the industry are dependent upon the external labour market, therefore the rationale for whatever internal structure that exists would be that it is the result of market forces.

What is a pay structure supposed to do?

Fundamentally, a pay structure has to be manageable and it has to be regarded as legitimate by employees. What is meant by a manageable structure? To answer this question, it is necessary to ask what a pay structure is supposed to do. It has four primary functions. First, to ensure that sufficient numbers of people are attracted to the organization from the labour market. Second, to encourage the internal labour market to function correctly so that incentives exist for promotion and training opportunities. Third, to ensure that feelings of inequity are not engendered. If, for example, a particular occupation was short staffed because the rate was not attractive to either external or internal candidates and could not be increased without causing problems elsewhere in the organization, then the structure is not doing its job and is interfering with the operation. Finally, to allow for the development of new jobs evolved through reorganization or the introduction of new technology.

Normally, pay structures grow up in a haphazard manner as a result of many pressures, such as the labour market, customs and practices, power bargaining and the boss's whim. The result, when looked at from the outside, appears idiosyncratic and illogical. There are likely to be distortions between job content and rewards, and distortion between the rewards for different jobs. However, what looks illogical from the outside, might make perfect sense to those within. Just because there are distortions, that does not imply that management automatically need to impose logic on a pay structure by such means as a job evaluation programme. Two pre-requisites suggest themselves: first, the existing pay structures must have become in some way unmanageable and second, the employees themselves must feel the inequity produced by the distortion. To change the wage structure in the absence of either of these two conditions runs the risk of creating more dissatisfaction.

Job evaluation

Job evaluation is about 'job content' and pay structures. It is not about levels of pay or pay systems, although it is closely associated with both. It is a technique by which relative value is given to jobs in order to confer legitimacy upon the pay structure and, more importantly, upon pay differentials. In other words, the work of job evaluation is to change the pay structure which normally means making it more logical and systematic. By pay structure is meant the hierarchy of differentials between jobs within an organization. There are only two questions pertinent to pay structures: 'what is the distance between jobs, and why?' Job evaluation attempts to answer them both by asking 'what should the distance be?'

It is worthy of restatement that job evaluation relates solely to pay structures. Therefore, management must analyse their problems carefully before embarking on such a scheme. They must be able to distinguish a problem of pay structure from other closely related ones such as income, pay systems, pay administration and labour market. Once it has been decided that job evaluation is needed, it might be supposed that it is just a matter of which method? However, this is far from the case and there are six major factors which have to be considered at the planning stage. These are:

- The existing pay structure.
- The selection of evaluators.
- The appeals system.
- The entrance of new jobs into the pay structure.
- The effect of job evaluation on communication in the organization as a whole.
- The system of job evaluation.

These factors must be considered separately, but they are in reality inseparable.

The existing pay structure

It is generally accepted by experienced practitioners in job evaluation that a new pay structure produced by job evaluation must bear some resemblance to the old pay structure. This is another way of saying that a change in pay structure can never be too radical unless you want a riot on your hands! The rationale for this is simply that although a pay structure may be illogical to an outsider, it has some meaning to those inside. Employees will have their own views on their own value, their own skill, the skill of others, the authority of others etc., and these perceptions are likely to be assailed by job evaluation. Therefore, it follows that management must justify the changes it proposes. The dictum of Barbara Wootton that 'change – always, everywhere, in everything – requires justification: the strength of conservatism is that it is held to justify itself' (*Social Foundations of Wage Policy* 1962, Allen & Unwin), was never more apt.

Here, the relationship between the pay structure and the authority structure is significant. The former supports the latter and, therefore, a change in either will be reflected in the other. Usually, the existing pay structure will be fairly close to the spread of authority, therefore restructuring has to be done with extreme care.

The selection of evaluators

In a sense, job evaluation is itself a 'justifying technique'; it lends respectability and authority to a process of restructuring. However, the technique itself cannot act alone if management argue 'well, you'll have to accept it, we used a recognized technique' as its sole justification – they could have problems. The other additional approach to lend 'acceptability' to the final outcome is to use job evaluation as part of a participation exercise.

At the outset, management must decide whether they maintain the job evaluation programme under their sole control and 'impose' its solution or let employees' representatives participate to improve the 'acceptability' of the result. The merits and disadvantages of one are the reverse of those of the other. However, there is a limit to the degree to which participation can take place. That limit is normally centred around the definitions of job content; the management alone must decide.

If a participative approach is adopted, there remains the key question of representation on the evaluation panel. An evaluation panel has to act independently, but independence does not confer the legitimacy necessary to the acceptance of its findings. For this reason, the constitution of the panel is a crucial factor. There are usually a number of key combination alternatives: outsiders/employees; unions/non-unions; by occupation; by level; by department. The problem with having every department represented is that 'interests' take over and the tendency is for the status quo to be preserved. Great care needs to be taken with the constitution of an evaluation panel. Who evaluates is as important as the method used.

It might be suggested that expertise in personnel, job evaluation or salary administration are necessary qualities for evaluators – this is not so. Access to expert advice on job evaluation is *essential* but the qualities needed for an evaluator are common sense and enough knowledge to be able to understand a job description – no more, no less.

The appeals system

The final outcome of any job evaluation scheme will be that someone will earn more or less than they did before the scheme, therefore an appeals procedure is an integral part of the overall scheme. There are two questions here: the constitution of the appeals panel, and the rules for appeal.

Normally the constitution of the appeals panel follows that of the evaluation panel, but it is advisable for some personnel to change so that there can be a fresh look at the job. The rules for appeal are important, because without them a job could be continuously rewritten until it passes the appeal panel. Phoney duties written in to gain a successful appeal bring the whole system into disrepute. It follows, therefore, that not only should management fix the job content, but that they should also decide how far a job must change before an appeal can be made. Other rules should include guidelines on evidence, advocacy and refer-back.

The entrance of new jobs into the pay structure

One of the reasons why pay structures are so often chaotic is that jobs continuously change. Pressures from the product market, from the labour market, from the abilities of incumbents, and from new technology all force changes in job content. Sometimes these changes occur imperceptibly, sometimes they are planned. In either case, the job evaluation system must accommodate such changes so that a new job can go through the system at any time without causing friction. The emphasis is always upon management to keep the initiative and a close eye on job content.

The effect of job evaluation on communication in the organization as a whole

The problem with job evaluation is that it is basically irreversible. In this sense, the introduction of job evaluation is a watershed for any organization. There is no going back once logic has entered the system; it cannot be returned to chaos at will. Only further job evaluation can change a pay structure based on job evaluation. It is this irreversible quality which makes management treat the technique with respect.

One thing job evaluation does is to make salaries public knowledge within the organization. If an organization is used to secrecy, job evaluation will bring a change which may promote less secrecy in other areas as well. Even if individual earnings remain confidential, grades and the salary ranges associated with those grades will have to be published. Employees will not only know their own grade and salary, but also those of others. It is for this reason that a 'consciousness' of the earnings of others is a pre-requisite of job evaluation. The technique itself will result in such a consciousness and if it was not there already, the effect could be traumatic. The message is that a job evaluation exercise at the point of instigation has a profound effect upon the communication system of an organization. It remoulds the relationships between individuals, between departments, and between the organization and its employees.

This effect is likely to have lasting repercussions and in this case the communication system is permanently remoulded.

The system of job evaluation

At the outset it is necessary to make clear that there is no ideal system to meet a particular organization's needs. It is always a case of the 'best fit' being applied after some crude analysis of the problems to be encountered. There are three basic approaches to job evaluation each of which offer a number of systems, these are:

1. Qualitative judgment alone:
   (a) Ranking (whole job comparison)
   (b) Job classification
2. Quantifying qualitative judgement:
   (a) Points system
   (b) Factor comparison
3. Comparing differences in decision making:
   (a) Castellion
   (b) Time span
   (c) Profile

The following is a brief description of the principal techniques in common use. No attempt is made to be comprehensive in this review and further study is advised. The selection of these particular techniques is based on their popularity and because they form the basis of many of the other techniques in use.

Job ranking

This is the simplest method of job evaluation and involves 'whole job comparison'. In other words, jobs are compared in their entirety without involving factor or specific criteria. Only general concepts such as value to the organization are used. Its principal merit is its simplicity, but its central weakness is its vagueness due to lack of specific criteria which leaves the result open to wide interpretation and consequently to altercation.

Step One

A set of approved job descriptions are studied by a panel of evaluators and sorted into a rough hierarchy.

Step Two

Each job is compared with every other job and jobs are formed into groups and a hierarchy determined.

Step Three (optional)

Numerical paired-comparison is applied to the hierarchy. To do this, a job scores 2 when it beats another job, 1 if it is valued the same and 0 if the other job is valued higher. In this way, the top job scores:

2 × number of jobs − 1

and the bottom job scores 0 as it was beaten by every other job. For example, ten jobs are ranked in Table 18.1

Table 18.1

Jobs		Score	*
A	222222222	18	18
B	12222222	15	14
C	12222222	15	14
D	111222	9	6
E	111222	9	6
F	111222	9	6
G	111222	9	6
H	22	4	4
I	2	2	2
J		0	0

* Note by using 0 for a draw, the distinctions become larger. This is an alternative scoring method.

Step Four

The pair comparison scores of each evaluator are aggregated together to produce a panel score.

Step Five

Job clusters are formed which might suggest grades. In the example, there appear to be four clusters.

```
A      − 18
BC     − 15
DEFT   − 9
HIJ    − 4−0
```

Step Six

The job evaluation exercise is now over (except for appeals). It is now necessary to convert the findings into a pay structure. It is very important to notice that pair-comparison does not measure the 'distance' between jobs, it only puts jobs in clusters. Therefore, we can say that BC is more valuable than DEFG *but not by how much*. If a pay structure is justified on pair comparison *scores*, it has no validity.

Comment

The chief advantage of job ranking is its simplicity and the fact that it can be applied to a fair number of jobs. However, it does rely on a substantial amount of goodwill to be successful. In addition, it has no direct means of transfer to a wage structure as it does not measure distance between jobs. There is also a tendency for job ranking to closely follow the existing authority structure; in other words to be very conservative.

Points method

Possibly the most commonly used method of job evaluation, its principal attractions are its flexibility and its use of specific criteria which lend some measure of justification to the final results. The disadvantages are first, that using specific criteria it is difficult to apply the method over a very wide range of jobs and second, that it is difficult to find suitable criteria which will be appropriate at the time of the initial exercise and later when appeal and new jobs come forward for evaluation.

Step One

The crucial step in the points method is the selection of criteria – those headings under which judgement will be applied. The choice of criteria must be governed by two practical considerations, first, the need for as few criteria as possible and second, the need for all criteria to actually apply to as many jobs as possible.

Examples of factors would be skill, effort, responsibility, working conditions and hours.

Step Two

After deciding upon a set of factors it is essential that each factor is unambiguously defined so that all the evaluators are using the same concepts. 'Responsibility', for example, is a factor which needs vigorous description before it is used. This is not a tedious semantic argument. If the evaluators are not sharing the same meaning of the word in question, then the result may be injustice and delay.

Step Three

Once definitions have been agreed it is necessary to divide the factor up by degrees. In other words, to create a scale of application for each factor, for example normal hours, fairly unsocial hours, very unsocial hours.

Step Four

Once factors have been chosen and degrees allotted to each factor, it remains to weight each factor and allocate points, for example:

Responsibility	120 points	(6 degrees)
Skill	100 points	(5 degrees)
Working conditions	60 points	(6 degrees)
Hours	100 points	(5 degrees)

Step Five

All the previous stages were preparatory steps in evaluating each job and evaluation will come to a points score. It is this point score which will allocate the job into the hierarchy which in turn will form the basis of the wage structure.

Step Six

The differences between the points method and whole job ranking is that the points method does measure the distance between jobs and, therefore, is more easily converted into a pay structure. *This is never an easy task*, but by allocating a sum of money to each point, it is possible to draw a pay curve for the organization (Figure 18.1).

By plotting pay against points divided into equal measures, it is possible to see how jobs fall into clusters and to see the distance between clusters. Having done this, it is necessary to form grades and there is no scientific way of doing this – the cluster and distances between them are only a guide.

Figure 18.1

Note the overlaps between grades. This is normal as it allows the wage structure to incorporate the workings of the pay system.

The Castellion method

This is a variation on the points method which uses decision making as its unit of comparison. As such, it is primarily used as a method of evaluating managerial jobs. The factors used are as follows:

a) The complexity of decision making
b) Pressure of work coefficient (a×b)
c) Numerical computations
d) Comprehensive ability
e) Vigilance
f) Consequence of errors
g) Education
h) Experience

A matter of degree is applied to each factor as per the points method. The relationship between factor a×b is recognition that the volume of a decision depends not just on its intrinsic difficulty, but also on the time pressure under which it is made, for example:

(a) Decision complexity:
 • simply requiring broad estimates only   60 points
(b) Pressure of work coefficient:
 • few decisions taken at leisure   1.10 points
                                             a×b   66 points

Proceed as for the points method.

Key jobs or benchmark jobs

Many practitioners advocate the pre-selection of certain jobs to be used in job evaluation in order to save time. Although precautions are taken to ensure that these jobs are representative of all the jobs to be evaluated, the principle is a dangerous one, particularly where job evaluation is being undertaken for the first time. Similarly, benchmark jobs are used to speed up the process of evaluating new jobs. By this means, a new job or an appeal is compared with the benchmark job for the particular grade to which the job aspires. Again, there is a great danger here from the ever-changing nature of job content. If benchmarks are to be used they must be constantly under review.

It is absolutely essential to 'write up' each stage of the job evaluation process so that the constitution rules, i.e. those referring to the selection of evaluators, evidence and the factor definitions are handed on to those who continue the job evaluation process. The use of new criteria or a new rule would defeat the object of the whole exercise.

A review

Perhaps the most important benefit of job evaluation is that it gives management a tool by which they can control their pay structure. The accent on job content means that management will be forced to be continually aware of employees' jobs and how they are changing – this can only contribute to the health of the organization. Furthermore, by giving the pay structure a logical character and a degree of legitimacy, job evaluation overcomes problems of differentials which cause dissent and friction amongst employees. In addition, job evaluation usually promotes more open communication within the organization so to achieve the purpose its results must be public knowledge. These then are the benefits.

However, all this presumes that the exercise has been carried out successfully, which basically means that everybody is happy with the results. This dependence for success on the acceptability of the results is the central weakness of job evaluation. It is, in fact, a pseudoscientific technique – its measurement being purely subjective (work study is subjective to a degree). The values it places on jobs and the distances it prescribes between jobs are abstract conceptions. They become 'reality' only if you are prepared to believe them. This is why faith in the system and trust in the evaluators is so vital to the success of any scheme. This weakness does not, however, invalidate the techniques.

A more serious criticism of job evaluation stems from a more general criticism of the true importance of pay structures. One of the major influences on the pay structure is the labour market, but is there any evidence to show that a logical pay structure is any less susceptible to pressure than an idiosyncratic one? Major movements in the labour market can distort a logical structure like any other but what is significant is that the sheer logic of systematic pay structures may make it difficult to respond to market pressures. A less organized scheme may have less difficulty in adjusting. Given the basic irreversibility of job evaluation, such rigidity may be a disadvantage. To put it simply, the value which a scheme gives to a job may not be that put on it by the labour market and sooner or later the two values will clash.

Pressures on job content: the danger and challenge for job evaluation

What changes?

- Objectives.
- Techniques and methods.
- Quantity.
- Quality.
- Priority of tasks.
- Degree of discretion.

How does it change?

- Market demand changes.
- Labour market changes.
- Incumbent: ability, motivation, preference for tasks.
- Supervision: ability, motivation, preference for tasks, degree of discretion.

- Power relations within the organization.

Possible consequences

- Misdirected effort.
- Creeping inefficiency.
- Management lose control.
- Job content of other jobs altered.

Pay structures and pay systems

As job evaluation is about job content, it does not concern itself with performance. It is concern for performance that forces a link between the pay grading structure produced by job evaluation and the pay system.

There must be a degree of overlap between pay grades to allow for seniority increments and merit increments. All organizations need some people to stay in their jobs and such requirements can be met by seniority or long service increments. As the person is doing the same job, they cannot be regraded, therefore the top limit of their grade must overlap the higher grade. Similarly, differences in merit should not be suffocated by the lower point of the grade above. Merit can exist without promotion possibilities, therefore merit increments should be able to overtake the lower points on the grade above. The greater the overlap of grades, the greater is the weight given to the incumbent of the job against the value of the job content.

Pay surveys

It is not uncommon to find managers baffled by the wage survey they themselves commissioned. Complex surveys do require a degree of statistical sophistication and expert interpretation. However, the situation often demands a simpler less ambitious form of survey.

What has to be accepted at the outset is that labour market surveys are a most difficult type of survey to conduct.

What do pay surveys measure?

Pay surveys measure the differences between occupations and organizations in a defined labour market area in terms of:

- Absolute value of pay.
- Increase or decrease in value over time.
- The rate of increase or decrease over time.

Obviously, the prime objective must be to find out what other firms are paying in the occupations you are interested in. However, that is not as simple as it sounds. A further objective must be to collect data in such a way that you can understand it and will be able to see the relationships you want. What you are looking for in a pay survey is the state of competition which will be revealed in the relationships between the figures you collect; but only if the information is collected with care.

There are basically three types of pay survey, each with a different capacity. These are:

1 Photographic shot

The most common form of survey is the one-off photographic shot, where the surveyors collect data just once and for a specific purpose.

This type of survey usually collects data on:

(a) The absolute value of pay by occupation and by firm and also, therefore,
(b) pay differentials by occupation and by firm.

2 Repeated survey

If a survey is repeated at intervals over time it can add other dimensions to the data.

Repeated surveys can show:

(a) Absolute value of pay by occupation and by firm.
(b) Pay differentials by occupation and by firm.
(c) Absolute value of the increase or decrease over the time period by occupation and by firm.
(d) Change in differentials by occupation and by firm.
(e) The 'rate' of increase or decrease.
(f) Differences in the 'rate' of increase or decrease.

3 Repeated surveys with indexation

The advantage of using indexation is that it shows the direction and rate of change more clearly than absolute figures.

The normal practice is to use *one year as the base year* (= 100) and let all other years be expressed as a percentage of that base year. Alternatively, it is possible to use *one occupation* as the base (= 100) and express all other values of pay against the base.

Example 1

Base year 1990 = 100

	1990	1991	1992	1993	1994
Occupation	110	120	130	145	160
Index	100	109	118	132	145

Example 2

Base occupation x = 100
                                                Index
                        Occupation x = 110 = 100
                        Occupation y = 150 = 136
                        Occupation z = 170 = 154

It is not difficult to see that both types of indexation can be usefully combined. The real value of using indexation is when the surveyor is more interested in the rate of change than in comparing the absolute value.

Some problems associated with setting up a pay survey

1 Defining the labour market you are trying to measure

If it is a local labour market, knowing the geographical parameters is essential. These are normally approximated by estimates of *travel to work times and costs*. In order to avoid wasted effort it is a good idea to know who the key firms are who represent competition. If a particular firm is known to be a pay 'leader' they must be included in the sample.

2 Like with like!

The basis of a survey, that is its whole validity which allows for interpretation, is that like is being compared with like.

If occupational pay is being compared, then the *occupations must be equivalent*. The same occupational title is not enough. In order to ensure occupations are equivalent, either of two conditions must prevail.

(a) The survey should use an *occupational classification*. The importance of this cannot be overstated.
(b) The surveyor should have enough knowledge of essential differences between occupations to interpret the data with accuracy.

It is also essential that the *units of measurement are equivalent*, basic pay = basic pay or total earnings = total earnings. Is the survey measuring starting pay or pay at some other point in time?

3 Understanding the manpower systems

At the very minimum, the surveyor must be aware of occupations which are linked in some way. Links can be for a variety of reasons, e.g.: occupations which compete for the same people or an occupation which is training for another.

The point about occupations that are linked is that pay differentials can be explained by the nature of the link and in some circumstances pay might be expected to move together.

4 Time coherence

In order to interpret your findings, certain additional data is essential:

- The date of the last increase.
- The date on which pay levels are set.
- The frequency of pay reviews.

Interpretation

Given that your survey has been properly produced so that occupational equivalence and unit of revenue of equivalence can be taken for granted, then interpretation is possible.

Value and increase differentials can be easily seen as their interpretation depends on the circumstances. Questions like 'Am I paying too much or too little?' and 'How much more would I need to pay?' should be guided by the figures.

It is, however, more difficult to interpret the state of competition from a pay survey. The key indicator is the spread or range of pay offered for the *same* occupation.

19 Grievance and dispute management

The problem of grievance procedures is that nobody loves them! The problem of grievances is that they are, for managers, so easy to disregard. In a sense, the first situation is a result of the latter. Managers find it all too easy to attribute grumbles to troublemakers or disputes to the 'six of one, half a dozen of the other' category, before investigation. To some, 'good people' don't have problems – but they do. To many managers the formal grievance procedure is an unwanted rival to their 'I'm always approachable' authority. Given the complexity of negative behaviour discussed in Chapter 8, some sympathy is due to management in this respect. However, managers cannot simply look the other way or rely entirely on their own busy resources.

At any one time in any organization there will always be a degree of dissatisfaction, and while it is impossible to eradicate grievances altogether, it is clearly management's task to minimize and contain such conflict. The problem facing management is not simply a matter of the complexity of grievances, but that they exist at numerous levels. To put it simply, there are individual, group and workforce grievances. Obviously as the scale of the problem varies the means of prevention and resolution also vary to scale.

Prevention is better than cure, but if you have a problem there must be some means of settling it without damaging the operation. The key elements in prevention are knowing the patterns of conflict (labour turnover, absenteeism, stoppages etc.); the behaviour of supervisors and junior managers; and the organization's operating policies, particularly personnel policies. The key element in resolution of conflict is the operation of an authentic dispute and grievance procedure.

Prevention

The pattern of conflict behaviour: the case of high labour turnover

The hotel and catering industry has a reputation for high levels of labour turnover – the facts confirm this. The levels are so high that consideration of any other form of conflict behaviour tends to be subsumed under this one problem. In Chapter 3, two cases were made that mitigate high levels of labour turnover; these were the need for numerical flexibility to match variations in demand and the need for skill accumulation by personal mobility. Accounting for these cases still leaves an awful lot of conflict-related labour turnover.

The first step to prevention is to recognize the type of problem that you have, which includes separating the preventable from the inevitable. In relation to preventable conflict, three areas of concern can be identified from research.

1. *The arbitrary behaviour of supervisors and managers* Because of the shift system and because standards are subjectively defined, employees face more than one supervisor, each with their own ideas about what they regard as good performance. Inconsistency is difficult to work with. This may be the background pattern of quitting, based on what is seen as unfair action by managers.
2. *The induction crisis* The induction crisis is endemic in the industry. Workers leave employers within a very short period because either the job is not what they thought it was going to be (see Chapter 6) or it is incompatible with their non-work life. While acknowledging that the pressure of the recruitment function is often extreme, there is always a premium on getting things as straight as possible at the outset. As a generalization, recruiters concentrate on the person's ability to do the job, but neglect to find out whether the person has *realistically thought out the job in terms of their domestic life for themselves*. Often an interviewee makes a mistake which costs the employer time and trouble.
3. *Distribution of effort and rewards* It was suggested in Chapter 3 that because productivity is though individual effort and does not increase with length of service, there is no point in rewarding seniority. While true in general, this argument loses some of its force on the ground. People expect to be rewarded for producing more or staying longer. With a workforce that contains both a transient population and a stable population, the lower levels of management are confronted with an enormous problem of how to distribute rewards and effort in such a way as to turn the transient population into permanence, while not upsetting the already permanent employees by denying them privileges. Matters like the distribution of days off have no economic impact, but have enormous significance for operational health.

The case of the junior managers

In the front line of people management are the supervisor and the junior levels of management. It is their behaviour that, to a large extent, determines the general level of morale and incidents of discontent. Given the discussion in Chapter 6 on how impressive labour contracts are for service workers, there is a greater than normal probability of misunderstanding and misinterpretation. It is difficult to manage service workers through a set of ambiguous rules. What is more, the occasion of shift overlap means that most workers have more than one manager which leads to a problem of inconsistency. All this points to the need for the training of supervisors and managers in people-handling skills. Uniformity would be impossible and undesirable, but a degree of consistency in actual skill can only be beneficial.

Policies that help

1. *Knowing the house rules* There are always some house rules and while it is usual to get them across through the induction process, people forget. Many problems occur over a misinterpretation of rules, therefore access to the rules and, if necessary, an independent interpretation (possibly by the Personnel Manager) would cut off

grievances before they start. It is the 'is he allowed to change my day off?' syndrome.
2 *Individual differences*   As productivity is individual productivity in this industry, it is wise to select carefully to avoid friction based on effort comparisons.
3 *Distribution of effort and rewards*   Give guidelines to departmental managers on distributing effort and rewards. Make clear divisions between the status of those under training and those accepted as competent performers. Give clear guidelines on the privileges of long service.
4 *Irregular hours of work*   Even if consumer demand is irregular, work can be organized on a continuous basis. Waiting around for work simply breeds gripes.
5 *Promotion and training*   Well-organized training and published opportunities.
6 *Pay system*   Easily understood and with legitimate differentials.
7 *Pay and benefits*   Competitive.

The goal of these policies is to try to eliminate unfair arbitrary management action, unstable and irregular work, inadequate employee status and recognition. The above policies don't, themselves, promote harmony, but they are the bedrock on which it is built.

Grievance and dispute procedures

There is a certain irony in the fact that neither managers nor workers are enthusiastic to use the formal grievance procedure. Managers see it as a slight on their authority and workers don't trust the system, because it always supports management authority. Looked at objectively, if workers do take their grievances to the system they are in fact affirming management authority. Grievance procedures are about justice, rough justice possibly, but justice nevertheless.

The real merits of formal procedure are, first, that by bringing the grievance out into the open they force resolutions to be on the lines of some fair principles or precedents. Second, this form of resolution is healthier for the organization in the long run than the alternative form of resolution, that is an informal settlement. Informal approaches are necessary and sometimes preferable, but not for everything. The danger of informal systems is that they use 'favours' and 'reciprocity' as the basis of resolution which are, by their very nature, secret and open to misinterpretation. There is plenty of evidence to show that when the informal settlement system dominates, it ends in an expensive mess with unofficial privileges having to be bought out! Settling a grumble with a bit of extra overtime solves nothing!

Impact of a procedure upon a grievance

- It helps to identify those to whom the grievance should be put and those who may be approached for assistance.
- It may help to clarify the issue if the grievant has to write it down or explain it to a representative.
- It may help to obtain appropriate information.

- It may speed up resolution insofar as it specifies time limits and ensures only those with the appropriate authority are involved.
- By requiring that records be kept it lessens the chances of ambiguous customs and practices becoming involved.
- It reduces the level of emotion involved.

Designing a procedure

There is a dilemma at the heart of any judicial procedures, and grievance and dispute procedures are no different. The problem is that *speed of resolution* is incompatible with *consistency of justice*. Anybody with a problem wants it resolved as soon as possible. This is natural. If everything was solved quickly that would mean everything would have to be settled at a low level of authority. This would mean inconsistent judgements which would, themselves, eventually become the source of conflict. Alternatively, if one person made all the judgements they would be consistent, but dangerously slow. This is the design problem of all procedures – how to reconcile speed with consistency.

Fundamentally, grievance procedures consist of a number of dimensions. These are first a number of stages following a set order. At each stage there is an attempt to resolve the grievance. Second, there are levels of authority which are superimposed onto the stages of the grievance procedure. For example, the first two stages may attempt to resolve the grievance at supervisory level, after which the remaining stages move to an ever higher authority level. The big element here is the terminal stage where the grievance must be resolved. Third, at any stage representation or arbitration may be superimposed. Fourth, there is the matter of formality; the degree to which the procedure is written down and rigidly applied. Finally, there are fixed time limits on the duration between each stage in order to prevent unfair delays.

Key issues in designing a procedure

1. Basic structure – number of stages.
2. Place of the terminal stage.
3. Time limits on stages.
4. Roles of participants.
5. Recording of procedure stages.
6. Scope of the procedure.
7. Representation.
8. Procedure differentiation (some problems may require different procedures).

None of this will work without someone making it work. This is usually a role for Personnel. Where a union is recognized, it is essential to specify the point in the system when union representation takes place and the point where the dispute can go to arbitration. These matters are the subject of negotiation.

20 Personnel administration

It might seem strange in the light of Chapter 3 that personnel management should still be considered important, yet it is. No matter how weak or strong the internal labour market, there is always a basic administrative function to be undertaken; whether this is done by someone called a Personnel Manager or by someone else, it still has to be done. Personnel is often seen as bureaucracy which is a little unfair. Such sentiments are really a substitute rationale for rejecting a strong internal labour market which is, in itself, perfectly legitimate. The real problem for personnel in the hotel and catering industry is that the normal unit size is far too small to carry a Personnel Manager, but someone still has to maintain some kind of personnel function. Often this function is delegated to an Assistant Manager who is responsible for other areas as well, or it is split between more than one person. In the case of large companies, the response of Head Office Personnel is to try to lay down guidelines in order to achieve a minimum standard of administration. This structural difficulty could easily be used as an excuse for poor administration, but it is really a very strong argument for actually doing it efficiently.

If one takes a close look at the role personnel management actually plays in the business, it is possible to identify four points of impact. First, in Chapter 6 it was suggested that the psychological contract was, at its inception, always imprecise. All the paraphernalia of job descriptions, good interviewing, good recruitment, trial periods, induction, etc. are, in effect, trying to make the agreement less imprecise. The more mutual the understanding can be between the new recruit and management, the greater the likelihood that the person will give the performance expected. This is, in effect, the second point of impact – supporting the economic objectives of the organization by trying to find the most productive people. This cannot be understated, because productivity in this industry is individual productivity. It will come as no surprise in the light of Chapter 3 that recruitment is a prominent feature of the personnel function, but it is important to realize that whoever is doing the recruiting is sitting at the interface between the internal and external markets and in fact controlling that relationship. The response of the external feed back into the internal is through the recruiter, because no one else knows what is happening in the external market. The last point of impact is in coping with the fallout when the relationship between management and worker goes wrong. Discipline, grievance handling and disputes procedures don't work automatically – they need handling. Being part of management does not compromise the need to make whatever procedures are agreed on actually work.

None of these four points of impact are actually precisely represented by particular roles, yet they are what personnel activities and roles should be doing.

- Making the relationship between manager and workers more precise, particularly in the initial stages.
- Recruiting the most productive people.
- Managing the relationship between the internal and external labour markets.
- Facilitating the resolution of conflict.

It is not that a Personnel Manager wakes up one morning and decides to make an employee's psychological contract more precise or relate the internal market to the external, but that is what he or she is actually doing in much of his or her daily activity.

If this is personnel management's role in the organization, what is the contribution of administration? All that paperwork – files, reports etc. – what is it for? The objectives of good personnel administration are:

- To provide sufficient information for management to make decisions affecting individuals, groups, departments, occupations and the workforce.
- To promote the feeling of equity of treatment.
- To give individual employees the feeling of confidence that their affairs with the organization are being administered correctly.
- To promote and maintain the goodwill and reputation of the organization in the labour market and with external institutions.

What is actually required to achieve these objectives will vary with circumstances, but there is a bare minimum which any organization cannot fall below. Every activity has its basic 'good housekeeping' rules and personnel administration is no exception.

Essential good habits in personnel administration

- Maintain all personal files on a comprehensive and 'active' basis. All files to be 'serviced' regularly.
- Maintain a management information system in respect to manpower.
- Ensure that all the basic 'processes' of personnel are efficiently operated, for example:
  – Recruitment
  – Selection
  – Engagement
- Ensure that all aspects of pay administration are efficient and in line with agreements and laws.
- Ensure that the organization confidentiality policy operates at all times.
- Pay attention to detail at all times.

All that talk of motivation in Chapter 7 counts for nothing if the Personnel Department loses files! News of sloppy administration soon gets around. Beyond a basic duty toward employees, there is an obligation to produce information to assist managerial decision making. In fact, the quality of aggregate information produced for management is, at least to an extent, dependent on the degree of vigilance over individual files.

Hard data/soft data

In any organization the Finance Department produces hard data, that is factual data e.g. cash levels, stock levels, revenue etc. Although this data is open to interpretation when presented together each piece of data is 'hard'. If a personnel file says a person was born on a certain date that is hard data. The number of people who leave the organization is hard data. In contrast, a note on a file which says that Mr X left because he was unhappy with his pay is soft data. It may be true, but there could be other reasons and, in itself, it is open to interpretation – so it is soft. Giving Mr X an appraisal rating of 'excellent' is soft data for the same reasons, it is subjective data.

The importance of distinguishing between hard and soft data is that personnel information tends to be a combination of both. Often they are confused and hard data is somehow seen as more valuable than soft. Soft data is subjective data, but that does not mean that it is less valuable. What matters is the integrity with which the data was collected. This means that soft data should not be generated by people with a vested interest in its interpretation. This is where the independence and integrity of personnel actually matters. An example would be useful.

Figure 20.1 is an extract from a labour turnover report. The numbers on the left and the right are hard data, but the reasons for leaving are soft.

					Dismissal			Resignation									TOTAL	Length of stay				END
Occupation	START	Recruited	Transfer in	Transfer out	Unsatisfactory	Poor conduct	Absent	Hours	Pay	Working conditions	Friction	Promotion	Emotion	Home	Illness	Studies	LEFT	Under 1 month	Under 3 months	Under 1 year	Over 1 year	
Day maids	23	48		1	2	2	9	3	8	3	1	1	1	10	1	3	44	17	17	6	4	29
Evening maids	10	22	1				3	3	4					8		4	22	12	6	2	2	10
Floor house-keepers	8	5		1			1		1	1				1			5		1	1	3	8

Figure 20.1

If the reasons for leaving were submitted by the department heads this is worthless data, but if they were the result of an exit interview conducted by personnel staff then they would be acceptable. Obviously, just one reason for leaving may be inadequate, but a degree of tolerance of the acceptability of soft data is made when the data collection instrument is being designed. Data doesn't have to be hard to be useful.

Principles of designing personnel data collection

- Define the purpose of the data collection, which means defining the activity or behaviour you are interested in.
- Decide whether you are interested in locating the problems within the organization in relation to this activity or monitoring long-term trends in the activity or both.

- Personnel data is not designed so that you can take action directly from the data, but should be designed to show what the problem is, where it is and suggest what questions you need to ask of those with authority in the identified area. From the data in Figure 20.1 you should want to know about selection interviewing given the number of maids leaving for home responsibilities and hours. You should also want to know about induction training and why there are so few transfers between day and evening?
- Ensure that soft data is collected in an unbiased way.

Day-to-day administration – policy guideline

In concluding Part Three, it might be useful just to list the activities that may require a guideline policy in the area. The list is not comprehensive and many more activities could be included. The important point in laying down guidelines is not to put people in straightjackets, but to give them flexibility while ensuring that people know who does what!

Documentation (what goes into, who has access to)

- Personal files
- Contracts of employment
- Job descriptions

Regular procedures

- Recruitment
- Selection
- Employment
- Termination
- Appraisal
- Promotion
- Status change
- Transfer

Occasional procedures

- Discipline
- Grievance
- Legal

Manning levels

- Performance standards
- Casual labour
- Overtime

Pay

- Grade structure
- Incremental structure
- Job evaluation
- Overtime
- Deductions
- Loans
- Advances
- Savings plan

Benefits

- Sick pay
- Holiday
- Discounts
- Entitlements
- Health plans

Training

- Induction
- Skills
- Supervisory
- Statutory
- Management

Security

- Locker inspection
- Security checks

Relationship with external bodies

- Government
- Education

Trade unions

- Recognition
- Agreement
- Bargaining structure

Individual recognition

- Seniority
- Long service awards
- Birthdays
- Retirement

Employee social activities

Staff accommodation

Seen as a list it looks daunting, but if the basic documentation is computerized, then many of the other functions become much easier to administer. The argument here is that if the basic things are done properly, then management strategies related to the business will have a greater chance of success.

21 *The costs of training*

One of the most difficult areas in management is to encourage training. At the heart of this problem is the fact that training outputs are often hard to quantify and that costs are difficult to allocate. One remedy would be to quantify the outcomes of training so that the benefits can be more easily seen and assessed. This is a matter for training policy and planning. In relation to costs, there are basically two approaches. The first is to take a simple line and allocate only directly attributable costs to the function. The second is to take an economic approach which involves quantifying benefits and bringing into the calculation production costs and performance costs. In other words, the costing of training can be made as simple or as complicated as you like. Perhaps what determines the approach is whether training in an organization is mainly a matter of short-term courses or one of continuous activity directly linked to performance.

The objectives of training organization

Well-designed training courses always have clear objectives. This is the first step to quantifying the benefits of training. However, the organization of training also has objectives. These relate to costs, to the effectiveness of delivery and to the achievement of productivity. The objectives of training organization are:

- To improve performance.
- To shorten the length of training time.
- To obtain better employee retention.
- To facilitate change.

The effect of training on performance has to be considered in three distinct but related aspects, which are: getting the newcomer up to the required performance as quickly as possible; raising the standard of all employees; and facilitating change through re-skilling. Perhaps the most obvious problem of evaluating training is that its effect is over time. Some results are fairly instantaneous but others are long term.

Effects of training through time

Short term
1. Change in training investment.
2. Change in attitude knowledge and skill of labour.
3. Potential change in the marginal product of labour.

Medium term
1. Change in the actual marginal product of labour.
2. Change in the organization's total output.

Long term
1 Change in the organization's total output.

Handling training costs

Despite the built-in difficulties of evaluating training, there are some very clear-cut issues that the organization has to rule on to develop a training policy:

- The nature of training in the organization – is it short term or continuous or both?
- Are the outcomes of the training short term or long term?
- Is the output change going to be measured? If yes, by means of a 'before and after' approach, or by monitoring continuous productivity, or both?
- Does the organization favour simplicity or complexity in its account approach?

Figure 21.1 illustrates the dimensions involved in devising a training cost accounting policy. The notion here is that the approach can either be simple or complex and that the key factor is whether or not training outcomes can be directly related to productivity.

Towards complexity in costing ↑	Continuous training connected to productivity	Continuous training not connected to productivity
	Not-continuous training connected to productivity	Not-continuous training not connected to productivity

Towards simplicity in costing →

Figure 21.1

To put it simply, if training can be quantified, then the accounting approach should be appropriate to that task. If, however, the training is for whatever reason hard to quantify, then a simpler approach is probably better. The key issues here are, is the training continuous and is the outcome of that training reflected in measured productivity changes? If this is the case, then the investment has to be closely monitored by the accounting system and the productivity controls. Alternatively, if the training is continuous but it is difficult to measure the outcomes, then control must be focused on the quality of the training rather than on its costs. In other words, it is more a matter of control on training performance than an accounting control issue.

Classification of costs

What should be included in training costs? The answer to this question will depend on the decisions made in relation to the issues discussed above. A possible list would include:

- Wages of trainees.
- Cost of recruiting trainees.
- Salaries of instructors.
- Instructional materials.
- Cost of external courses.
- Costs of training centre.
- Cost of errors or spoilage.
- Output foregone.

If the organization is involved in continuous, or long-term, training where the outcome can be measured through changes in productivity, then the following list of cost items is appropriate:

- Cost of initiating the training function.
- Cost of running the training function.
- Cost of training capital.
- Cost of training working capital.
- Cost of instruction.
- Wage cost of trainees net of output.

Evaluating training when output can be measured

Notwithstanding the problems of measuring output and using it as a means of evaluating training, if an output measure does exist then the effectiveness of training may be measured in a number of useful ways; for example, by changes in the marginal product after training. Alternatively, a comparative approach may be taken in which the output of the trainees can be measured against that of an experienced worker and the effectiveness of training gauged by the time it takes trainees to reach the experienced worker standard (EWS).

(a) Training times

In this approach the performance of the trainees is measured against EWS and the objective of the training is to achieve EWS standards in the shortest possible time.

Figure 21.2 shows output ranged against time with the EWS indicated as the target. The trainee's progress over time is charted (WT is the wage rate for the trainee, OT is the objective of the training, and t is the time).

The starting point of t depends upon the level of skill recruited. Charting raw recruits against recruits with experience is a measure of the adaptability of the training function. However, the main point is always to increase the slope of the line and thus shorten the time period.

154 *Human Resource Management in the Hospitality and Tourism Industry*

Figure 21.2

Comparing two methods of training

Figure 21.3 uses six pieces of information to show how two training schemes (A,B) can be compared. The information it uses is as follows:

W = wages
EWS = output standard
t_1 = duration of training of scheme A
t_2 = duration of training of scheme B
ΔR = average retention time
MP = marginal product of labour which is the point at which increased output equals increased labour input
X = the time between finishing training and leaving the company. The point to note here is that the wages paid in both schemes are the same and that there is no difference in wages after training.

Figure 21.3

Scheme A trained people to the point where wages matched output at EWS in time t_1. Scheme B trained people to pass the EWS standard in t_2 and go on to a higher level of output and marginal product. The retention time of scheme B is X_2 which exceeds that of scheme A.

Scheme B is clearly more effective. It must be noted, however, that if the higher output of scheme B leads to higher wages, then some of the benefits of the scheme are lost.

22 Questionnaire design

Managing people is not just about people. It is also about information and data. Guessing what people think is a dangerous game. Why not ask them? Communication with employees, customers and other organizations often involves collecting data. The questionnaire is now part of the manager's life. It must be done well. The kind of surveys conducted by human resource managers include employee opinion surveys, inter-firm surveys, pay surveys and employee attitude surveys (see Chapter 12).

The problem of questionnaire design is that there are no guaranteed formulas for success. Though a difficult task, it is one which becomes easier with practice. Among its many attributes the questionnaire is an especially good tool for collecting information on facts and opinions from large numbers of people.

Think before you start to design the questionnaire

Once you are committed to a questionnaire you are involved in two processes: a creative process of writing questions and a design process of devising a structure which is rational in terms of the questionnaire's objective and intended subjects.

As in most aspects of management, if the objectives are not clear then the results will be as unclear as the objectives. Before even starting to design your questionnaire, a number of aspects of your topic have to be considered and clarified. Some of these aspects will appear to be obvious, but elementary mistakes are even more harmful than errors in design detail.

Put simply, there are three fundamentals that you have to get straight before you start:

- What do you want to know?
- How much do your intended subjects know?
- What are you actually measuring?

What do you want to know?

1. What people think about a subject – their opinion.
2. What proportion of people hold a particular view?
3. Is something important to people?
4. How much do people know about a particular subject?
5. How do people feel about a subject?
6. Do people believe in a particular subject?
7. How important is the subject compared with something else?
8. What are people's expectations?
9. Do people expect change?

The list is not exhaustive and it is easy to see how such topics as job satisfaction, opinions on pay and reactions to change could benefit from asking these basic questions before you start.

How much do your intended subjects know?

It would be ridiculous to ask people questions on subjects they know nothing about. It happens! This is an area where expert assumptions have to be made. In other words, the manager has to have a rough idea of how much the intended subjects know of the topic. However, these assumptions are not just about knowledge. Some thought has to be given to how your subjects learnt their knowledge of the topic. Did they learn it through some form of education or from experience or both. There is a connection between how one remembers something and the way it was learnt originally. Is it remembered for what it is, or is it remembered by association or comparison with something else? If you ask people their opinions on something, you have to have grounds for suspecting that they will know about it and have feelings towards it.

Assuming your subjects know about your topic, some thought needs to be given as to the form in which they hold this knowledge. Three dangers lie in wait here: nostalgia, reality and 'ought' modals. To put it another way, your subject can be seen 'through rose-tinted glasses', 'through self-constructed reality' and 'by reference to how it ought to be rather than how it is'.

These aspects are not matters of interpretation to be applied to data once it has been collected; they are aspects that can be accommodated by a questionnaire and need to be part of preliminary thinking.

What are you actually measuring?

Questionnaires can take many forms, particularly when psychological aspects are being measured. While it is beyond the scope of this chapter to review every type of questionnaire, it must be clearly understood that you must be certain as to what is being measured and accept, that in most circumstances, only one form of response can be measured by one questionnaire. It must also be accepted that in some cases there is a need to seek expert opinion. If the project involves psychological measurement, then having the project undertaken by specialists is the advisable course of action.

Are you measuring: knowledge, some aspect of behaviour, opinions, priorities, attitudes, beliefs, values, perceptions, feelings, evaluations?

Seeing opinions and attitudes as the same thing is a common error.

Questions to be considered at the planning stage

Everyone worries about the response rate of their questionnaire. The sample size has been calculated, but will I make it? It is not a matter of luck! Questionnaire design plays a part in the success and it is not just a case of making it look pretty!

In designing the structure of a questionnaire, you have three questions to consider.

First, how to induce people to fill it in; secondly, how are the responses to be aggregated; thirdly, and most importantly, will it achieve the objectives? These questions are in fact criteria by which you could judge your questionnaire design.

Alas, there are no firm rules you can apply to questionnaire design – circumstance dictates. However, it is possible to identify the kind of design decisions that have to be made. The list below is not exhaustive.

Design questions

1 The length of the questionnaire.
2 Where to put personal details.
3 The degree of disguise.
4 Whether to fire blanks.
5 Whether to use check questions.
6 Running order or sequence.
7 The need to aggregate the data.
8 The need to compare the data with other data.
9 The need to computerize the data.

The best way to answer these questions is to imagine yourself filling in a questionnaire. This is where a degree of awareness of the subject's knowledge can contribute. That said, there is no substitute for piloting the questionnaire.

Writing questions

There are no easy answers here, only pitfalls to avoid. As in the case of design, question writing is aided by the ability to think out what information you are seeking and the ability to visualize how your intended subjects might perceive your topic.

Remember any question is supposed to:

- Raise attention.
- Focus.
- Eliminate alternatives.
- Draw an unambiguous response.

These criteria presuppose that the subject is interested, aware and has knowledge of, or about, the subject you are surveying.

Types of question

There are basically two types of question – open-ended and closed.

The closed question restricts the answers to a small set of responses and requires the questionnaire designer to have a fair knowledge of the range of options the subjects might have in this area. It does, however, generate precise answers.

Questionnaire design

The open-ended question has the merit of not imposing restrictions as to the possible answer, but is harder to aggregate and computerize. It has the merit of offering richer and deeper responses.

Wording pitfalls

Here are some common pitfalls to be avoided:

1. Avoid vague wording, e.g. Frequently, Normally.
2. Avoid belief. Questions should not depend on the subject believing in the question, e.g. Healthy eating is good for you, How much do you spend on vegetables in a week?
3. Avoid leading questions, e.g. Most people think . . . ?
4. Avoid typical examples.
5. Avoid letting the subject answer 'It depends on'.

Some common problems

In broad terms, the commonest problems fall into three categories which are, first, phrasing questions, secondly, determining the levels of classification of choices blocks and, thirdly, handling the possibility of 'don't know'. There are, alas, many more pitfalls.

Problems of phrasing questions

In what direction do you phrase factual questions? Do you ask: 'How long have you lived at your present address?' or do you ask 'When did you move into your present address?'

The first question is easier to answer, but will be less accurate than the second.

Problems of expressing levels of degree of a choice set

Problem 1 The key decisions
Often, questionnaires contain choice sets like the following example containing classes of numbers:

    100–199
    200–299
    300–399
    400+

If this choice set is to work, you have made certain important decisions, which are:

1. Do you need equal intervals?
2. How wide should the classes be?
3. How many intervals do you need?
4. Where do you set the boundaries?
5. The last category needs special consideration. If it is open-ended, then calculations become difficult. If it is closed, the implication is that a finite limit exists which may not be how your subjects interpret the questions.

Problem 2 Handling the unspecified
What do you do when the classification you are using cannot contain all possibilities? The answer is you need to ask about 'other' categories. If you need to ask 'Other?', you also need to ask the subjects to specify what it is, which means a supplementary question.

The possibility of having to use the 'Other' category has to be considered very seriously, because it may have implications for some other part of your questionnaire. If a large proportion of answers fall into the 'Other' category, then the questionnaire itself is less valid.

Problem 3 Handling rogue items
In setting out a classification you often come across items that do not fit easily into the mainstream of your class boundaries. There are a number of options here, such as:

- Combine the item into another class and tell the reader.
- Tell the reader it is not to be considered at all.
- Use the 'Other' device.

Handling the possibility of 'Don't know'

It was suggested earlier that part of the initial thinking process was to access how much your intended subjects actually knew about or cared about your topic. If there is any reason to think that their knowledge might not be comprehensive or that their attachment might be variable, then the questionnaire must build in the opportunity to express this with a 'Don't know' option. This avoids the possibility of subjects inventing answers to questions they find difficult or spoiling their questionnaire out of frustration.

Simple commonsense rules

Although there are no hard-and-fast rules, experience has taught us to apply common sense to the task:

- Use simple and concise language.
- Do not make unrealistic demands of those who are to fill in the questionnaire.
- Each question should ask about one 'thing' only.
- Each question should have no escape route, i.e. 'Don't know', 'No comment', 'It depends'.

- Be polite.
- Be straightforward and guard against double meanings.
- Get the question order right.
- Make the layout easy to follow.
- Give clear instructions.
- Test the questionnaire first.

Planning a survey

The whole task of creating a questionnaire must be seen as part of a larger process which involves its application. This is the survey process. It too can be designed.

Survey design

There are many approaches to designing a survey, and variation will depend to a large extent on the complexity of the subject. The list below is a suggested process:

Stage one: Identify the subject and set some objectives.
Stage two: Pilot a questionnaire to find out what people know and what they see as the important issues.
Stage three: List the areas of information needed and refine the objective.
Stage four: Review the responses to the pilot.
Stage five: Finalize the objective.
Stage six: Write the questionnaire.
Stage seven: Re-pilot the questionnaire.
Stage eight: Finalize the questionnaire.
Stage nine: Code the questionnaire.

Survey administration

Stage one: Select the sample.
Stage two: Prepare the mailing system. This requires the questionnaire to be numbered, a return date set and mailing facilities to be organized.

Coding a questionnaire

The purpose of coding a questionnaire is to allow a computer to undertake the hard work of aggregating the answers. The principle behind coding is based on two concepts – the variable and the range of possible answers.

Every question or part of a question represents a variable; for example:

Gender – male/female (one variable).
Nationality (one variable).

Furthermore, questions may have more than one answer. Answers may be as simple as 'Yes' or 'No', but they may also be a wide range of possibilities. Therefore we need to tell the computer to recognize and place the whole range of possible answers in separate codes.

The numbers used in codes usually begin with 0 or 1, then follow a sequence, e.g. 1,2,3, . . . 10, etc. They are normally written as 000, 001, 002, etc.

When a code is assigned to a variable, every possible outcome must be coded. For example, the variables Gender and Nationality:

Gender: Male = 1
               Female = 2
Nationality: = British = 1
               French = 2
               German = 3
               Other = 4

Entered on the computer, it would look as follows:

Question No.	Variable 1 (Gender)	Variable 2 (Nationality)	Description
1	1	2	Male, French
2	1	3	Male, German
3	2	2	Female, French

Part Four

Human Resource Management and Quality

23 Commitment, job satisfaction and labour turnover

Introduction

The moment an organization adopts a policy which emphasizes quality, then it has to rethink its approach to motivation. In a service industry where customers are dealt with face to face, there can be no question of high quality coexisting with high levels of labour turnover. Even when there is an efficient training function, the constant appearance of new faces prevents a degree of continuity taking root. Such continuity is essential to good-quality service. It is a concern for quality that has refocused the perspective from 'the problems and benefits of high labour turnover' towards the idea of employee commitment. In other words, emphasis is now on how we can keep our valued employees. Keeping them automatically implies the question, how can we motivate them to a level of performance beyond what might be expected from secure employment to a level based on taking responsibility and being actively involved? To have this greater expectation of employees is essential, because continuity alone does not make for quality service. There is always the chance that the performance of a stable workforce can go stale.

Commitment by employees automatically means greater commitment from managers who must possess a wider range of motivational techniques than was the case with a workforce that was ever changing. It is true that in most service organizations there are always stable and unstable elements in the workforce. However, it is clear from the analysis of the labour markets of labour-intensive service industries that managers have, in the past, chosen to manage the whole workforce in a style appropriate to an unstable element of that workforce. This changes once quality becomes a priority. Management policies must then have a style and content that suits the needs of a stable workforce.

While it is easy to imagine the relationship between job satisfaction and labour turnover, the relationship between job satisfaction and commitment is more complex and is, in some respects, rather surprising. One would expect labour turnover to decline as job satisfaction and commitment increase. However, what is the direction of influence between job satisfaction and commitment? If an employee is more satisfied are they also more committed or does commitment cause satisfaction?

To understand the relationship between this trio of concepts it is necessary to start with one behavioural aspect, that of people leaving. Whether they leave or stay does act as an indicator of both job satisfaction and commitment. However, the key to this matter is the pivotal concept of job satisfaction. It is pivotal because it will be shown that both labour turnover and commitment are dependent upon it. If a new perspective is taken on job satisfaction, one which is not concerned with questions of what motivates, then the role of job satisfaction becomes clearer. The new perspective is to see it as a *process*, not just as content which gratifies needs.

Labour turnover – reversing the question

Why do people stay with an organization?
1 Habit? A comfortable feeling like an old overcoat.
2 The self-justifying nature of routine.
3 What you do you come to believe in eventually, no matter what you thought at first?
4 A need for social identity.
5 A reciprocal exchange with an organization.
6 A calculative-instrumental exchange.
7 Fear of change and new horizons.
8 A need for purposeful life activity.

These reasons are not mutually exclusive and often their boundaries are blurred. Nor are people always aware of the reasons for staying. Almost by definition the rationale becomes a habit.

Job satisfaction as a process

Motivation theory shows us what elements of employment and work can motivate. In motivational theory, individual differences between people and changes within the same person in different circumstances and over time are explained by different levels of individual need and changes in those needs. What has to be explained is how changes come about. In other words, accepting changes in personal need, how does the individual construe these changes? There must be a process at work here involving both personal needs and situational variables. Note what is being said here, that job satisfaction is not just a matter of satisfying needs but also of making the social and physical environment work for them.

Every individual makes his or her own satisfaction. The individual puts together their psychological and social needs with all the elements of the situation as they find it and produces a concept of job satisfaction of their own. In other words, job satisfaction is manufactured. Very much a bespoke creation. The assumption is that, even if individuals are not rational or realistic, the situation imposes both on them. Whatever satisfaction there is to be had must lie in their objective situation. In other words, it is only their situation which can satisfy their actual needs. It cannot come from anywhere else. Even ambitions and dreams have their centre of gravity in the person's current situation. The expression 'Where do I go from here?' captures this notion of things being rooted in the reality of the present. This is not to say that everybody will be able to create an acceptable level of job satisfaction. For some the level of satisfaction created remains unsatisfactory, which may in turn lead to labour turnover.

There are five processes that enable people to create their own satisfaction. Each of them works through either changes of needs or are responses to stimuli from the work environment. The processes are:

- Information processing.
- Selecting particular attributes.
- Ordering attributes.
- Trade-offs.
- Reselection and reordering over time.

For the purposes of understanding these processes, it would be useful to work from a hypothetical example. An individual has some personal needs which relate to work. These needs are expressed in a range of job attributes which they look for in selecting a job and hope to find in the job. Not all attributes of a job are selected and those that are, exist in a rank order of some kind, for example, working in a stimulating group comes before pay which ranks above interesting tasks, etc. All very well, but how does it actually work? As the sole source of satisfaction is the working environment, the individual takes in the information that is there, then reassesses their range and rank of favoured job attributes. No good wanting autonomy if the place runs on close supervision!

What then happens when some of the favoured job attributes are not available in that particular environment? One solution is to leave, but another is to 'trade-off' the costs and benefits in order to get a 'working set of job attribute satisfiers'. For example, the pay is poor but the boss is nice, the group is attractive even if the work is boring, etc. In this way, job satisfaction is manufactured by the individual. It must be said that if there are particular and intensely felt needs that are not available, then the most likely form of behaviour is to leave.

What is commitment?

Commitment is a conscious affirmation of loyalty to something or somebody. As commitment in secret is rather a redundant idea, the concept implies some form of behaviour which substantiates this state of loyalty. It may be as mundane as not leaving or something more affirmative such as extra motivation. A further complication comes with the focus of commitment. Within the work environment there are many potential targets:

- Job commitment.
- Tasks within a job.
- Occupational commitment.
- Career commitment.
- Organizational commitment.
- Work group attachment.
- Commitment to a profession.

It would be easy to fall into the trap of thinking that because the organization is the actual situation for all these types of commitment, they are all variations on the theme of organizational commitment. They are not. If the primary aim is to create organizational commitment, then loyalty to a task, an occupation, a profession, or to personal advancement, can run counter to the concept of the organization as the emotional home and source of stimulus.

What is organizational commitment?

Definitions abound, but perhaps the clearest way to describe organizational commitment is to draw a picture of the behaviour that is likely to be found in an employee who is specifically committed to an organization.

Beyond the obvious likelihood of punctuality, reliability and cooperativeness, three deeper aspects of commitment may be present and visible. These are:

1 An emotional attachment to the aims and values of the organization. This attachment is often expressed through pride in the name of the company.
2 A willingness that goes beyond normative expectations.
3 Being prepared to push instrumentality into the background. Notice, pushing it away from performance but not abandoning it!

In a sense, commitment has one advantage for management over motivation, in that while motivation has to be demonstrated to be acknowledged, commitment actually has to be openly declared in some way by both parties. Commitment implies going public.

The definitions themselves, while various, are fairly coherent. Some emphasize the connection between organization and personality and between group and personality. For example:

> 'The willingness of social actors to give their energy and loyalty to social systems, the attachment of personality systems to social systems to social relations which are seen as self expressive.' (Kantor)

One element expressed in all the definitions is congruence, the process by which the goals of the organization and those of the individual become increasingly integrated or congruent. For example:

> 'A partisan, affective attachment to the goals and values of an organization, to one's role in relation to goals and values, and to the organization for its own sake apart from its purely instrumental worth.' (Buchanan)

However, some writers recognize that the instrumental worth of an organization can never be dismissed.

A common theme that runs through the ideas on commitment is the concept of exchange, that is, giving energy and time in return for rewards.

This brings together the basic ideas of motivation theory with ideas on work environment, in that people come to organizations with needs, desires and skills. If the organization provides the opportunity for abilities to be utilized and for some needs to be satisfied in a consistent and dependable way, then the possibility of commitment is enhanced. By contrast, when this is not the case, then the chance of achieving commitment is diminished.

This idea of exchange not only reconfirms that the instrumental nature of employment is never far from the surface but also that it fits exactly into one of the key elements of the job satisfaction process – that of exchanging attributes. Here we have stumbled upon the link between job satisfaction and commitment.

The exchange idea must, in operation, be a judgement made after some time; for example: 'Let's take a rain check. I'm giving this much and I'm getting this back. Yes, it's worth committing, no it is not worth it.' The process of forming a judgement by summing up both sides of an equation is only possible through the job satisfaction process itself. In other words, only after manipulating and altering valued attributes through an exchange process and then seeing if satisfaction is attainable is a decision to commit made. If this is true, then we would expect to see *commitment following job satisfaction with perhaps a small time lag*. This is indeed the case, but there is an extra twist in the tail.

If the progress of an employee is examined over a period of time, starting from the moment they agree to join the organization, then a pattern emerges that slightly changes the relationship between job satisfaction and commitment just described. At this point two new terms are introduced – entrenchment and re-commitment.

A brief overview of the progress of a newcomer into an organization would be through a series of stages:

Stage	Behaviour
(a) Pre-entry stage	Anticipation
(b) Early stage	Initiation through socialization
(c) Settling in	Time to evaluate job satisfaction
(d) Settled in	If job satisfaction is high, then the employee re-commits
	If job satisfaction is low, then the employee does not re-commit.

What is happening here is that commitment is dependent not just on job satisfaction but on job satisfaction being maintained to the time when a reappraisal or 'taking a rain check' takes place. In other words, achieving job satisfaction at the very beginning is good but not a precursor of commitment. If, and only if, job satisfaction is maintained does the employee commit. What follows this commitment is a form of entrenchment whereby the employee, so to speak, puts down roots.

What is the psychological value of commitment?

The real value of organizational commitment is in its capacity to facilitate change. If the individual is focused on the organization rather than the job or the career or profession, then the reception accorded to change is slightly different than if commitment was not present.

If we expand the concept of motivation a little, a number of questions appear. When applying an incentive, what are we trying to achieve? To get people to work harder? Be more loyal? Be flexible? Be prepared to abandon old skills? Be prepared to learn new skills?

The last three objectives all carry the fear of change and require cooperation. The committed environment has an advantage over mere 'good motivational practices' in this important area.

The lessons for managers

The main point for managers is that, given that they want a stable workforce, job satisfaction must be a goal. However, the strategy must be to encourage satisfaction at the outset through a good induction process, but more importantly to have an early appraisal at between four and six months to see if satisfaction has been maintained. The actual point in time when the employee considers commitment and entrenchment cannot be known, but it is almost certain to be within the first six months.

If commitment is a desired aim, then it can be reinforced by policies which make the employee a stakeholder in the organization. Profit-sharing and shareholding schemes work well in the context of commitment. In a sense they are the 'public' commitment of management to the committed employee.

24 Empowerment

If the trend towards organization commitment is seen as a means to create a new organizational context, then the 'active principle' within that context is the concept of *empowerment*. In fact, the ideas of commitment and empowerment work in tandem and form the basis of the concept of 'quality'. In order to understand what empowerment is, it is necessary to recognize that it is about organizational behaviour and about change. It is a new form of organizational behaviour and structure which has come about because of a perceived need for organizational responsiveness and which is itself the mechanism that enables organizations to be responsive.

The idea of empowerment is perhaps often misunderstood. Such misunderstanding has led to cynicism about the 'authenticity' of empowerment schemes. Responsibility without power is one cynical view. In a sense, this scepticism is justified because to work properly empowerment has to be done well. This requires management to realize what an enormous change is required of the incumbent of an empowered role. For empowerment to work properly, both managers and workers have to understand the real implications of what the change actually means.

What is empowerment?

Empowerment is incorporating into an employee's role the authority and means to be responsive to customer requirements. It enables the employees to be responsive by ensuring that the necessary rules of order within the organization do not interfere with the performance of a task which the customer requires.

Put simply, this means that empowerment is giving the employees the right to 'break the rules' to serve the customer. In a real sense this is a risky strategy for management because 'rules' are always necessary to an organization. It is a balance between organizational rules and discretion which must be available quickly.

The idea that employees should have authority and take responsibility for their actions is not new, but it has never before been allied to a business objective, that is, ensuring customers receive a defined quality of product or service. What is new about the empowerment movement is that it takes a basic idea from motivation theory, that is, that employees respond to autonomy and achievement, and places it in an overall design of the production or service. Here human performance is built-in to the product or service itself, rather than being just a factor of production like working capital.

The logic of empowerment

Perhaps the best way to see the differences in philosophies between straightforward good management of workers and the empowerment idea is to see how the empowerment movement came about. The logic of giving employees authority stems directly from three factors which have come together simultaneously. These are:

1 The advances in computer and telecommunication systems have led to an increased ability to communicate and an increased ability to specify and control the content of people's jobs.
2 Technology has granted the ability to specify and therefore to standardize a product or service. At the same time, market competition has led to the need to use that ability to specify and standardize to create product differentiation through added value.
3 A desire to get closer to the customer. The idea that companies must understand the needs of their customers has led to the simple conclusion that means getting close to them.

These three 'big' ideas have led to a number of organizational changes:

(a) The height of the organizational pyramid is being lowered. Organizations are getting flatter, with fewer and fewer levels of authority between the strategy decision-makers and the shop floor.
(b) If being able to respond to customer needs is the aim, then flexible work practices are essential. The implication here is that roles need to be defined broadly and must 'not be set in stone'.
(c) If understanding the customers' needs is the aim, then those people who deal directly with the customers are important employees. The new emphasis is to focus on the performance of those employees who deal directly with customers.
(d) To take advantage of the flatter organization, the flexible work practices and the feedback from customers there has to be an organization culture that values change.

In a sense, these organizational changes are 'the context' of empowerment rather than leading directly to it. What the organizational changes imply is good human relations management with a focus on development and on individuals. What leads directly to the notion of empowerment is the realization that it is *never easy for an organization to be responsive* and that there is *no one ideal structure that will guarantee such responsiveness*. Organization theory has in the past suggested two polar types of organization: the bureaucratic structure and the organic structure. While the former is 'rule bound,' the latter is more open, less rule bound, and capable of rapid change. Obviously the organic model is more responsive than the bureaucratic one. However, the question remains, is it responsive enough?

The modern answer to this question is No! Organizational structures need rules, need goals of order, otherwise nothing can be achieved. By definition this places a limit on how rapidly a structure can change itself. It is this reasoning that has led to the conclusion that people can be more responsive than structures and that therefore to 'go that extra mile' for the customer requires a personal response rather than an organization response. This is the heart of empowerment. This is the logic that leads to the idea of giving people the ability to override organizational rules and norms to meet specific customer needs.

The limits of empowerment

It must be clear from the context that empowerment is not about management giving up their responsibility and giving away their authority to employees who can do what they like. This is a recipe for chaos. What empowerment is about is giving employees authority and decision-making power within parameters defined by two variables, which are:

- The definition and nature of the actual product and service being offered.
- The boundaries of customer perception of that product or service and the probable range of discrepancy between the organization's definition of product and service and the customers' definition.

In other words, the employee cannot change the product or service but they can intervene between the organization's idea of what the product or service is and the customer's perception of it. Where they disagree is where the responsiveness of empowerment plays its major role. Differences in expectations, the requirement for minor changes and for minor additions, the idiosyncratic nature of feedback on satisfaction, all these aspects are best handled by a person rather than by a set of rules and roles.

The real limits on empowerment come in two forms:

- Control over resources.
- The scope of the product and service itself.

Phony empowerment is when the employee only has the 'power' to make a profuse 'apology' but cannot put the problem right. There must be sufficient resources under the control of the person to be able to put things right. The danger here is that they may promise more than can be delivered or that they may extend the product or service beyond that laid down (and costed) by management. The resource problem in the context of empowerment requires a closer relationship between managers and workers.

The management–worker relationship in the context of empowerment

Clearly there is a strong element of trust required by the idea of empowerment. This is why the concept is so closely linked to the policy of encouraging organizational commitment from employees. Commitment and trust come out of the same knapsack. Where there is a blurring of boundaries and rules and where there is a high level of subjectivity, trust becomes the significant element in the manager–worker response to the customer.

However, trust is not all that is required: knowledge of the product/service and knowledge of the organization form the background to trust.

If an employee is going to respond to a customer, they must know:

- What the product or service is! This means knowing its limits and its position in relation to other products or services.
- What the organization can and cannot do! False promises end in tears. There are limits in terms of production and its terms of costs.
- The rules and norms of the organization. To be sensitive to the areas of discretion.

This knowledge cannot come about by accident. It requires careful role definition and training.

Change and learning

It was suggested earlier that the logic of empowerment is based on the idea that organizations, even organic organizations, cannot be quickly responsive to customers. There are limits to how adaptive an organization can be. This is also true of individual managers. They cannot do everything, know everything. It follows therefore that encouraging learning by employees takes away from managers the potential burden of knowledge overload. Even if they have the knowledge, managers cannot remember or be aware of everything at the moment it becomes required by a customer.

In terms of technical production, the normal situation would be managers laying down the product and system, and faults being picked up as they occur. This is a 'deficiency based' approach to quality. The problem is that it is 'backwards facing'. When a problem occurs, it is handled. The empowerment approach is the key to prevent problems, to be proactive in terms of quality. The approach required here is one of continuous learning by the employee. The development of this learning begins with training employees to reflect on the quality of their own work. This is followed by giving them the authority to change their own work methods to improve the product. The final stage is to incorporate the capacity to reflect and change into the definition of the product or service itself.

25 Functional flexibility and the service organization of the future

The third key concept of modern human resource mangement is functional flexibility. Along with empowerment and commitment it is a contribution of human resource management to the achievement of quality of service and product. This concept belongs to a quartet of forms of flexibility, which are: flexible people, numerical flexibility, remuneration or earnings flexibility, and functional flexibility.

Flexible people

A set of people who are multi-skilled and who are willing to change their job content on a contingency basis. This kind of constant change provides interest and challenge for the worker who has to cope without diminishing standards. In reality, flexible workers have to be able to cope emotionally with moving from a pleasant skilled task to, perhaps, even a demeaning unskilled task. This kind of demand on workers makes their attitude as important as their skills and training. For this reason, the concept of flexible people is linked with that of empowerment.

Numerical flexibility

Numerical flexibility meets the need to adjust short-term labour supply by such means as:

- Temporary workers.
- Part-time workers.
- Overtime.

Earnings flexibility

Here, adjustments in labour supply are achieved by linking pay to performance. In this way the cost of labour is automatically adjusted to the level of business. Tipping can be seen in this light.

Functional flexibility

Functional flexibility meets the needs for adjustment to demand by adjusting the content of jobs:

- Boundaries between jobs are broken down.
- Related jobs are joined together by common skills.
- People are trained to perform a wide range of skills (flexible people).

In a very real sense functional flexibility is the tough one because the others are easier to implement and often act as a deterrent for introducing functional flexibility. If any organization is operating with a weak internal labour market (see Chapter 3), then it finds altering numbers of workers by manipulation recruitment and labour turnover and having a self-adjusting pay system very easy to implement and very successful. The problem is that numerical and earnings flexibility are possible enemies of quality. Think of the tired chambermaid on overtime cutting corners to get home. It is the ideas of flexible people and functional flexibility that connect to quality in a positive way. In other words, these four forms of flexibility are not always compatible and are in fact rivals, with numerical and earnings lining up against people and functional.

When variations and fluctuations in customer demand are extreme, such as when there are daily, or even hourly, fluctuations, then from the point of view of the manager, the task of juggling people, jobs, skills and costs, while trying to maintain quality, is a difficult one. It requires a coping strategy. This volatile contingency behaviour is associated with direct service industries such as retailing, hotel and catering, and various forms of tourism business. One argument, which is discussed later, is that functional flexibility begins life as another item to juggle, part of coping, *but which over time becomes a stabilizing strategy* which decreases the variance of labour supply and reduces the need for the alternative forms of extended labour supply such as casual labour and overtime.

Indeed, the rationale for functional flexibility is that it provides an alternative form of coping with business variation to numerical flexibility, which alters numbers employed, and to earnings flexibility, which alters individuals' pay.

There are two forms of functional flexibility. These are, first, *whole job substitution* where workers take over other jobs when required and, secondly, *boundary-loosing approaches* where parts of jobs become merged so that the task can be moved from person to person instead of the person moving to the task.

Barriers to functional flexibility

Functional flexibility is about changing people's jobs! There is always a resistance to change, but this in itself is not the main barrier. There are three serious problems with loosening an organization's job boundaries:

- The skill mix.
- The size of skill differentials.
- Group competition.

It is easy to talk about multi-skilling, but it is not so easy to apply. If the skills of the proposed 'merged jobs' are numerous and of high contrast and variety, then it may be difficult to train people in so many tasks. A mixture of manual skills, people skills and data skills at several levels might make for interesting work but it may give recruiters and trainers headaches!

If there is a wide gap between skilled occupations and unskilled occupations it may be impossible to 'merge' jobs across such a gap. In this case the organization has to accept that functional flexibility can only occur within particular areas.

A more human barrier comes with the existence of groups who function competitively within an organization. Work processes often range groups of workers against each other. For example, reception want the rooms *now*, housekeeping want them really clean! Drivers of excursion coaches much leave on time, guides do not want to hassle their clients! This kind of pressure is natural, but it does not make it easy to merge jobs.

Substitution, quality and strategy

While functional flexibility forms the overall framework, the operational concept is that of substitutability. By this is meant the degree to which one employee in a job can be substituted by another. The principle relating technology to external labour markets is known as the substitution principle. However, exactly the same principles apply within an organization's internal labour market. This is problematic for a strategy which encompasses standards of quality, because some of the principles of substitution have the effect of pushing quality downwards.

The argument here is that as substitution presents dangers to quality, they need to be encompassed within the same strategy.

An organization's ability to substitute one person for another increases when the following apply:

- The more unskilled the job.
- The more training is offered by the organization.
- The more personal attributes count in a job.
- The less dependent the job is on previous knowledge.
- The more knowledge can be substituted by information.
- The less the degree of specificity.

In a real sense the second of these principles, that of training, can – if it is contained within a strategy – offset the adverse effects of the others. The danger is, however, that without planning and without specifying what is required in terms of knowledge, skill and personal attributes, these aspects will be determined by market forces and cost reduction economics. It is worth pointing out that quality strategies have to be able to defend themselves from economic imperatives. One such argument from economics would suggest that functional flexibility has to be cheaper than its more established alternatives. Even if this were possible in the long term, it is an unfair argument because, unlike numerical and earnings flexibility, functional flexibility is umbilically linked to the mainenance of quality. *Quality measures and functional flexibility must both share the same policy and strategy framework because they are mutually dependent.*

Strategy for implementation: plan or let it happen organically?

Two interesting choices exist here. First is the requirement for training. In this approach, multi-skilling is done through training. This requires planning and careful application. Someone who does a job occasionally needs to be as good as someone who does just that job every day. The second approach is more organic and suggests that boundary loosening is the easier way to overcome barriers and that after a time the new flexibility becomes institutionalized not through policy but through daily experience. Here the approach is to encourage people to do part of each other's work, so that gradually everyone can do everybody else's job. In a way this is a dangerous approach because it is difficult to control. It does, however, have the merit of getting the concept accepted without the negotiation that would be required by the planned approach and without engendering the fear that follows the public announcement of change.

From coping to stability

The theoretical framework for the idea that a once highly volatile situation can be turned into a stable one comes from some experience of seeing it happen to an external labour market. Unstable labour markets can gradually be tamed by increasing bureaucracy within organizations. This argument is founded on the idea that people become more responsible when they are managed more responsibly. There are parallels here – enhanced skill and empowerment may have the same taming effect.

Once functional flexibility takes hold, it can overcome the many barriers that confront it and directly challenge economic arguments, not on the grounds of being the cheapest form of enhanced labour supply but by its ability to reduce the fluctuations within labour supply. If consumer demand and labour supply are seen as conflicting, then functional flexibility can be seen as a conflict resolution mechanism, being so automatic as to be almost unnoticeable.

The starting point of training

The planned approach to a commitment to functional flexibility means a planning process and training.

The planning process

1. Identify which jobs can be part of the programme.
2. Sort the jobs into broad levels of skill. This banding ensures that people can be matched to their right level.
3. Within each job, identify: systems and sequences, technical knowledge, routine and variable tasks, and tasks containing a degree of personal judgement and decision-making.
4. Identify common tasks between jobs.
5. Identify common knowledge between jobs.
6. Identify core skills and knowledge.

The service organization wage structure of the future?

If functional flexibility is achieved, then the organization structure and, more particularly, the wage structure will change radically. To speculate on this requires the abandonment of two accepted ideas and their replacement with two others. If we abandon the concept of the job as a defined occupation, and if we abandon the idea of people choosing a job being based mainly on job content, and instead substitute the idea of the flexible job and add that job selection may be as much influenced by the convenience of the hours of work as by the job content, then the wage and skill structure simply has to change.

The skill and wage structure of the service organization of the future may look like Figure 25.1.

Figure 25.1

Contrast the pyramid on the left, which has a traditional structure of pay differential based on occupations and their skills, against the one on the right where there are only three skill levels. Within the lower level the differentials are based on time at which the work takes place. It is the acceptance of the concept of unsocial hours which is so important to the reform of pay in labour-intensive service industries.

Part Five

Management at the Corporate Level

26 Career management

Introduction

Every organization is concerned with the quality of its managers. Irrespective of whether the organization operates a strong or weak internal labour market for its workforce (see Chapter 2), there is always a desire for some continuity in management, therefore, to a degree, companies always operate a strong internal labour market for managers. This means that while recruitment from the external labour market is used, it runs alongside a system of internal promotion. To an extent, all organizations are dependent on a group of aspirants to guarantee continuity of its management functions.

Put at a general level, career management is about matching the organizational needs with employee aspiration while keeping one eye on the external labour market supply conditions. But in more practical terms, it is about 'traffic' management – matching opportunities to potential, and identifying growth factors – what causes potential to be realized later? In other words, there are two inseparable concepts involved in career management – *planning* and *management development*. These concepts come together when someone says 'who have we got to take over?' and someone else says 'how about X?' to which the response is probably 'are they ready?'

What is illustrated here is that each concept has its own special problems. In the case of career planning, the long term meets the immediacy of a vacancy and rarely is the timing perfect so potential rarely dovetails perfectly. So it is not just a case of identifying potential but 'storing' it. In a sense, 'storage and growth' is the key concept in career planning. It is pointless having people with potential waiting around in jobs that do not develop them towards their potential. The special problem of management development is recognizing potential, and what causes it to grow, against the background of young managers recruited from the labour market doing very different jobs from the jobs of senior managers in the organization. The interests of planning and management development coincide in identifying jobs which contribute both the storage and growth functions of careers.

Career planning

The career planner needs to have information in four key areas:

- Organization pay structure.
- Pay levels of competitors.
- Business plans and their impact on opportunities.
- Identified potential.

Putting aside, for a moment, all considerations of quality, what the planner needs to know in respect of identified potential is:

- The number of people identified as having potential.
- Where these people are in the organization.
- How old they are.
- What they earn.
- The existing channels of promotion.
- The key stages in development
- How long people stay at each stage of a career path.
- Dead-ends or blockages.

If a career planner had all this knowledge it would still lack direction. What gives it all meaning is having *target occupations*. It is no good talking about future managers – what are they doing? You need to specify the target occupations you are engineering paths and devising personal development programmes for, for example unit management, financial controller, sales manager etc. These targets are not ceilings for the individuals concerned, but do give the system some focus without being inflexible.

What has to be understood is, first, that whether or not an organization has a formal promotion policy, one will exist through custom and practice, second, that single promotion affects all other promotions and finally, that even in the most organized scheme there will always be a difference between the policies and what happens in reality. It follows from this that the first task for the career planner is to find out what is going on. All this points to the need for some career analysis.

Like other functions, career analysis needs some clear information including:

1. What is happening at the moment (examination of current labour supply and the working of promotion criteria)?
2. How effective are the organization promotion policies?
3. How realistic are the promises made to aspirants?
4. What is the effect of existing policies and intended policies on all other personnel policies such as pay structure, pensions and status?

Career analysis: some useful techniques

Manpower flow approach

The best guide to analysis is to examine the career of the target occupation. When this is compared with some hypothetical career path it is even more effective. If, for example, it is assumed that all the sales managers in a hotel company come from a reception background because of the experience that would give them of handling customers, and that they would also have had a hotel school education, then this can be tested by focusing on the career histories of those in the position. The result is a comparison **between two manpower flows. Figure 26.1(a) depicts what was intended, but Figure 26.1(b) what was actually happening.**

An example is shown in Figure 26.1. Historically, it would seem that sales managers were always recruited from outside the organization. This kind of analysis tells you what kind of career path actually exists, whether intended or not.

Figure 26.1 *(a) Internal manpower; (b) Actual manpower flow*

Age distributions

An age distribution is simply a way of distributing a population between defined and meaningful grades or levels on the basis of age. It uses proportions of people in grades at particular ages to describe the population.

Figure 26.2 is an example which shows the proportion of employees in each of four levels at each age. It is basically a photograph of the organization, like a school photograph with the juniors at the bottom going through each year to the senior grades at the top. The difference here is that the photograph works from left to right. Such a display is useful in the analysis of careers.

Figure 26.2

The basic needs of career planning are to display paths, identify stages of development and indicate timespan. Figure 26.2 is limited in this respect, but it does indicate the stages of progression by identifying the latest age at which people move up. Here, for example, if you haven't progressed from grade 1 to grade 2 by the time you are thirty-five, you are unlikely to do so. A more useful form of the age distribution is the biographical age distribution. The great advantage of this technique is that it is independent of rates of mobility and, therefore, can operate at any velocity of labour turnover.

Biographical age distribution

Here, the conditions are changed from describing different people of different ages in different grades to describing the same people at different ages in different grades. In other words, the distribution now looks backwards over the career histories of a sample

Figure 26.3

of a target occupation. To bring that order to this distribution two conditions are desirable: first, that the sample is all in the same occupational level or grade, and second, that the sample should be the same age. By these means, the distribution has a standardized starting point. However, the first condition is easy to meet, but the second is almost impossible. This means that the sample will decline to the right of the distribution. This in itself is harmless, but it does mean that the capacity of the sample to answer questions is limited to the *left of the age of the youngest member of the sample.*

Figure 26.3 shows details taken from a larger distribution, which has been reduced to the youngest member of the sample which is, in this case, thirty-eight years of age. The target group is hotel managers.

The target group is represented by the white space. What is important here, is how quickly people become assistant hotel managers, which appears to be the only route to becoming a general manager. In this form of analysis, the longer a person stays in a particular grade, the more important it is deemed to be as a development stage. By this token, department heads and supervisors stand little chance of making it and these roles are not seen as development roles.

The merits of this form of age distribution are that it:

- Identifies career path.
- Identifies stages which are crucial to development.
- Is independent of levels of mobility.
- Is an investigation technique.

The danger of this technique, however, is that it does not measure the recent past. If things have changed dramatically in the target occupation this technique will miss them.

Management development

The real problem with management development is that it is never easy to say what it is that constitutes good performance. In other words, what is a good manager? It is easier to point out good managers than it is to say why they are good. It is even harder to generalize what you see in good individuals into something you can select for or develop people towards.

There are so many types of manager and they do so many different things, how can we pull out some common factors? In fact, management development is really an organizational concept because at least when placed within this framework it might be possible to judge good performance. Management development varies between companies because their jobs are different, their needs are different and their assessment of performance will be different.

While it is obvious that the knowledge base of someone at the junior level of management will be different from a very senior manager and that, at least in theory, the difference could be made up by training, what concerns management development is being able to identify those people who can change sufficiently to become capable of managing at the higher level. In its early days, management development tried to identify psychological traits which were common between aspirants and successful managers. A less ambitious and more practical approach is to look for skills. Like anything else skills have levels, but at least some will be common to both junior and senior managers and their application to different levels of management can be measured. If there is a criticism to be made of this approach, it is that there has been a bias towards people-handling skills rather than decision-taking and analytical skills. The problem for investigation is always that the type of decision tends to change with the level of authority. In a sense, this is a clue to how skills can be revealed.

The focus of attention must be the target job and the skills they use. Techniques are available for investigating management skills, but the basis must be to find out what the superiors of the target job consider to be the attributes of good performance. The approach to this problem which follows is in two stages.

Stage 1

1. Find out how the superiors of the target job differentiate between existing incumbents of this job.
2. Test to see which dimensions are related to good performance by asking the superior to rank the present incumbents or to use similar data from the appraisal system.
3. Check for the degree of consensus between the superiors.

Stage 2

1. Investigate the actual work of the target job by:
   (a) Observation.
   (b) Critical incident technique.
2. Use superiors to identify what would constitute good and bad practice.
3. Ask superiors to identify what skill would be necessary to achieve good practice.

Stage 1 looks at people and stage 2 at jobs. When brought together they should help to identify and authenticate required skills and good and bad performance of those skills. It must not be overlooked, however, that management is not just a bag of skills, there is the question of knowledge and can it be implanted by experience or education and training.

So far, there has been a tendency to overlook the actual human being who is trying to build a career. While the goal of the planner and the developer might be to have any person with potential in the right job, getting satisfaction, growing and not being tempted by the labour market, individuals may perceive their own careers in a variety of ways. Motivation again is central to the concept of management development.

Schein: career anchors

A case has already been made in Chapter 7 for self-identity forming a basis for motivation and being likely to embrace an occupational identity. Schein suggests that for those with a career orientation, as against those with a particular job, the identity is formed from a self-assessment of their own abilities, their motives, their attitudes and their values. He argues that these congeal into a basic orientation from a period of search and discovery in the early years of a career. He calls these basic orientation career anchors and suggests five types: technical competence; managerial competence; security; autonomy; and creativity. In his discussion on the need for independence and the desire to build something, he makes an important and perhaps surprising contribution to our knowledge of entrepreneurs. These anchors are essential self-descriptions borne out of experience which harmonize ourselves to our work.

Schein, E. H. (1978), *Career Dynamics: Matching Individual and Organisational Needs*, Addison Wesley.

The basis of Schein's argument is the experience of work which people have and which forms their orientations. Three other pressures on personal aspirations can be identified:

- The compatibility of the career with the style of life the person desires.
- How far they have already travelled. Satisfaction with career is often correlated with how far back they started.
- People always remember what attracted them into the career in the first place. Often motives for behaviour can be traced back to those original purposes.

Careers in the hotel and catering industry

Management careers exhibit a number of conspicuous features:

- There are a lot of career opportunities in management. The industry displays a rate of promotion to management far in excess of most industries.
- There are two streams of management – those based on experience only and those based on vocational education and experience.
- Careers tend to be developed through a mixture of company career structures and labour market mobility.
- Because there are two streams of management career with one offering the opportunity to rise from the lower ranks the salaries of all junior ranks tend to be pulled down by this connection to the working ranks (see Chapter 3).
- This restriction does not apply to levels higher than junior managers and management salaries show a wide dispersion.
- Career structures vary from company to company.

Perhaps the most obvious structural feature of the hotel and catering industry is its fragmented small unit structure. To understand what this means in terms of careers, we have to superimpose the skill model from Chapter 3 on to the industrial structure and, while doing so, slightly recast the mould of the basic skill proportion pyramid. We also have to add another vital variable: companies or organizations. While most companies mimic the structure of the industry in that they have numbers of units plus a head office with perhaps some intervening levels of management, how they actually operate in terms of how authority and responsibility are distributed and how roles are prescribed is likely to vary from company to company.

Influence of structures

Given the structure of the industry, the obvious target occupation for careers would be unit management: hotel manager, restaurant manager, catering manager etc. This is clearly a large proportion of the management population of the industry, but the opportunities don't stop there as line management extends up to the corporate level.

Functional specialisms at head office and within larger units offer alternative careers. However, functional specialization is, by its nature, a smaller population than line management. To understand career paths to unit management it is helpful to recast the skill pyramid showing the direction of the flows (Figure 26.4).

Figure 26.4

Two points need to be made here.

First, the 'store and grow' stage is clearly the role of the assistant manager. Second, and of great importance, is the assumption which underlies the whole edifice, which is that some of the knowledge at the bottom is needed at the top, or to put it another way, managers have to have technical knowledge of the operation they are managing.

Influence of role changes

This assumption is coming under pressure from two fronts – a business orientation and technology. Information technology is allowing more things to be controlled in terms of the unit by head office and by the manager within the unit. To use the benefit of this technology managers are being granted autonomy within specified parameters and hotel activities are being turned into cost centres. In tandem with this is an emphasis on selling.

The result of these changes could be a change in organization structure, with autonomy being given to department heads reporting directly to the manager. This diminishes the role of the assistant manager. It is possible to envisage a generalized customer care role here. The point here is that if you change a job, you change the knowledge base of the job and, therefore, you change the career path needed to reach it. Organizational change produces career changes. Similarly, changes in the unit–head office relationship affect the role given to functional specialists such as marketing, finance and personnel. Examples can be found of companies which favour head office as the locus of these functions and others that deploy them in the units or area office. The message is basically that variations in company philosophy on organizational structure produce variations in role description, which alter career paths. However, it is worth considering whether the changes discussed above are changes or additions to the knowledge base of managers. Does the need for increased business skill and information technology skill deny the need for the technical skills of hotel and catering?

The assistant manager: a development analysis

Notwithstanding the pressures for change, the industry is, to a very large extent, reliant upon the assistant manager to provide its stock of managers. Most managers have served three appointments as assistants, but the jump from assistant to sole charge is always a large one. No matter what technical knowledge and people-handling skills are accumulated on the way up, the individual's ability to grow as a decision maker will not develop unless he or she is given the chance to make decisions.

It is at this point that corporate development plans are in the hands of existing unit managers. A corporate culture of development, delegation and appraisal is essential if the 'unassertive copilot syndrome' is to be avoided. If the assistant simply carries out decisions already taken, the assertiveness so essential to sole charge will simply wither. It is worth exploring this idea further.

As in any activity, speculation abounds as to the merits of the past versus the future. Such speculation usually uses stereotypes as its currency. In the hotel industry the 'old-fashioned' manager is ranged against a modern business person with ideas about standardization and costs. Sometimes this comes out as an amateur versus professional argument. A more detailed version suggests that the host spends too much time making the guest happy at the expense of profits and that the manager of the future would be in the office doing some long-term thinking and planning. These kind of arguments infiltrate the dialogue between industry and education. Like many of its kind this debate is based on the false premise that these approaches are mutually exclusive. They are not.

These aspects of looking after guests and doing some business planning are simply two parts of one activity – managing. They are only separated by size of operation. The hotel manager of the future has to have traditional knowledge of the profession and modern business skills. As illustration, the style of English hotel based on the notion of the nineteenth century 'country house' has very traditional standards but needs modern marketing to bring in the customers. What links both the so-called, traditional knowledge with the modern world is innovation and imagination. If we say that, the modern manager should:

- Know how customers differentiate between hotels.
- Be able to lead customer taste.
- Know how to design a system.
- Be able to assess the capacity of people, groups, systems and machines.

That is, know what is possible; what can be done.

These capabilities can be achieved solely by experience (a lot!) and solely by scientific management (market research, systems design, work study etc.) but *they are best activated by both*. This argument is an advert for both experience and education but there is something missing! How do you know that you need these capabilities? The answer is you won't know unless you have an imagination and are an innovative person. To a very large extent innovation is dependent upon assertiveness.

Some recent work in management development has classified managers in terms of innovators and adaptors. The first are not dependent on existing knowledge to handle situations and are prepared to go outside the known parameters for a solution. The adaptor uses initiative but thinks within the known constraints. Both require willpower and assertiveness.

To return to the assistant manager, if he or she cannot change something, cannot exert their will, then eventually they will begin not to see the need for change. Seen as a development process, lack of assertiveness can turn an innovator into an adaptor. Taken to its logical conclusion a lack of assertiveness makes a person leave management altogether.

Kirton

Kirton observed that people produce different solutions to similar problems. He distinguished between those who 'do things better' from those who 'do things differently'. The difference is whether or not the structure surrounding a problem is incorporated in the solution. If it is, then the outcome will be innovative. If it is accepted and placed outside the problem then the solution will be adaptive. Kirton felt that managers could be classified into innovators and adaptors and he developed a scale for measuring this differentiation. This interesting work addresses both questions of change and organizational effectiveness.

Kirton, M. (1976), 'Adapters and Innovators: A Description and Measure', *Journal of Applied Psychology*, vol. 61, no. 3, pp. 622–629.

The point being made here is that the role of the assistant manager only works as a development process *if it is made to work in this way*.

The problem is that the role contains tendencies that *can* work against personal development.

First, and most obviously, if the manager has not given the assistant responsibility and authority then the young person's opportunity to develop assertiveness and decision-making ability will simply be choked off.

Second, and quite independent of the attitude of the manager, is the 'here and now' nature of the work. Constant pressure from guests with problems and staff with problems can make the assistant manager see their role and management itself as a problem-solving, short-term activity. This process is reinforced by the variety of the work being in itself an attractive aspect of the work. Constant variety and 'never a dull moment' can be fun but there is a drawback if it makes the person forget the long term.

Finally, assistant managers need eyes in the back of their heads! The sheer complexity of running at least four types of work process (cleaning rooms, serving drinks, serving food and producing food) and undertaking probably several managerial functions (sales, personnel, training and accounting) all in the same day would make adaptors of us all! With such variety the assistant manager is dependent on systems and procedures but as has been said many times before, standards are subjective and therefore the qualitative control of standards requires constant judgements. It doesn't have to happen but all these characteristics can lower the person's perspective.

What the role is good at is developing people-handling skills. Constantly talking to guests and staff should instil both confidence and skill into an individual's make-up. It is sometimes argued that these skills are only for junior ranks and are not necessary for higher management. This of course is nonsense. To take just two aspects, listening and persuasiveness are skills as much in use by company chairmen as by junior managers. However, whether a person becomes good at handling people is dependent on whether they are given clear authority to decide matters.

In reality, the problem is not so much that the assistant manager does not get the chance to make decisions but that these decisions are confined to guest relations and operational tuning problems. When do they learn about business? Exactly when or how these skills are developed are important questions for career planners. The use of managerial assessment is helpful in this respect because it tells the planner how far individuals have developed.

The question of how far managers need to know the *technical* aspects of running their operation is often debated. This question is part of the wider debate referred to earlier. In fact, it is quite obvious that managers must know about what they are managing and the depth of technical knowledge only improves their capacity to make good business decisions. At the very least technical knowledge has four distinct roles:

- It forms part of the basis of personal authority.
- It forms a central part of the individual's occupational identity.
- It grants the ability to assess the personal capacity of workers in an industry where personal productivity matters.
- It grants the ability to recognize the open-ended aspects of business such as service and food and beverage and how they can be developed to increase sales.

27 Organizational change

No-one doubts that organizations change. Sometimes the change is in the nature of an upheaval and at other times it happens gradually. Change can be deliberate and planned but it can also be enforced and reactive. Not too many years ago the academic discipline of organization theory used to concern itself with two broad modals, the bureaucratic form with its rules and defined roles and the organic form which was less rigid. To a large extent these forms are still the basic currency of organizational structure, but the plot has changed. It has become more complicated. The idea of thinking of organization structure as the result of influence by other factors has not changed, but our thinking about what constitutes 'structure' has changed. It can no longer be confined to elements such as hierarchy, roles, power, authority, groups. Now we must also think of less tangible dimensions such as culture, leadership, information, behaviour. Structure, meaning form, is now only one of many ways of perceiving organizations. Indeed, change itself has become a focus of attention, suggesting that organizational change is the result of larger changes in the social and industrial worlds.

What is the point of studying organizations?

Organizations are the entity which conducts the transactions which make up the economic activity in all its forms. It is in organizations that goods and services are produced, work provided and value enhanced. Such is the complexity of technology, markets and finance that no one individual can cope with the attention they require. To cope with such a division of labour requires a unified entity, which is the organization. Organizations are also social entities which contain relationships of various types. Life within organizations contrasts with social life despite both pervading the other's territory. We speak of organization decision-making but, in a purist sense, only people can make decisions! Yet, such is the significance of the context of organizations that we can indeed speak of them in decision-making terms.

When individuals make decisions in organizations they are, to paraphrase Abraham Lincoln, for the organization, by the organization. Organizations like individuals, have self-interests, the most important of which are to survive and grow.

What is organization theory?

Organizational theory is a body of knowledge which attempts to explain the structure of organization, the behaviour of organizations and the behaviour of people within organizations. It combines ideas of form and structure with human factors and environmental factors such as markets, society, law and politics. At its centre is a concern to explain how the work involved in making things and supplying services is organized. By inference, there is the suggestion that it is also concerned with how things should be organized. The idea of an 'ideal' modal is always around. More suggestive than prescriptive.

The main concepts in organizational theory are:

- The division of labour, the complexity of the production task and the degree of specialization.
- Centralization or decentralization of authority.
- Communication and information distribution.
- Technology, task scope routineness.
- Labour and labour cost.
- The degree of environmental complexity and uncertainty.
- The degree of competitiveness and cooperativeness in the environment.
- Culture and values.

All these dimensions can be studied in a number of ways. For example:

(a) We can take an intra-organizational perspective.
(b) We can adopt inter-organizational approaches which are concerned with competition and integration and, in a comparative sense, with diversity versus convergence.
(c) We can look at organizations in their social and political environments by looking at how organizations adapt to changes in the market, technological and political environments.

Although change is a matter of intra-organizational concern, in effect the concept of change cuts across all these perspectives. The need to change may stem from within, but may equally be caused by something external – it may be initiated by the organization or by outside forces, it may be voluntary or inevitable.

For the management of any organization there are always two types of goals based on a concern with, on the one hand, 'order' within the organization and, on the other, with expansion and productivity. These might be termed *goals of order* and *goals of productivity*. Clearly they are related. Nothing can be produced in chaos and indiscipline. A degree of order is always necessary. Productivity itself is a source of order as it brings economic benefits. These two goals can be incompatible when the value of production is not distributed in some acceptable way.

Goals of order concern such aspects as fairness and equity in the distribution of rewards and in the application of authority, group identity, competition, values, discipline. Goals of productivity concern incentives, motivation, leadership, job design, differentials. Both sets of goals overlap in terms of organizational structure and human resource management policy.

Organizational change

Organizational change is an approach to the study of organizations which embraces all the branches of the subject. Whether change is initiated by the organization itself or is forced upon it, pressure for change is ever present. There are two central practical issues which need to be addressed. First, how is organizational change achieved? Secondly, how is the resistance to change overcome? Notice that resistance is assumed.

The pressures to change

External factors

Changes in the economic, legal, political and technological worlds can force change on an organization. However, it must be said that organizations themselves are part of the environment they live in and continuously attempt to exert influence.

Internal factors

- Inadequate output.
- Inadequate profits.
- Competition.
- Technological change.
- Low performance in terms of innovation, efficiency and adaptiveness.
- Inadequate utilization of plant, support systems or maintenance.
- Low morale.

Achieving change

Putting aside for a moment the actual causes and purposes of change, it is possible to make some assumptions about organizations:

1. How organizations are structured affects performance and outputs.
2. The values of the dominant coalition also affect performance and outputs.
3. The environment sets limits on how organizations are structured.
4. People who lose status or power resist change.
5. The more exposure to change, the more the acceptance of it.

The opportunity to start from scratch is rare, so organizational change is always a matter of some form of *intervention* in the status quo. The nature of this intervention is the material for strategy. There is, however, an original sin in the field of organization change which is, to expect training to do all the work. It is a very common occurrence to find a belief that training alone will change attitudes and thus enable other changes to take place. This is a fallacy. Training can never be that powerful and it can never work alone. In fact, no single technique can work on its own. In a way, it is not surprising that so much faith is placed in training because at a very fundamental level change is about job redesign, new attitudes and new expectations.

Approaches to organization change and key issues

- Changing attitudes through training.
- Redesigning jobs.
- Redesigning the structure and therefore roles within it.
- Strategic vision and will.
- Out of chaos; letting the organization change in an organic unplanned way.
- Making structure serve objectives.
- Preparation for responsiveness; making ready for unspecified change.
- Changing people and/or skills; technological change and human capital.
- Changing key people.

No single one of these approaches can affect change. Strategy has to encompass a coalition of these approaches. However, some approaches are always there. All strategic approaches are dependent on three main components. First, is the vision and willpower of top management. Without this, very little will actually happen and strategy may remain at the level of plans. Secondly, there must be a change in key people and thirdly a role change. It is an inevitable outcome of organization change that roles will change.

At its simplest, strategy has five tools which it can use to implement change:

1. Policies.
2. Structural changes.
3. Appointing new people.
4. Procedures, systems and plans.
5. Tactical interventions.

These are the means, the active ingredients of strategy. It is likely that they will all be used within a strategy. For example, the very purpose of appointing a new person would be the expectation that they would have new policies, change existing systems, change roles and make new appointments of their own.

At the general level, however, the key debate is between the school of thought that argues that attitudes and behaviour will change when roles are altered and the school which argues that when roles change attitudes and behaviour remain the same unless role change is accompanied by training.

Organizational change usually implies an intervention which covers the whole organization, though this is not necessarily always the case. It follows that if the whole organization is changed, then the relationships it has with other organizations will be changed as a consequence.

The human task in achieving change

It is one thing to see change in organizational terms but change is, at heart, a human task. Somebody has to devise the change strategy and make it happen. People have to be persuaded, induced and even forced to change. Enemies have to be friends, interests have to be reconciled and the past has to be discounted. All these tasks are essential human aspects of change. The person instigating change has to influence other people.

The human process of influencing change

A change 'agent' has to work to achieve change and does so by being sensitive to the needs and desires of others and being sensitive to the alliances and coalitions they make as part of organizational life. Persuasion is a word which conceals an enormous amount of effort. Persuasion has numerous tasks, which include:

- Sense needs.
- Amplify understanding.
- Build awareness.
- Create credibility.
- Legitimize viewpoints.
- Generate partial solutions to problems.
- Broaden support.
- Identify opposition.
- Identify areas of indifference.
- Clarify the risks.
- Encourage flexibility.
- Put forward trial concepts, i.e. fly kites.
- Create supportive groups.
- Eliminate undesirable alternatives.
- Crystallize the issues and the debate.
- Seek consensus.
- Establish and maintain coalitions.
- Formalize what is agreed.

This is what persuasion actually entails! It is not surprising that it is so often associated with leadership.

Resistance to change

It is easy to imagine that change is greeted by resistance. It is also wrong. Often change is welcomed. It depends on the culture of the organization and on the degree of threat implied by the change and on society's general attitude towards change. A conceptual framework, ofter referred to as the 'iron cage', sums up the dimensions of resistance. Figure 27.1 depicts the concept. The key 'enforcers' of this attitude are investment in training and society's approval or disapproval of change.

In behavioural terms, resistance can be more complicated. Behavioural reactions can include:

- Enthusiasm.
- Disillusionment.
- Panic.

```
                    ┌─────────────────────────────────┐
                    │ Assault on personal values      │  Reinforced
                    │ Assault on professional skills  │  by society;
                    │ Assault on organization values  │  negative
                    │ Dreaded consequences for client │  attitude
                    │ Feared personal consequences    │
                    └─────────────────────────────────┘
                         Reinforced by betrayed
                         investment in training
```

Figure 27.1 *The 'iron age' of resistance*

- A search for the guilty who support change.
- Punishment of those who sit on the fence.
- Praise for those who resist.

The key to understanding reactions to change lies in timing. There is a clear distinction between first reactions and reflection and between the hope that it may not happen and the acceptance of its inevitability. Action taken too early could be damaging.

The positive acceptance of change depends upon the degree of insecurity which accompanies it and with the degree of investment made in the 'old ways'. Management have to appreciate that when workers have made sacrifices to learn skills they are unlikely to surrender them without regret. The policy implications of this are:

1. There has to be a culture of change based on openness.
2. Consultation is a part of the change process.
3. Incentives have to be built into retraining packages.

It is also necessary for managers to realize that the acceptance of change does not automatically mean that the old ways are forgotten. Regret about 'the old days and old ways' is a serious motivational issue, and not one that can be ignored.

28 Developing labour strategies

Labour strategy and the business

In Chapter 14 we discussed how to relate the number of people employed to the fluctuations in business demand. This only serves to emphasize that labour strategies are largely dependent on business strategies. The business strategy decrees to the labour strategy:

- How many workers are needed.
- The proportion of fixed to variable employment.
- The proportion of added value available for wages.
- The type of people the business needs.
- The type of skills the business needs.

Two factors dominate the relationship between business strategy and labour strategy, these are:

- The pattern of demand by customers.
- Technological change.

Yet, despite this relationship, labour strategy has a life of its own quite distinct from business strategy. You don't change your staff every time your business strategy changes, nor do you restructure your organization with every change of plan. In other words, labour is usually more permanent than the duration of business plans and it is for this reason that the problems of attracting, retaining, sustaining and motivating a workforce need consideration independently in their own right.

What is strategy?

Usually the word strategy is associated with the word planning. This is correct, but strategy means more than designing a programme of action for the future. Such programmes require objectives – where do these objectives come from? For the business, it may well be that the objectives come from alternatives derived from market information. But here, strategy comes from the pursuit of targets. This is not the case with labour strategy. Here the concern is with continuity and change and in this respect labour strategy is more architectural in tone. The central element to all strategy, which precedes the planning process, is the creation of a vision. Put simple – 'what do I want my organization to look like in the future?'

The creation of a vision is never easy. Common sense and 'reality' get in the way, but we move towards what we can see, therefore all planning processes require a model to head towards. Only when the model is in place can you see what must change. In the case of labour strategy, we are concerned with people, skills, motivation, knowledge, how work should be organized, control and authority. These are the bricks that make up any organization. Like any building their quality and quantity are interrelated and interdependent, therefore any vision and consequent design must examine the interconnections between all these parts of the organization. What is more, organizations live in labour markets, therefore the vision should embrace the relationship between the organization and its labour markets.

To pick your way through this maze requires a particular questioning technique, which at its simplest argues that the objectives of your labour strategy come from asking:

- What do I want?
- Why do I want it?
- What does it assume about technology, labour markets and the behaviour or people?
- What would need to change from the present position?

These questions need to be addressed across a range of organizational issues.

Strategy and coherence

In Chapter 7 we discussed that terrible question – what motivates? It is of perennial importance, but so difficult to answer. One reasonably safe bet is to bypass all the issues on motivation and to say that whatever you are doing to motivate your staff only has a chance of success if it makes sense to the individual employee. If your labour strategies are coherent, then the individual is more likely to 'sense' what you are doing than if he or she is being pulled in two different directions at the same time. If, for example, an individual is given close supervision and is expected to show initiative, or has insecure tenure of employment and is expected to be committed to the organization. Such contradictions are often only apparent to the individuals concerned, but they undercut management's efforts to motivate. The case for coherence in labour strategies is that eventually the employee will sense it and will be able to 'make sense' of what is expected of them. In other words, whatever you do is more likely to work if all the messages tell the same story. This gives one criterion by which we might judge labour strategy – coherence.

The process of developing labour strategies

There are three major stages in developing labour strategies. The first two are directly concerned with the business strategy but the third is concerned with the type of organization which will meet the needs of the business strategy. The stages are:

1 Review the pattern of demand

This first stage involves reviewing the pattern of demand for the product or service in terms of fixed and variable labour supply.

2 Review the pattern of technological change

It is important to be clear about what is meant by 'technological' in this context. Here the word is used to describe any work process not necessarily done by a machine. To change the service in a restaurant from silver service to a self-service buffet is a change in work process and is as much a technological change as replacing manual work by machine.

The *technological assessment* which precedes labour strategy development has, itself, three components each with a different significance for strategy.

Technological change

Looking into the future, what rate and type of change do you envisage:

- Steady state (i.e. no change).
- Gradual change built on existing knowledge and skills.
- Gradual change based on new knowledge and skills.
- Incremental change built on existing knowledge and skills.
- Incremental change built on new knowledge and skills.
- Revolutionary change.

Examples of incremental change might be computerized reservation systems, sous vide and microwave cookers. The impact of these changes is not just on the numbers of people employed, but on the type and depth of skill required.

Technology and the labour market

As has been discussed in Chapter 16, the nature of jobs determines their labour market characteristics, therefore what has to be assessed is the nature of the jobs to be done, because such an assessment is the primary influence on future recruitment policies.

What has to be assessed for each work category is:

- The degree of specificity to the organization.
- The level of training, education and experience.
- How far personal characteristics count.
- How far knowledge can be substituted by information.

Technology and control

In Chapter 6 we discussed how the nature of a job influences how management applies control. The assessment here is primarily concerned with how far performance standards can be measured and what value management place upon employee autonomy and initiative.

3 Develop strategies for organizational behaviour – attracting, sustaining and motivating the workforce

At the heart of this approach to developing strategies is a questioning framework. The assumption of this framework is that strategies begin with the question 'what do I want?'. This emphasizes the importance of managerial 'will' in strategy. It also argues

Original values and purposes	What should my organization look like?
Rationale for the original values and purposes	Why should I want it?
Assumptions	What does my vision assume about technology, labour markets and people?
Assessment of change	What has to change from the present?
Objectives	What must I do?
Strategies	How can I do it?
Check for constraints	Is it legal? Can I afford it?
Check for consistency	Is it consistent with other strategies?

Figure 28.1

that the starting point is a vision of what the organization ought to be like in the future. **The emphasis is on values and primary purposes.** Figure 28.1 is a model which shows the progression of the question and answer sequence.

Note also that the planning process in the conventional sense begins at the fifth point and that 'means' enter at the next stage. The means can be structures, systems, specific appointments, policies etc.

Remember that this framework is simply a sequence of questions, but what are these questions about? Where do you start?

What you are trying to do is to get to the fundamentals then to examine your position on the fundamentals of organizational design. There are six, which are:

- *Stability* Concerned with the mobility of the workforce and the relationship between the organization and its labour markets.
- *Incentive* Concerned with rewards – attraction, motivation and retention.
- *Control* Concerned with style of authority and questions of autonomy.
- *Order* Concerned with differentials of all types between members of the workforce.
- *Communication* Concerned with the degree of openness and knowledge distribution.
- *Location* Concerned with significance of the location of the organization in the local society.

All this does is identify areas of concern – how do we get at meaningful questions? The technique recommended here is to take, for each area, *extreme policy options* (EPOs). Examples would be high job security policy, or pay market leadership, or strong worker autonomy or single status. By taking an extreme policy option you can explore your thinking in each area. An example would be appropriate at this point.

Example: An extreme position on stability

Original purposes and values

I want a stable organization with a constant workforce and minimal labour wastage.
This requires a strategy to produce job security for the workforce.

Rationale for the original purpose and values

Why do I want stability?

- I don't anticipate fluctuations in demand.
- I anticipate regular technological change.
- I need to increase the value of human capital because the new technology develops from existing knowledge.
- Existing skills are very specific to the organization.
- I want to avoid a difficult labour market and heavy recruitment costs.
- I want to avoid high training costs.
- I want loyalty and commitment.
- I think that I will get an emphasis on quality if I offer security.
- I want flexibility and adaptability in my workforce.

Assumptions

What does the desire for stability and its policy arm – job security – assume?

About people

- That the investment already made in skill is not a barrier to learning or, if it is, that a job security policy will overcome it.
- That people will be prepared to pass on their skills to others – willingly. Again, the relationship between their own investment and job security policy is crucial.
- That by taking the sacrifice out of learning people will be prepared to abandon old skills for new.
- That by feeling secure people will show more commitment to their work and to the firm. In other words, security motivates.
- That in the long term people will find their own ways of doing things, therefore detailed specification of end (quality and quantity) is probably better than tight control of means.
- That there is a danger of dependency which matters if technology grants workers a degree of autonomy.
- That people will value long-term personal relationships with co-workers.
- That the culture and values of the workplace will be continuously re-enforced and will, therefore, be stronger.
- That people will either consciously or unconsciously, forgo their labour market power – weaken it in return for security.

About the labour market

- That you won't be able to find the skills you need at a price you are prepared to pay.
- That the jobs you have cannot easily be substituted by people with different skills.
- That after a while your firm will not be 'visible' in the marketplace.
- That you forgo the 'fresh air' principle.
- That you can attract sufficient people at your prescribed port of entry. If the port of entry is subject to fierce market competition it might endanger the strong internal labour market you need to construct.
- That internal training produces better skills than the open market.

About technology

- That the type and rate of change can be handled by workforce.
- That no revolutionary change is on the way.

Objectives

What must I do?

- Ensure I have a retraining capacity.
- Ensure that productivity improves consistently.
- Apply pay levels that will prevent temptation to leave. (Do I want to become a market leader?)
- Offer a package which is unconditional on performance.

- Ensure managerial control over the deployment of skills.
- Promote from within.
- Reduce ports of entry to the necessary minimum.
- Negotiate a flexible union agreement.
- Lower manning levels.
- Possibly build a buffer of non-secure part-time employment to account for fluctuation in demand.
- Grant a degree of autonomy as to means while keeping controls of ends.
- Develop a style of supervision suitable for long-term relationships.
- Develop a communication policy that assumes that people are interested and involved.

A complete review of strategy requires this process to be carried out across all the fundamentals of organization design using, in each case, appropriate extreme policy options (EPO). Figure 28.2 illustrates this process by suggesting some key questions and some possible EPOs in each area. *There are many more questions that could be asked.*

The whole purpose of following the exercise is to make your labour strategies coherent. Extremes are valuable in two ways. First, they point out the underlying assumptions about behaviour so that you can cross compare these assumptions to see that they don't contradict each other. Second, you modify your position from the extreme but do so with the knowledge that you know the implications. In the example given you may not really want a high job security policy, but a more moderate version of it, but you are clear now as to why you want it and what it implies.

In real terms, you are likely to have strategies in areas like recruitment, pay, status, promotion, selection and training. Although they exist in their own right, these strategies should flow from the analysis of the fundamental. That way they should display coherence.

What about the means?

Once you have decided what you want and why you want it, and have refined this down to some objectives, then one additional consideration arises – by what means are these objectives to be achieved? Obviously, the actual means used will depend on the objectives, but broadly speaking labour strategies can be implemented in a variety of ways.

- Through policies, procedures, systems and plans.
- By altering the organizational structure.
- By appointing specific people to implement objectives.
- By making tactical interventions without altering policies or structures.

Thinking the matter through is one thing, but once you reach the point of considering means then simultaneously you have reached the point when you have to consider how to communicate the strategy. We have discussed in Chapter 6 that all management behaviour communicates. The great danger with strategic matter is that it is long term and it is about change, there is simply more time available for misinterpretation by the workforce. In other words, whatever the strategy, the communication of it, both intended and unintended, must be thought through. So far, the only criterion for judging a labour strategy has been coherence, but as everything depends upon the

Questions to uncover original values and purposes	Possible EPO
Stability	
How much fluctuation in demand is anticipated? How much technological change is anticipated? Can technological change be built on existing human capital? Just how specific are the skills I need? To what extent do I need employees to be flexible? What is the training capacity of the firm?	Job security, high wastage, core/periphery
Control	
How far can I measure performance standards? How much do I value personal merit? What role do personal characteristics play in the job? What style of supervision most suits my technology?	Bureaucratic control, structured participation, informal/occasional control
Order	
On what basis do I distribute rewards? Should the focus of policy be on the individual, the group or the workforce? Would competition within or between groups be beneficial? What benefits would accrue from homogenous groups? How interdependent are the workers and their groups? How divisible is the workforce in terms of employment status, sex, age and skills?	Single status, customer skills valued higher, technical skills valued higher, core/periphery
Incentives	
How far can I measure performance? How does productivity depend on motivation? Do incentives increase the size of the labour market? Can I buy loyalty? Does loyalty lead to flexibility?	Market leadership, PBR, all benefits on selection
Communication	
How much do they need to know to do their work? Would giving more information enhance management authority? Would more information prevent or promote conflict? How far can knowledge be substituted by information?	Worker participation in all decisions, all salaries known, openness

Figure 28.2

authority of management, this too could be a minimum requirement of any strategy – that it enhances the authority of management.

Believing in what you are doing

This chapter has not advocated any particular labour strategy, it has only pointed out a questioning process of development. It has, however, built the process on the assumption that it is the whole package, that is everything about the job that counts. The philosophy of the process is simply that a strategy is more likely to work if you believe in it and you will believe in it if you find your own judgements convincing. The process advocated here is designed to help you think through to that conviction.

A direction for HRM

It will be recalled that right at the beginning of this book there was a lot of talk about the 'immediacy' of the industry – the focus on the here and now. Yet, here we are at the end talking about strategy. In fact, there is nothing incompatible here. True, strategy is commonly associated with the long term, but it *always embraces the immediate*. It is a fatal flaw to think of strategy as long term and in broad outline. Real strategic thinking and planning starts from where you are now and projects where you want to go to. If there is a real criticism to be made of labour management, whether it is in the guise of personnel management, industrial relations, manpower planning or whatever, it is its failure to achieve completeness. The failure to think and plan in detail. In a sense, trying to answer unanswerable questions like what motivates and what the industry needs in terms of specific workforce requirements, have prevented management from trying everything and from trying to give everything a coherence. Giving workers a gleaming new canteen, plenty of scope in their work, harsh supervision and poor pay, is not telling the same story; neither is good pay, no autonomy, poor conditions and good supervision. They cannot have everything! Maybe, but if what they have points in the same direction, is coherent, then management's motivational exhortations may stand a better chance of getting a response. If it is a game of chance and you don't want to bet on all the horses, at least you can make it a handicapped race! Applied motivation in the future is likely to be about putting attributes together into employment and motivational packages which tell a story to the worker. Without doubt, the technique of the future will be employee attitude surveys. If convenience is going to be a major factor in the decision to work in a leisure society, then 'motivational packages' will be built with regard to how people live as well as what they do at work. The industry values part-time workers, because they are convenient to the economics of labour supply, but such workers will have to be valued for much more than this. They are at the cutting edge of productivity. Time and effort spent in motivation here is well spent. Perhaps the future is organizing different employment packages for skilled full time, unskilled full time and unskilled part time, irrespective of what job they do.

To some experienced recruiters the argument of the model in Chapter 3 that hotel and catering units almost always exist in a labour market surplus might strike a discordant note. Running around hoping to keep up with the labour turnover doesn't 'feel' like a surplus. Yet it is. The labour market is tough enough without making it harder for yourself with stereotyped notions of what you want. The search for 'good people' is not helped by a myopic vision of 'willing flexible souls'. Looking for good people means constantly looking at job content. It is not just the person to fit the job, but the job itself to allow the person to be maximally effective. If a genuine shortage exists in the labour market then management are forced to look at job content, but a modern approach to HRM embraces this as naturally as expert selection procedures. When it comes to evaluating competence and effectiveness, the focus is on job content rather than the personal qualities anyway. Why not make it a central focus in recruitment and selection?

One of the more tedious debates which permeates the industry and vocational education is whether the skills of managing are more important than knowledge of hotel and catering operations. The argument is destructive because both are necessary and complementary. Paying attention to the skills of managing has the advantage of overriding not only technical knowledge, but also functionalism (marketing, personnel, finance etc.). Good practice in HRM assumes that everyone who manages has the skills to do so. HRM has contributed to these skills by devising methods of measuring competence. This process is linked to managing by objectives, but the future will go beyond setting objectives and measuring defined competences to researching and prescribing 'how' things are to be achieved. Again, we see detailed thinking coming to the aid of effectiveness. This is not Taylorism making a comeback in a suit and tie, but a balance between researched methods of achieving objectives in management and encouraging managers to have initiative to go on and find even better ways. One thing is certain, the structure of the industry being as it is, *nothing can be achieved in HRM strategy without stable, motivated and skilled unit managers.*

There is undoubtedly an HRM movement in corporate life – uncodified but nevertheless an observable trend towards an emphasis on the long term, on getting commitment from people, and encouraging flexibility and quality in general. Having argued that the hotel and catering industry is, in some ways, unique, does this mean that it is, therefore, outside such a movement?

The answer is no, because the HRM movement itself is, to a degree, a reaction to labour market forces – an experience not unknown to the hotel and catering industry. Table 28.1 summarizes the direction of the drift towards HRM in the future.

Table 28.1

Area of activity	From	To
Time perspective	Short term	Long term
Planning	Reactive	Pro-active
Management–worker psychological relationship	Compliance	Commitment
Evaluative criterion	Cost minimization	Maximization of labour utility
Motivation	What motivates	Make it all work (employment packages)

People perspective	Groups from which individuals emerge (have we got a waiter who would make a good X?)	Individuals and their group context (X will work well, be happy and grow in that group)
Selection	Looking for good people (we know the type of person we want)	Examine the job content as well as looking for good people (let's get the job right first then go for what we want)
Functionalism	Clear boundaries	Integrated with operations
Communication	Walking the job, assessing morale	Attitude surveys
Management skills	Measuring competence	Researching and prescribing 'how'.

What all this means, is recognition of the value of employees and a determination to make them effective.

Further reading

This section has two purposes: to give the reader a lead into the deeper study of the topics and to introduce more applied readings which are directly relevant to the hotel and catering industry.

Chapter 1

Medlik, S. and Airey, D. W. (1978), *Profile of the Hotel and Catering Industry*, Butterworth-Heinemann.

Chapter 2

The model suggested in Chapter 3 is founded on the notion of internal labour markets and their relationship to the external labour market. This relationship is explained in detail by Doeringer and Piore and given a broader and alternative interpretation by Edwards. A direct application to a small sample of hotels is found in Simms et al.

Doeringer, P. B. and Piore, M. J. (1971), *Internal Labour Markets and Manpower Analysis*, Heath Lexington.
Edwards, R. (1979), *Contested Terrain*, Heinemann.
Simms, J., Hales, C. and Riley, M. (1988), 'An Examination of the Concept of Internal Labour Markets in UK Hotels', *Tourism Management*, vol. 19, no. 1, pp. 3–12.

Chapter 3

A detailed analysis of the model is presented in Riley 1991, with the significance of consumer taste and spending power highlighted in Riley 1981. Given the importance to the model of occupational rigidity, the direct consequences of job content to external labour market characters are given a theoretical treatment by Hage. This text is relevant for understanding the recruitment process. Any consideration of hotel and catering labour markets must include the role of minimum wage legislation, which is considered in depth by Alpert who analyses American data on the restaurant industry. An application of core periphery theory is found in Guerrier and Lockwood.

Alpert, W. T. (1986), *The minimum wage in the Restaurant Industry*, Praeger.
Guerrier, Y. and Lockwood, A. (1989), 'Core and Peripheral Employees in Hotel Operations', *Personnel Review*, vol. 18, no. 1, pp. 9–15.
Hage, J. (1989), 'The Sociology of Traditional Economic Problems: Product and Labour Markets', *Work and Occupations*, vol. 16, no. 4, pp. 416–445.

HCITB (1984), *Manpower Flows in the Hotel and Catering Industry*, HCITB, Wembley.

Kelly, T. R. (1982), 'Research into the Vocational Education and Training Requirements of the Hotel and Catering Industry in the UK', *Journal of Travel Research*, vol. 21, part 2, pp. 22–26.

Riley, M. (1981), 'Declining Hotel Standards and the Skill Trap', *International Journal of Tourism Management*, June, pp. 95–104.

Riley, M. (1991), *An Analysis of Hotel Labour Markets in Progress in Tourism Recreation and Hospitality Management*, Pinter Publications.

Chapter 4

Although a real 'chestnut', the piece by Roy has not lost its power or relevance in showing how things can get out of control.

Roy, D. (1955), 'Making Out: A Worker's Counter System of Control of Work Situations and Relationships' in Burns, T. (1955), *Industrial Man*, Penguin.

Worland, D. and Wilson, K. (1988), 'Employment and Labour Costs in the Hotel Industry: Evidence from Victoria, Australia', *International Journal of Hospitality Management*, vol. 7, no. 4, pp. 363–377.

Chapter 5

The principal theoretical model used here is attribution theory. Among the many good texts on this subject Brown provides not only a clear explanation, but also some excellent examples.

Brown, R. (1986), *Social Psychology* (2nd edn), The Free Press, Macmillan.

Chapter 6

In order to highlight the very imprecise labour contracts applied in the hotel and catering industry, Mars and Mitchell set it in the context of more mainstream industrial relations. Hales and Nightingale point out that what managers are supposed to do, and what they actually do, may not be the same.

Hales, C. and Nightingale, M. (1986), 'What Are Unit Managers Supposed to Do? A Contingent Methodology for Investigating Management Role Requirements', *International Journal of Hospitality Management*, vol. 5, no. 1, pp. 3–11.

Mars, G. and Mitchell, P. (1976), *Room For Reform? A Case Study of Industrial Relations in the Hotel Industry*, Open University Press.

Chapter 7

For a text which sees motivation through the management process see Vecchio but for greater detail of explanation read Handy. All the theories of motivation have some basis in research and the Vroom text remains the best summary of that research. Drawing on the ideas of Goldthorpe, Watson takes the problems of motivation into the wider context of society.

Handy, C. B. (1976), *Understanding Organisations*, Penguin edn, Chapter 2.
Vecchio, R. P. (1988), *Organisational Behaviour*, The Dryden Press, Chapters 6 and 7.
Vroom, V. and Deci, E. L. (eds) (1970), *Management and Motivation*, Penguin.
Watson, J. (1980), *Sociology, Work and Industry*, Routledge Kegan Paul, Chapter 4.

Chapter 8

Festinger is the only place to start here. Study of negative behaviour leads towards reading in interpersonal behaviour with its emphasis on defence mechanisms.

Festinger, L. (1957), *A Theory of Cognitive Dissonance*, Stamford University Press.
Gowler, D. and Legge, K. (1973), 'Perceptions, the "Principles of Cumulation" and the supply of labour' in Warner, M. (1973), *The Sociology of the Workplace*, Allen & Unwin.

Chapter 9

For a good short summary of group process read Handy, but for a deeper analysis the reader should turn to Brown. For an introduction to the psychology of intergroup relations read Tajfel and Frazer which will draw you towards Festinger.

Brown, R. (1986), *Social Psychology* (2nd edn), The Free Press, Chapter 6.
Festinger, L. (1954), 'A Theory of Social Comparison Processes', *Human Relations*, vol. 7, pp. 117–140.
Handy, C. (1976), *Understanding Organisations*, Penguin edn, Chapter 6.
Tajfel, H. and Frazer, C. (1978), *Introducing Social Psychology*, Penguin edn, Chapter 7.

Chapter 10

A good review of equity theory is given by Brown, while Lawler reviews most of the conventional wisdom on pay and motivation. Gower and Legge provide the theoretical framework for the type of behavioural pattern so often observed in the hotel and catering industry.

Brown, K. (1979), 'Social Determinants of Pay' in Stephenson, T. E. and Brotherton, C. (1979), *Industrial Relations; A Social Psychological Approach*, Wiley.
Gower, D. and Legge, K. (1970), 'The Wage Payment System' in Robinson D. (1970), *Local Labour Markets and Wage Structures*, Gower.
Lawler, E. E. (1971), *Pay and Effectiveness; A Psychological View*, McGraw Hill.

Chapter 11

Shamir is very much the starting point for a debate which describes hotels as organizations in terms of bureaucracy or adhocracy.

Shamir, B. (1978), 'Between Bureacracy and Hospitality; Some Organisational Characteristics of Hotels', *Journal of Management Studies*, vol. 15, pp. 285–307.

Chapter 12

Eisner, J. and Van der Pligt, P. (1988), *Attitudes and Decisions*, London, Routledge.

Chapter 13

Hochschild, A. R. (1983), *The Managed Heart: Commercialization of Human Feeling*, Berkeley CA, University of California Press.

Riley, M. (1986), 'A Social Psychological Framework for Customer Service Training', *Tourism Management*, vol. 7, no. 2, pp. 103–112.

Chapter 14

Although a complicated book aimed at manufacturing industry, Chapter 2 of Eilon outlines a conceptual framework for all productivity. Casson is a set of case studies, all of which have relevance for the hotel and catering industry.

Casson, J. (1976), *Manpower Planning at Work: Some Practical Experiences*, IMS.

Eilon, S., Gold, B. and Soesan, J. (1976), *Applied Productivity Analysis for Industry*, Pergamon.

Chapter 15

Johnson has written extensively on the problems of labour turnover in the hotel and catering industry. Bowey provides a method for measuring stability.

Bowey, A. W. (1969), 'Labour Stability Curves and a Labour Stability Index', *British Journal of Industrial Relations*, vol. 7, pp. 71–83.

Johnson, K. (1981), 'Towards an Understanding of Labour Turnover', *Service Industries Review*, vol. 1, no. 1, pp. 4–17.

Chapter 16

For a general but thorough approach, read Torrington. However, for a highly focused text on selection and interviewing, Eder and Ferris is recommended.

Eder, R. W. and Ferris, G. R. (1989), *The Employment Interview*, Sage.
Torrington, D. and Hall, L. (1987), *Personnel Management: A New Approach*, Prentice Hall, Chapters 14, 15, 16.

Chapter 17

Torrington, D. and Hall, L. (1987), *Personnel Management: A New Approach*, Prentice Hall, Chapter 24.

Chapter 18

The great merit of Greenhill's book is that it starts with the construction of basic pay schemes and works towards very advanced ones. At every stage there are good examples. Mars *et al.* reveal the intricates of hotel pay systems.

Greenhill, R. T. (1988), *Performance Related Pay*, Director Books.
Mars, T., Bryant, D. and Mitchell, P. (1979), *Manpower Problems in the Hotel and Catering Industry*, Saxon House, Chapter 1.

Chapter 19

For thoroughness and attention to detail, Thompson and Murray is recommended.

Thompson, A. W. J. and Murray, V. V. (1976), *Grievance Procedures*, Saxon House, Lexington Books.

Chapter 20

Torrington and Hall is comprehensive and well written, but Livy is less functional and more policy orientated. Both are recommended.

Livy, B. (1988), *Corporate Personnel Management*, Pitman.
Torrington, D. and Hall, L. (1987), *Personnel Management: A New Approach*, Prentice Hall International.

Chapter 22

Ghauri, P., Gronhaug, K. and Kristanslund, I. (1995), *Research Methods in Business Studies*, London, Prentice-Hall.

Chapter 23

Lincoln, J. and Kalleberg, A. (1990), *A Culture Control and Commitment*, Cambridge, Cambridge University Press.

Chapter 26

Although it is based on corporations with fairly stable workforces, Bennison and Casson is a text which carries a lot of important ideas and techniques. Smith is concerned with applying useful forms of analysis and of particular relevance here is the chapter on the Camel Model. Careers are about individual motivations and organizational needs and these are brought together by Schein. An application of the techniques suggested by these texts to the hotel industry is found in Riley, and Guerrier considers the situation for women managers.

Bennison, M. and Casson, J. (1984), *The Manpower Planning Handbook*, McGraw-Hill.
Guerrier, Y. (1986), 'Hotel Manager: An Unsuitable Job for a Woman?', *Service Industries Journal*, vol. 6, no. 2, pp. 227–240.
Riley, M. (1990), 'The Role of Age Distributions in Career Path Analysis', *Tourism Management*, vol. 11, no. 1, pp. 38–44.
Riley, M. (1995), 'The Analysis of Managerial Experience: Integrating Career Analysis with Labour Market Dynamics', *British Journal of Management*, vol. 6, pp. 195–203.
Schein, E. H. (1978), *Career Dynamics: Matching Individual and Organisational Needs*, Addison-Wesley.
Smith, A. R. (ed.) (1980), *Corporate Manpower Planning*, Gower Press.

Chapter 27

Burnes, B. (1993), *Managing Change*, Glasgow, Pitman.
Hendry, C. (1995), *Human Resource Management*, Oxford, Butterworth-Heinemann.
Hoecklin, L. (1994), *Managing Cultural Differences*, London, Addison Wesley.
Wood, R. (1994), *Organizational Behaviour for Hospitality Management*, Oxford, Butterworth-Heinemann.

Other useful texts

Bowey, A. (1976), *A Sociology of Organisations*, Hodder and Stoughton.
Knight, I. B. (1971), *Patterns of Mobility in the Hotel and Catering Industry*, HCITB, London.
Riley, M. (1984), 'Hotels and Group Identity', *Tourism Management*, June.

Index

Adair, J., 65
Adams, J. S., 49
Advertising, 113
Age distributions, 186
Anatomy of hotel and catering labour market, 15–25
Anxiety, 87
Appraisal, 123
Appraisal interview, 126
Appraisal, systems, ambiguity in, 123–4
Attitudes:
   and behaviour, 77–8
   components of, 76–7
   scaling, 80–3
   social norm, 78
Attribution biases, 36–7
Attribution theory, 34–5
Authority:
   and communication, 73
   perceptions of, 69
   and power, 72–3
   sources of, 70–1
   and structure, 71–2

Bureaucracy and authority, 41, 71–2
   and personal service, 42–3

Career analysis, 184–7
Career motivational factors, 187–9
Career, structure in hotel and catering industry, 189–93
Commitment:
   entrenchment, 169
   and job satisfaction, 165–7
   and labour turnover, 165–7
   types of, 167
Communication:
   and authority, 73
   and management behaviour, 41–2
Conflicts, prevention policies, 141–2
Consumer demand, nature of, 1–2, 21–2
Co-orientation model, 85
Customer–service relations, 84

Data collection, in personnel, 147–8
Distortion of grievances, 55–6

Earnings flexibility, 175
Elasticity of demand 8–9
Employment interview:
   format of, 115
   objectives of, 114
   structure of, 114
Empowerment, 171
Episodic questions, 118
Exchange model, 86
Expectancy theory, 48
Extreme policy options, 204, 206

Festinger, L., 55–6
Fishbein, M., 78
Formal control systems, dangers of, 42–3
Full-time employment, estimating levels of, 99–100
Functional flexibility, 175

Goldthorpe, J. A., 51
Gouldner, A., 41
Gratuity systems, 68
Grievances:
   and management authority, 141–2
   managerial approach to, 58
Grievance procedures:
   design of, 144
   merits of formality, 58, 141–2
Group behaviour, 60
Group identity, 62–3
Group process, 61–2

Hard data/soft data, 146–7
Herzberg, F., 45–6
Hierarchy of standards, 18–19
Hiring standards, 12, 96, 111–12
Hochschild, A. R., 88
Hotel and catering industry, unique features of, 1–3
HRM – future directions, 208

Indexation, of pay, 138–9
Integration principle, 52
Intensity of feelings, dilution of, 56–7
Intergroup behaviour, 63
Internal labour markets, dimensions of, 12

Job alignment, 124–5
Job characteristics and labour markets, 109–10
Job choice and motivation, 50
Job content, pressure to change, 136–7
Job evaluation, 128–36
Job satisfaction:
  sources of, 46
  and unskilled work, 50

Kirton 192
KSA, 115–17

Labour contract, psychological nature, 38–40
Labour market characteristics, 7–9, 109–10
Labour productivity, basis of, 71
Labour stability, measurement of, 107–8
Labour supply adjustment mechanisms, 101
Labour turnover:
  calculation of rate of, 106–7
  as conflict behaviour, 141–2
  costs of, 27–9
  and recruitment, 9–11
Labour utilization, 95
Leadership of groups, 64–5
Length of a vacancy, 27–9
Location factors and work values, 52

McGregor, D., 53
Management development, 187–9
Management pay, 23, 189
Maslow, A., 45
Mobility and structure, 18–19
Motivation, 44

Negative behaviour, 55
Numerical flexibility, 175

Occupational rigidity, 19, 23
Occupational structure, 17
Orientations to work, 51

Organization theory, 194–5
Organizational change:
  pressures for, 196
  resistance to, 198–9
Orwell, G., 42
Overtime, behavioural implications of, 26–7

Pay administration, 127
  comparisons, 67–8
  differentials, influences on, 25
  and leisure, 66
  rate, influences on, 20, 24
Pay structures, purpose of, 127–8
Pay surveys, 137–40
Pay systems and grievances, 26–7
  related to structure, 137
Performance standards:
  and accounting systems, 100
  need for, 95–6
  purposes of, 96
Personnel administration:
  objectives of, 145
  good habits, 146
  policy guidelines, 148–50
Planning, strategy, 200–8
Power and authority, 72–3
Pre-interview material, 119–20
Productivity, actual versus forecast, 100–1
Psychological contract, 38–40

Question strategy, 117–19
Question technique, 117–19
Questionnaire design, 156

Rational choice model, 78
Recruitment and labour turnover, 9–11
  strategies, 113
Responsibility and occupational identity, 71
Role conflict, 42–3

Sales forecast and labour demand, 96–7
Self theory, 46–7
Skill model, 16–21
Skill proportions, estimate of, 18
Smith, A., 8
Snyder, R., 47
Social emulation, 88

Social hours, labour market, 23–4
Social skills training, 90
Soft data/hard data, 146–7
Stability index, calculation of, 107–8
Strategy, defined, 200–1
   conceptual framework for, 201–8
Subjective nature of standards, 2
Substitution principle, 111, 177
Supply curve for labour, 66
Survey administration, 161
Survey coding, 161

Tajfel, H., 62–3
Technological change and strategy, 202
Theory X, 53

Theory Y, 53
Training costs, 151

Understanding people, problems of, 33–4
Unsocial hours labour market, 23–4

Vocational education and careers, 190
   and weak internal labour markets, 23

Williams, R., 47
Work scheduling, 102
Work study, 102–5
Workload analysis, 97–100